OFFICIAL

Netscape JavaBeans

Developer's Guide

Windows 95/NT & Macintosh

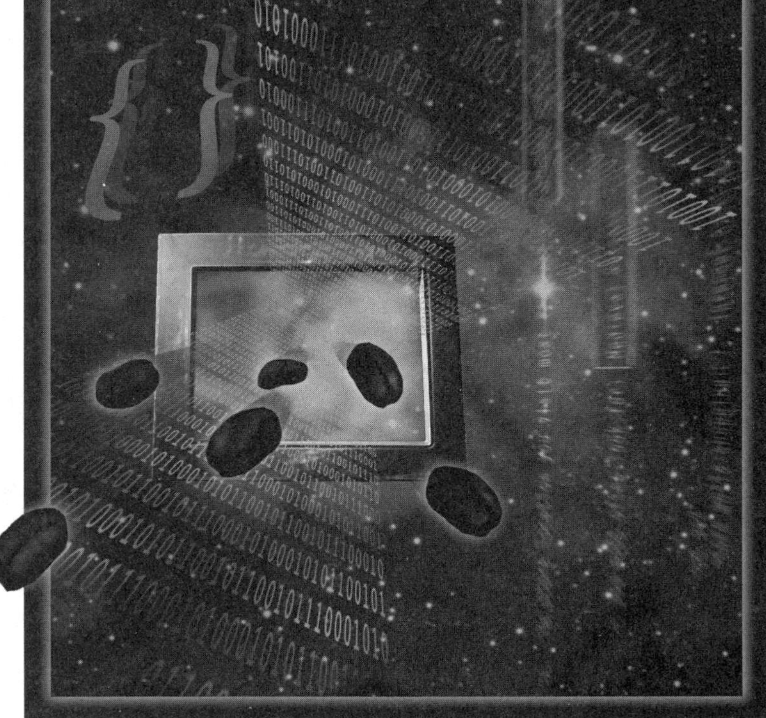

Creating & Integrating Cross-Platform Components With Netscape ONE Tools

Doug Nickerson

Ventana

Official Netscape JavaBeans Developer's Guide

Library of Congress Cataloging-in-Publication Data

[Insert CIP data here—if there is only a number, and not full data, use this format:
Library of Congress Catalog Card Number: 96-xxxxx]

First Edition 9 8 7 6 5 4 3 2 1

Printed in the United States of America

Published and distributed to the trade by Ventana Communications Group
P.O. Box 13964, Research Triangle Park, NC 27709-3964
919.544.9404
FAX 919.544.9472
http://www.vmedia.com

Ventana Communications Group is a division of International Thomson Publishing.

Netscape Publishing Relations
Suzanne C. Anthony
Netscape Communications Corporation
501 E. Middlefield Rd.
Mountain View, CA 94043
http://home.netscape.com

President
Michael E. Moran

Associate Publisher
Robert Kern

Editorial Operations Manager
Kerry L. B. Foster

Production Manager
Jaimie Livingston

Brand Manager
Jamie Jaeger Fiocco

Art Director
Marcia Webb

Creative Services Manager
Diane Lennox

Acquisitions Editor
Neweleen A. Trebnik

Project Editor
Amy E. Moyers

Development Editor
Laura Berry

Copy Editor
Ellen Strader

CD-ROM Specialist
Ginny Phelps

Technical Reviewer
Richard Jessup

Desktop Publisher
Kristin Miller

Proofreader
Apryl Lamb

Indexer
Richard T. Evans, Infodex

Interior Designer
Patrick Berry

Cover Illustrator
Leigh-Erin M. Salmon

About the Author

Doug Nickerson works as a software engineer, primarily in C and C++. He has been interested in computers since 1985, when he bought his first computer—a Commodore 64—on which he used to write music programs. He holds a degree in computer science from the University of Massachusetts at Amherst. Doug has programmed professionally in C/C++ for about seven years, in the fields of electronic catalogs and data logging equipment. He has written about Java and C++ in the computer press, including *C/C++ Users Journal*, *Dr. Dobb's Journal*, *Windows Tech Journal*, and the *C++ Report*. Doug is also an experienced musician who occasionally performs classical music and Bossa Nova on the guitar. He lives in Massachusetts with his wife and two small sons.

Acknowledgments

First I'd like to acknowledge my agent, Bill Adler Jr., for his unflappable attitude. And a thank you goes to the editors of the earliest incarnation of the book, Lisa Bucki and Amy Hayworth. Amy especially helped me out by acting as if book writing was normal. Also at Ventana: Amy Moyers, Laura Berry ("maybe it would help if you..."), Richard Jessup, Ginny Phelps, Diane Lennox, Clark McCabe, Neweleen Trebnik. My colleagues Jim Dodd, Mark Hruska, Tom Mignone, Amy Kaye, Dawn Stowers, Peter Mularski, and Lon Hocker helped with their suggestions and computer expertise. Martin Rinehart and Megan Newman shared their valuable insights into the publishing world. Most of all I'm grateful to my wife, Maria, who supported me gracefully during the nights and weekends spent preparing the book.

—Doug Nickerson

Dedication

To my wife, Maria.

Contents

Introduction

Welcome to the *Official Netscape JavaBeans Developer's Guide*. You may be familiar with the programming language Java. If you are, you've heard about its cross-platform capabilities and its adaptability for the Internet and the World Wide Web. JavaBeans, a component architecture from Sun Microsystems, is the most exciting thing to happen in the Java world since the development of Java itself. JavaBeans is exciting for two reasons:

- JavaBeans builds upon an idea whose time, many people feel, has come: component software.
- The JavaBeans architecture is based upon Java.

Component software may very well realize what has become a dream for many people: reusable software components that can be strung together to create a complete application, run in many operating systems and environments, and make software development faster, more reliable, and cheaper. And what's the significance of JavaBeans's being based upon Java? Sun has followed a very simple and natural approach to creating software components. A simple JavaBean is simply a Java class that follows some additional rules, mostly simple naming conventions. And nothing in the specification limits you from creating more complex JavaBeans. JavaBeans are portable where Java is, which is anywhere the Java Virtual Machine is implemented.

Netscape has committed itself to the support of JavaBeans in their present and future products. Communicator 4 supports the JDK 1.1 JavaBeans specification. This commitment is important not only because it leads toward industry adoption of the JavaBeans model, but also because JavaBeans integrates well with Netscape ONE—Netscape's existing group of tools for intranet/Internet development. In conjunction with JavaBeans, Netscape has added new component types that can be linked with JavaBeans to create *crossware* applications. One new component type created by Netscape is JavaScript beans, objects that are based upon beans, written in JavaScript, and loaded into Netscape's new crossware development tool: Visual JavaScript. These new component types give intranet/Internet developers even more options for developing crossware applications.

Who Should Use This Book?

You as a reader are interested in the Internet. You likely have some programming experience. You may be a Webmaster or person responsible for researching Internet technologies for a large or small company. You may use and be familiar with other Netscape products and technologies such as Communicator, JavaScript, or LiveConnect.

Before reading the book, you could always benefit by gaining some background on Java (1.0 or 1.1) and its libraries, especially some familiarity with the AWT. I definitely have not assumed you know the newer features of Java 1.1; I take the viewpoint of a reader whose Java knowledge ends at Java 1.0, who may need pointers on how Java 1.1 is different, and who wants to know what JavaBeans is all about. I matched this reader profile myself at the beginning of this book. (In some ways I still do!)

I also provide some introductory material about component architectures and how they relate to other types of programming; these sections may be useful to anyone interested in modern computing issues.

What's Inside?

I organized two threads in this book, JavaBeans from Sun Microsystems, and Netscape ONE components—that is, types of components developed by Netscape to work with Netscape ONE, such as the new JavaScript beans, CORBA components, and Composer plug-ins. These two threads had to be synchronized and to cooperate without deadlock. (If you understand that computer "joke," you'll certainly have no difficulty with the rest of this book.)

The first six chapters describe JavaBeans and the JavaBeans API from Sun Microsystems. Starting with Chapter 7, I introduce technologies from Netscape. This includes some material about Visual JavaScript, JavaScript beans, CORBA, and Composer plug-ins. The last part of the book contains a reference to the JavaBeans API and information on persistence and working with Java Archive files (Jar files). Overall I've tried to organize topics in the book from the simple to the complex, covering general information about component architectures before getting into the details of the JavaBeans API, for example. Here's a chapter-by-chapter sampling of topics:

Chapter 1 is an overview of component architectures, what they are, and what they're good for. It also contains some material about ActiveX, OLE, CORBA/IIOP, and Netscape.

Chapter 2 is a "First Look" at JavaBeans. It describes how some of the features of component architectures are used in JavaBeans—to give you a fast head start.

Chapter 3 discusses the BeanBox from Sun. The BeanBox is a container environment for beans that lets you load beans and connect them together.

Chapter 4 is a programming example. It focuses largely on the details of creating a new event type to get two beans to cooperate.

Chapter 5 is a detailed look at the *Property API*, the support in the JavaBeans API for properties—including simple, bound, and constrained properties, and design patterns.

Chapter 6 is a similarly detailed look at events. The event model in JDK 1.1 has been restructured from a new perspective (from JDK 1.0). The new approach is not difficult, but it's new and different enough to make a detailed understanding crucial.

Chapter 7 begins the discussion of Netscape components and tools; it is an introduction to Visual JavaScript and Netscape's Component Development Kit (CDK).

Chapter 8 is a description of the new JavaScript beans from Netscape, and a look at their new file format, the JSB file.

Chapter 9 is a description of CORBA components for use with Visual JavaScript from Netscape. It also contains some introductory information about CORBA and Object Request Brokers (ORBs).

Chapter 10 covers some other objects that can be used with Visual JavaScript, such as plug-ins created in Java, Customizers, and PropertyEditors.

Chapter 11 is a look at persistence and synchronization, the storing of beans, and the prevention of deadlock and races in code containing multiple threads.

Chapter 12 is a reference chapter to the new JDK 1.1 package containing most of the JavaBeans support: java.beans.

Chapter 13 is a list of examples from Visual JavaScript and the Component Development Kit.

Chapter 14 looks at the new way to archive applets and beans and pass them around the Internet: the Jar file format.

I'm sure there could be many other organizations of this material. In fact, one of the unexpected pleasures of writing is realizing that more than one arrangement of a topic is possible. An overall goal is to help you learn about component architectures and how they might be used in intranet/Internet environments; I hope my organization brings that out.

About JDK 1.1

You need the JDK 1.1 to develop JavaBeans. This gives you the ability to compile code for Java 1.1. The JDK 1.1 and the Beans Development Kit (BDK) are included on the Companion CD-ROM. You install the JDK and BDK by running the self-extracting file from the Windows Explorer. This starts an installation wizard that will ask you pertinent questions such as to where one must install. For a root directory, I prefer drivename: \JDK11 for the JDK, and drivename: \BDK for the Beans Development Kit. The examples in the text were tested in Windows 95 on both a 486DX2/50 machine and a Pentium 100.

For Chapters 7 through 10, you'll need Netscape's Visual JavaScript and Netscape's Component Development Kit. You can read Chapters 7 through 10 without these tools, but you need them if you want to run any tests of your own. These are downloadable from http://developer.netscape.com. If you have a version of Netscape Communicator on your machine, it will let you preview your Visual JavaScript scripts in Navigator. Also, this is not a book on CORBA, but Chapter 9 does contain some information about Netscape's CORBA components. Using these components requires that you have access to an Enterprise Server 3 installation.

One can develop JavaBeans under the JDK 1.02 specification. Sun has provided some guidelines for these that they call "transitional" beans. As I began this book, some software vendors had come on board with full JDK 1.1 support; others had not. As I finish the book, most Java development tools are supporting JDK 1.1, and support for beans developed in JDK 1.1 has been added to most environments, including Netscape Communicator. For these reasons I haven't emphasized developing beans for JDK 1.02 in this book. I speak of Java 1.0 in this book not as a dead thing, but as a necessary jumping-off point for Java 1.1.

The Never Ending Story

A prognosticator, reading tea leaves or consulting a crystal ball, would not be far off with the prediction: "change will come to the software field." The prevalence of change in software languages and systems reminds me of the title of a film from the 1980s, *The Never Ending Story*. (I've not seen this movie recently since my three-year old son's taste in movies runs more to *Gumby* and *Sammy—the Way Out Seal*.)

So look for Java and JavaBeans to change and evolve. Look for Netscape to evolve their idea of crossware development and add more tools and technologies to Netscape ONE. Look for further cooperation between Netscape and Sun Microsystems, resulting in further improvements to tools for the component developer, for example, the Java Foundation Classes. And look for Microsoft to keep trying to change Java under the auspices of making it run better under Windows. Change keeps developers and users of computer software interested and authors like myself most cheerfully employed.

Doug Nickerson
doug_nickerson@onsetcomp.com

An Introduction to Component Software

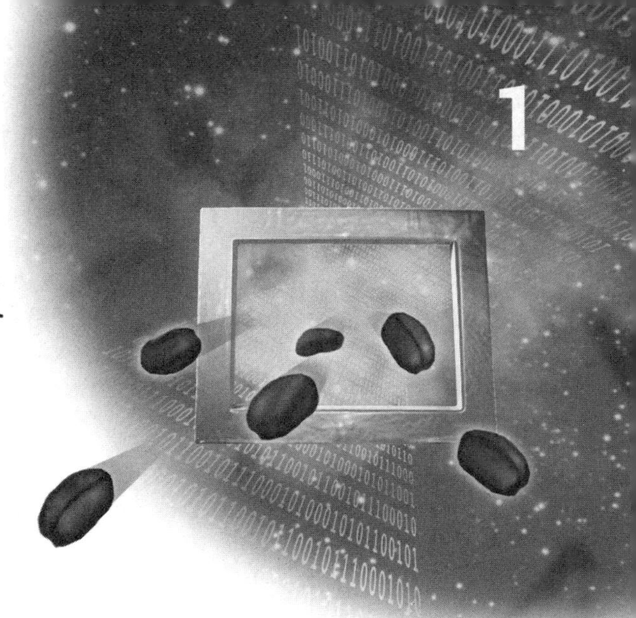

Netscape has long been dedicated to the idea of open systems development. Its Open Network Environment (ONE) technologies form a group of tools and services that assist the developer in creating cross-platform applications for the Internet. Indeed, Netscape has called their vision of cross-platform software built upon widely supported open Internet protocols "crossware." And Java fits well with any vision of cross-platform development.

Java programming language can enliven World Wide Web sites with sound and animation and provide plug-in functionality (via applets) without the worries usually caused by cross-platform dependencies. Netscape began to support Java applets starting with Netscape Navigator 2.0. Netscape and many other vendors have supported Java either with development environments or libraries to support Java development.

For example, part of the Netscape ONE technologies is the Internet Foundation Classes (IFC). Written in Java, these classes provide a programming environment 'on top of' Java's native Abstract Windows toolkit (AWT). Recently, Sun and Netscape have announced the Java Foundation Classes (JFC), which will leverage the experience of both Netscape and Sun in the area of Internet development.

With Netscape's announcement of its intention to support JavaBeans in present and future products, it has added another brick to its building of easily developed crossware applications. Before JavaBeans, Java did not have a generalized component architecture that enabled Java classes to be used as building blocks for rapid application development. The JavaBeans component architecture from Sun Microsystems fills this need while inheriting Java's simplicity, flexibility, and crossware capabilities.

To understand JavaBeans, first let's get an idea of what component architectures are and what problems they try to solve. This chapter introduces component software and discusses the following:

- What is a component?
- What is a component architecture (or model)?
- What makes component software different from traditional procedural or object-oriented software?

I'll try to answer these questions. Also, to illustrate features of real-world component architectures, I'll include background information on Visual Basic Extensions (VBXs), Component Object Model/Object Linking and Embedding (COM/OLE), and ActiveX.

Support for and interoperability with Common Object Request Broker Architecture (CORBA) is also important to Netscape (and to Sun); CORBA and Internet Inter-ORB Protocol (IIOP) will be covered in a later section.

The last sections discuss JavaBeans and Netscape's support and vision for it.

What Led Up to Components?

The history of software development has been a history of managing complexity. Consider the history of programming languages. A list of language developments in the programming language field is as follows:

- Machine language
- Pseudo-code interpreters
- Assembly code
- High-level languages
- Object-oriented languages

Each successive language development managed more and more complexity than the one before it, leaving the programmer free to think about 'higher-level' issues. For example, machine language (ML) required programmers to remember numbers, often in octal or hexadecimal. Pseudo-code interpreters took certain often-used ML routines and converted them to a single code that could be called as a subroutine. Assembly code introduced mnemonics to represent ML instructions and "pseudo-ops" (instructions to the assembler) that managed the structure of a machine language program.

Assembly languages were followed by high-level languages, such as FORTRAN, ALGOL, PL-1, C, and Pascal. High-level languages added named variables, control structures such as if and while, block structure, and subroutines to the programmer's bag of tricks. Using these languages, the programmer could think about problems at a higher level of abstraction. Data could be structured and separated from the procedures that operated on them.

Next came the development of object-oriented languages which are at the heart of the topic of this book. The JavaBeans Application Programming Interface (API) is written in Java, an object-oriented language that owes something to both Smalltalk and C. Simula and Smalltalk introduced the ideas of classes and objects. In object-oriented languages, data is not passed among procedures; it has a home—it is bound with the procedures into an *object*.

Object-oriented languages provided the features of *encapsulation, inheritance,* and *polymorphism*. The binding of the data and procedures just noted is an example of encapsulation. Also, data can be made public or private, and an object can expose only those functions that it needs to provide an interface to its data. Inheritance is the ability of one object to derive some of its functionality from another, and to inherit functions and data fields. This is a benefit because it enables code re-use.

Polymorphism is the hardest feature to describe. The word roughly means many shapes. Polymorphism lets you call the same function on different objects and have the object decide for itself how it wants to 'behave,' (which function it actually calls).

Object-oriented languages made it possible for programmers to create libraries of objects designed to implement a certain task, which other programmers could then re-use or extend as they wished.

Where do components fit into this scheme? It is possible to see components as the next-in-line development on the 'managing/encapsulating complexity' scale. Next, let's look at what problem components are trying to solve.

Components & the Tight Binding Problem

Object-oriented software encapsulates procedures with data into an object. This is an improvement, but objects have not necessarily become as easy to use as integrated circuits are for the hardware designer. One reason for this is the 'tight binding' between an object and an operating system. A team of programmers can share a C++ library of objects between them fairly well if they are all working in the same environment. Across operating systems, C++ can be shared at the source code level, each person recompiling the objects for his or her own computer system.

Sharing an object or an object library at the binary level is more difficult. Even on one platform such as Windows on PCs, there can be problems if the library was not compiled with the same compiler that's being used for the development. This is a reason, I think, why C++ libraries such as Microsoft Foundation Classes (MFC) and Borland's Object Windows Library (OWL) have been successful. They target a specific task—building applications for Windows, a single operating environment, and often a single compiler.

Tight Binding

The programming field has an abundance of terms that describe types of connections between objects in a program or code and an operating system. In addition to tight binding, there are 'late' and 'early binding.' The last two are particularly applicable to object-oriented programming. Late binding means that a method called on an object instance isn't determined until run time. This fact is closely related to polymorphism. Early binding, on the other hand, is what happens when you compile a C program; the functions to be called are bound at compile-time.

These terms all say something about the 'when' or 'how much' of connections between computer objects of some sort.

What Is a Component?

Components overcome the tight binding problem by putting a layer that acts as 'middleware' between the component and the operating system. Thus, when asking for a service, the component doesn't address the operating system directly; it follows a protocol. Different operating systems are responsible for supporting this protocol if they want to interact with the component. The protocol is provided by a component architecture.

Taking the foregoing into account, one definition of a component would be as follows: a component is a software feature that is made up of binary code that accomplishes some computing task, can operate in different software environments, and can link up with other components to form a complete application.

That is, components let you integrate and mix and match separate building blocks such that your application development is much easier. And, in the case of a component architecture like JavaBeans, they work cross-platform in the client/server environment represented by the Internet.

For example, there might be a JavaBean intended to access a remote database. A developer using a development environment supporting JavaBeans might use this bean, along with HyperText Markup Language (HTML), other beans, and Graphical User Interface (GUI) elements such as buttons and text fields to create a front end to a database. Once the application is deployed, the end user works with the front end to generate a query, and the bean processes it (perhaps turning it into SQL) and sends it to the database for processing.

Components encapsulate data, for which they provide an interface, but also address the tight binding between most operating systems and the code that runs in them. They do this by following a protocol or architecture. The next section looks at component architectures and the features they typically provide.

Component Architectures & Their Features

Components do much of what objects do and, they work in many different operating systems with many different computer types. How do they do this? By following the conventions of a component architecture. The following list includes features that are typically provided:

- **Properties** are also called attributes, these describe a feature of a particular component. For example, a button in a GUI might have a "color" property or a "name" property. Often, the client program has some means to change the value of these properties, although properties can be 'read-only' too.
- **Methods** are the services a component offers. People familiar with object-oriented programming know about calling methods on objects—or the other way of saying it: 'sending a message to an object.' Methods can do computational work, affect the appearance of the component, or access the properties. Particularly important to component models, methods can be 'targeted' by other components—called by other components to perform useful work.
- **Events** are the means of linking up components. Events, which will be familiar to users of GUIs like Windows, can be produced (or fired) by a component. And most importantly, these events can cause actions in other components, by calling a target method on those other components. The preceding are features of a component alone. The following are features that are provided by the component architecture itself:
    - **Publishing:** In order for a component to be used in various container applications, there must be some way for it to tell the world what capabilities it offers. This is often called publishing. What needs to be published? Properties, methods, and events. An application, usually an application 'builder,' needs to be able to provide a list of properties, methods, and events so that the user can modify a property or connect up the 'fire-event' code of one component with a target method on another.

- **Graphical editing:** There may be a way to edit or affect a component in a graphical user interface. An example would be the resizing of a button component to make it fit a dialog box or form.
- **Customization:** In addition to graphical editing, the component architecture might make possible the customization of a component behind the scenes by a programming language. As we'll see later, JavaBeans's Customizer interface provides support of this type. Customization could be used to support wizards, letting a developer design an application builder to step through bean development.

What's a Wizard?

Wizard is an automated tool that walks a user through the development of an application. It usually presents a series of dialog boxes which allow the customization of the application. Visual C++'s App-Wizard was probably one of the first such tools, but the term has come to be more general.

- **Persistence:** Components need to be saved or stored. When working with components in an application builder environment, a developer will need to be able to make changes to a component and save those changes with the component. This feature of persistence needs to be supported by the architecture.

Some Current Component Architectures

I now want to describe some architectures or models that provide a way to build, use, and store components. The intention of this section is to provide an introduction to how real-world component systems implement the features I've been talking about. Entire books could be and have been written about each architecture; I hope the little bit of history and description here will give you some context when it comes to understanding JavaBeans itself.

Visual Basic Extensions (VBXs)

Visual Basic Extensions (VBXs), introduced in Microsoft's Visual Basic 1.0, are primarily controls. Programs for MS Windows get much of their functionality and their unique look from various types of controls. Windows programmers will be familiar with the following control types: BUTTON, EDIT, STATIC, LISTBOX, COMBOBOX, and so on. Much of the time spent developing for Windows (at least the user interface code) is spent laying out these controls on dialog boxes and windows, often using some sort of resource editor.

Visual Basic was one of the first environments to let the developer create Microsoft Windows applications visually. The Visual Basic environment provided access to the usual Windows controls but let the developer add additional ones. Programming in Visual Basic centers around the paradigm of a Visual Basic form—which basically looks like a blank window. VBXs are presented in a toolbar, from which the developer can select buttons, text fields, icons, and so forth, and place them on the form. When the developer selects the control on the form, a property window displays the available properties for the control. These properties can be things like the color of a button or arrow control, or the size of the border around the control.

Visual Basic also supports events. Selecting a control, the user is presented with a code template for code to respond to a button click or mouse down, for example. Persistence was a feature of VBXs because the controls could be saved with some context and used in other Visual Basic applications.

VBXs have some limitations, however. They weren't designed to be a generalized model for component software. The most obvious limitation is that they were available only in Visual Basic. They worked with Windows and certainly weren't designed for client/server environments like the World Wide Web. Microsoft is sure to have realized these limitations. They had already been working on Object Linking and Embedding (OLE), which was built upon a more generalized object model, the Component Object Model (COM). COM is the basis of not only OLE, but also of many other technologies that Microsoft provides, including ActiveX. As part of its migration toward all things OLE, VB-4 VBX controls were replaced by the OLE Control specification (OCX) . COM is the unifying thread in the OLE/ActiveX landscape, so before looking at OLE and ActiveX, let's take a look at COM.

The Component Object Model (COM)

COM is an attempt to solve the problems we've been talking about: it supports components that are accessed in a standard way and that are not bound to a particular operating system. The foundation of OLE and ActiveX is COM, and the linchpin of COM is the COM object.

A COM object has most, but not all, features in common with an object in object-oriented programming. A COM object implements one or more 'interfaces'; more than one is typical. Interfaces contain methods and group related functionality together. For example, if we were to provide a COM object that accessed a customer database, one interface might have methods such as the following: LookupCustomerName( ), GetAddress( ), and GetOrderNumber( ). Another interface, part of the same COM object, focused upon area code data and phone numbers, might provide methods: GetPhoneNumber( ), GetAreaCode( ), AddPhoneNumber( ), and SortByAreaCode( ).

Interfaces have both an internal name or ID, called a GUID, and a name more suitable for use by people. The human readable names usually begin with the letter "I". The example interfaces above thus might have the names ICustomerData and IPhoneBook. The GUID is implemented as a 16-byte number.

In order to work with the COM model in a program, the developer first interacts with the COM library. The library must be initialized before using any COM facilities. This initialization takes the form of a function call. The COM library provides housekeeping services—without it, the interfaces of the COM object would not be available.

How does a client program gain access to interfaces? Before using the methods of a certain interface, such as the preceding ICustomerData interface, the client initializes the COM library, then fetches a pointer to the ICustomerData interface. From this pointer (really a pointer to a pointer to a list of functions) the client can call the methods available in the ICustomerData interface.

The insides of the COM object are in binary. The client program (the user of the COM object) doesn't have access to them. For this reason, the object can work in many different operating systems, as long as the rules are followed for how to access the COM features. Also, the object could have originally been written in a different language than the client program using it. In addition, COM puts restrictions upon modifications to an interface. Once an interface is released by a vendor, no modifications are allowed. If the supplier of the object needs more functions, such as a new way to track customer data in the ICustomerData interface, a new interface must be created. Therefore running programs that use a certain COM object are not affected when a software supplier wants to add more features. Client programs can continue to use the old COM objects or upgrade to the new ones.

COM objects actually run in something called a COM server. The server implements the methods provided by the various interfaces. The server also manages the list of function pointers by which the client uses the COM interfaces. A server must be started before a COM object can be used. One of the COM library's responsibilities is to start up such a server. (See Figure 1-1.)

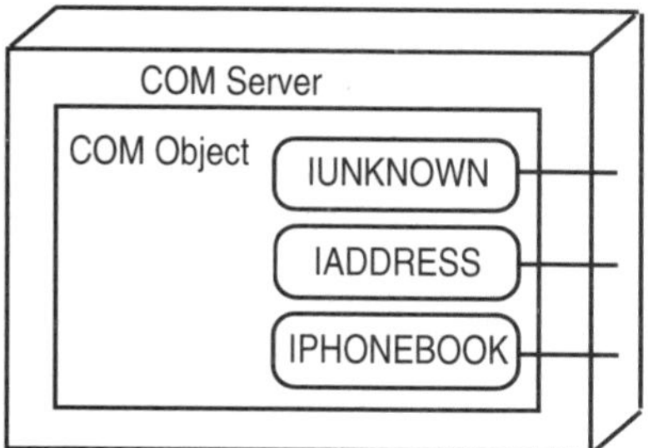

Figure 1-1: A COM object with its interfaces, running inside a COM server.

As I mentioned, many different technologies have been implemented using COM. The various types of technologies called OLE are among them, but Microsoft continues to base products upon this generalized object model, including ActiveX. First, a look at some of the technologies called OLE.

OLE: Object Linking & Embedding and Beyond

OLE was originally an acronym for Object Linking and Embedding. And, in the beginning, that's what it was: a way to embed an object, like an Excel spreadsheet, in a Microsoft Word document. Objects could not only be embedded, but linked. That is, changes to the original spreadsheet data would be reflected in the Word document. Microsoft has continued to improve OLE and add new functionality with each new version. Starting with OLE 2, Microsoft no longer referred to it as Object Linking and Embedding, but simply as OLE.

OLE

OLE 2 was evolving into a more generalized way to share software between various applications and systems, so the terms that defined the acronym and the version number were dropped. The technology is now simply called OLE. (Microsoft tried to encourage people to pronounce this like a word you would hear at a Spanish bullfight, but not everyone does. I heard a member of the Visual C++ team, quite knowledgeable about OLE, pronounce it many times by sounding out the individual letters: "O," "L," "E.")

OLE is thought to be complex, but it is also powerful. It is complex largely because of the vast number of services that it tries to provide. No longer simply Object Linking, some of the following technologies fall into this area of system software:

- OLE compound documents
- OLE Controls
- OLE Automation
- OLE Extended Messaging Applications Programming Interface

OLE compound document support is what was provided by OLE 1. The idea was that people could work with different applications, embed one inside the other, and work as if they were using a single application. OLE controls are the same as OCXs, a GUI element like a button or text box. The OLE control specification also required that the control provide its own user interface, let a container application request its properties (color or size for example), and have the ability to send events to which there could be response. This made them similar to VBXs. OLE Automation objects export macro primitives. Besides the areas previously listed, there's an OLE service in Windows 95 called the Rich Edit control, a type of dialog box that supports compound document capabilities.

The services simply illustrate the wide range of technologies that have been implemented on top of the Component Object Model. Each also has complexities that need to be understood by a developer using the technologies. Perhaps more interesting to the user of JavaBeans are the controls now called ActiveX, which I'll discuss next.

ActiveX: Formerly Known as OLE

Around the beginning of 1996, Microsoft began using the name ActiveX to "signify a technology with connections to the Internet or the World Wide Web" (David Chappell, in *Understanding ActiveX and OLE*). At the same time, Microsoft needed some technologies to compete in the developing field of the Web. Microsoft renamed OLE controls ActiveX. But ActiveX is not the same as OLE controls. The specification was simplified. At least, the qualifications for being an ActiveX control are fewer than for OLE controls.

As I mentioned in the section on OLE, an OLE control was required to have quite a bit of functionality. In the language of COM, it was required to implement several interfaces to fit the definition of an OLE control. It had to be able to draw its own user interface, produce events (similar to VBXs), and let a container application access its properties. ActiveX controls are only required to implement one interface (called IUnknown) and be able to register themselves—in the Windows system registry. Of course, the ActiveX specification describes how an ActiveX control can fire events, let a container get and set its properties, or display a user interface, but it is no longer required to.

The ActiveX specification was simplified primarily to shrink the size of ActiveX controls. Since ActiveX controls are meant to be downloaded on the Web (and connections can sometimes be slow), the often large code size of OLE controls would be a problem. ActiveX controls are limited to platforms that support Windows. (Windows 95 and Windows NT are supported as of this writing.)

OLE Naming: A Name Is a Name

As a note on naming, at first OLE referred to just Object Linking and Embedding; then it was applied to a whole range of different technologies. Now the term ActiveX refers to most things that were once OLE, and OLE now refers to Object Linking and Embedding, as it originally did. By the way, Java has no such identity crises in terms of its name. (It does, however, suffer occasionally from an overabundance of coffee metaphors.)

Distributed Components

I've glossed over a distinction in this discussion of component architectures. Components such as VBXs and the later OCXs essentially reside on one system. CORBA, which I'll discuss later in Chapter 1, and DCOM are distributed component architectures. These architectures provide facilities for the sharing of components between systems located on local or wide area networks. The CORBA specification in particular was designed with client/server systems in mind. CORBA's Object Request Broker (ORB) lets applications deal with objects transparently. To an application requesting an object to provide some service, it doesn't matter whether that object is found on a far away network server or on a local system.

One of the more popular client/server environments today is the World Wide Web. So, it's important that any component technology that is to work on the Web support the distribution of components across networks. Among the technologies we've looked at together, ActiveX fits this description. And JavaBeans, of course, was designed to be a distributed system from the ground up.

The key difference to the user is that older models like VBXs, which were often written in C, were specifically designed for Visual Basic (VB). Had Web browsers been available when Visual Basic 1 was introduced, there still would not have been a way to enliven your Web page with VBXs. This is not a fault of the technology; VBXs were just not designed as generalized distributed models.

In the intervening years between the introduction of VB and the current explosion of the Web, many technological developments have happened on the distributed component front. Microsoft created the COM model and based their OLE technologies on it. VBXs, now based on COM, became OCXs. Microsoft introduced a distributed version of COM (DCOM) in 1996. And CORBA has had the distribution of objects/components as a goal from the start.

CORBA

The Common Object Request Broker Architecture (CORBA) is a product of the Object Management Group (OMG), a consortium of over 650 companies. CORBA is an attempt to provide an industry standard *middleware* in client/server environments. Middleware refers to the software protocols between systems—it is sometimes called the Object Bus.

CORBA attempts all of the things we've talked about and more. It's an attempt to standardize the distribution of business objects between different operating systems and computers—on the same computer or across a network. Three things about CORBA are important to this overview:

- Interface Definition Language (IDL)
- Object Request Brokers (ORB)
- Internet Inter-ORB Protocol (IIOP)

The Interface Definition Language (IDL) acts as a contract between components and their clients. IDL is not coded in any particular programming language. In a C++ like syntax, it specifies the interfaces of a component and tells a component's clients what to expect. Once specified, an interface definition in IDL can be implemented in a number of languages; this makes no difference to the client using the services.

Object Request Brokers (ORBs) are the intermediaries that let CORBA-specified objects communicate among systems or across networks. The ORB works conceptually as an Object Bus, managing requests from one object to another, thereby providing transparency among different systems. If one object invokes a method on another, the ORB finds another object to satisfy the request. The other object might be on the same machine or across a network.

For client/server systems this means when a client application requests an object to perform a service, the ORB is responsible for finding that object (the object may reside on any number of servers). (See Figure 1-2.)

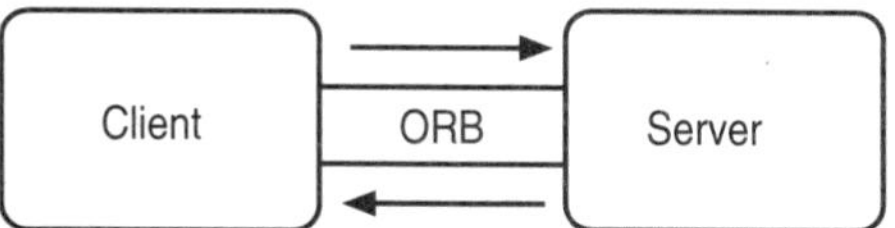

Figure 1-2: The CORBA ORB acts as an intermediary between clients and servers.

Of particular interest to users of Netscape is the Internet Inter-ORB Protocol, often called IIOP. This protocol can be viewed as an ORB specialized for the Internet. Netscape's support of this protocol will make the development of crossware that use CORBA services much easier. It will also make access to legacy systems and multi-platform databases possible.

Incidentally, the OMG doesn't implement the software to support CORBA. It solicits proposals from members of the consortium. Members submit proposals based upon existing technology. The consortium members represent a wide cross-section of the computer industry. Microsoft is not a member, but introduced a competing specification called the Distributed Component Object Model (DCOM) in 1996. DCOM provides the services of a CORBA ORB and has its own IDL.

JavaBeans

JavaBeans is a new component architecture from Sun Microsystems. The specification for JavaBeans was finalized in October 1996. Sun received the input of a number of other companies while developing JavaBeans. These companies included Novell, IBM, Apple, Sybase, Powersoft, Borland, and Symantec. Sun's goals for this project were to extend its 'write once, run anywhere' goal from Java to the world of components.

Unlike ActiveX (which was based upon COM/OLE and OCXs), JavaBeans was designed from the ground up to be a component model and to integrate well with Web pages and the Internet. JavaBeans's beginnings are reflected in its simplicity and cross-platform capabilities.

Simplicity

Notions of simplicity are somewhat subjective. People very familiar with a certain programming environment—whether a language, application program, or operating system—often find that language simple. There are some objective comparisons to be made between JavaBeans and ActiveX though. JavaBeans is simple because it is integrated with Java. A Java class that has public methods is already a JavaBean as is—albeit a bean that may not have much functionality.

This simplicity makes JavaBeans easier to learn it's always easier to learn something that builds upon what you already know. (I'm sure I'm not the first to discover this principle!) OLE and ActiveX, for example, require you to learn a whole new set of concepts, new interfaces, and a set of new macros for dealing with these interfaces. JavaBeans's new concepts are those of component software, and those are the same throughout all component architectures. JavaBeans does require you to become acquainted with the java.beans package, but this can be done gradually, and simple beans don't require a huge investment in learning new features. A Java class is already a bean. One cannot say the same about a simple class written in C++.

Cross-Platform

Java is cross-platform. Any computer that implements the Java virtual machine can run Java. Beans are written in Java; they are no different than Java classes, which makes beans portable anywhere Java is. Java is compiled into a platform-neutral form called bytecodes; then the bytecodes are interpreted by the Java virtual machine. Companies license the right to implement the virtual machine from Sun. The virtual machine has been implemented on Windows 95/NT, Macintosh, and Sun Solaris operating systems, as well as HP-UX (a Hewlett-Packard operating system).

Beans have all the characteristics of the component architectures we've been talking about: they implement properties, methods, and events, and they run in any environment. There are now bridges to other component technologies—a bridge to ActiveX is available, with other bridges to follow—that will let JavaBeans interoperate with other component architectures. The Java IDL project is well on its way to making Java interoperate with CORBA. And Netscape's support of JavaBeans and CORBA's IIOP is here now.

Currently, there are a few ways to write ActiveX controls (Visual Basic, C++), but only one way to run them: Windows. ActiveX runs under Windows (95/NT); porting to other environments, like the Macintosh, was predicted in late 1996. Microsoft is in the operating systems business, so they have much more impetus to add extensions to ActiveX controls that optimize performance for their operating systems than they do to make them 'write once, run anywhere.'

In addition to being limited to Microsoft operating systems, ActiveX has also been criticized for its lack of security. ActiveX controls can operate outside the 'sandbox,' letting them write to a local disk (for example) after being downloaded from the Internet.

Netscape & JavaBeans

Netscape has announced its support for JavaBeans. This means that JavaBeans will be supported in various Netscape products such as Communicator and Enterprise Server. Perhaps more importantly, Netscape is committed to supporting JavaBeans in the future. The JavaBeans architecture fits in well with Netscape's vision of "Crossware Applications for the Networked Enterprise."

End users and developers can look forward to support in Netscape products for pre-packaged and home-grown JavaBeans. Netscape also will make services available as JavaBeans. Netscape views JavaBeans as delivering some of the same functionality as Visual Basic (building applications with components), but extending this model to the Internet. Some of the roles Netscape has in mind for JavaBeans are:

- Services in Communicator 4.0, such as the mail service, and messaging will be implemented as JavaBeans.
- Remote services across intranets or the Internet will be accessed with JavaBeans. For example, the Netscape Directory Server lets developers access its functions via a JavaBean.
- All services that are made available as JavaBeans will be usable as drag-and-drop components from application builder tools such as Netscape's own Visual JavaScript.
- CORBA services that are turned into Beans can be used in Visual JavaScript and other builder tools.
- JavaBean use will break up into two main areas: client-side Beans like Charts and GUI elements, and server-side Beans for features such as remote database access. (See Figure 1-3.)
- JavaScript will let the developer create 'objects' that will be usable like JavaBeans in Visual JavaScript. These components created in JavaScript are called JavaScript Beans (JSBs).

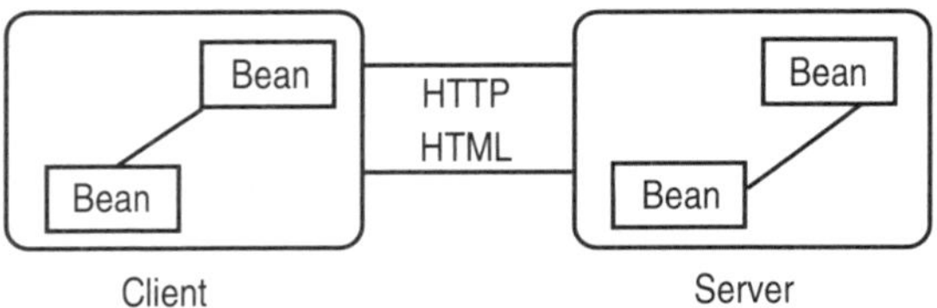

Figure 1-3: JavaBeans running on a client application and on a back-end server.

So, there will be a tight integration between the existing Netscape ONE tools such as HTML, Java, JavaScript, Netscape plug-ins, and JavaBeans. Users should be able to leverage their previous knowledge of Java and JavaScript to easily create crossware applications.

Moving On

I covered a lot of ground about component software in this chapter. Let's take a look at the topics reviewed here.

I reviewed the history of programming languages and showed how developments in languages often came about to manage complexity. The review covered everything from machine language to object-oriented languages. You then learned that components can be viewed as the next logical step in managing complexity.

Components have the following features: properties, methods, and events. Publishing, customization, and persistence are other services provided by component architectures. I reviewed some real-life component architectures and discussed distributed components like CORBA as well as Netscape's support of CORBA IIOP.

That brought us to JavaBeans. JavaBeans was designed from the ground up to be a component architecture and to be 'Internet-aware.' You then saw how Netscape plans to integrate JavaBeans into its plans for crossware, both now and in the future.

In the next chapter, I'll take a first look at JavaBeans. The focus will be on how JavaBeans implements the typical component features discussed in this chapter. We'll also look at the Java code for a simple bean.

JavaBeans, First Look

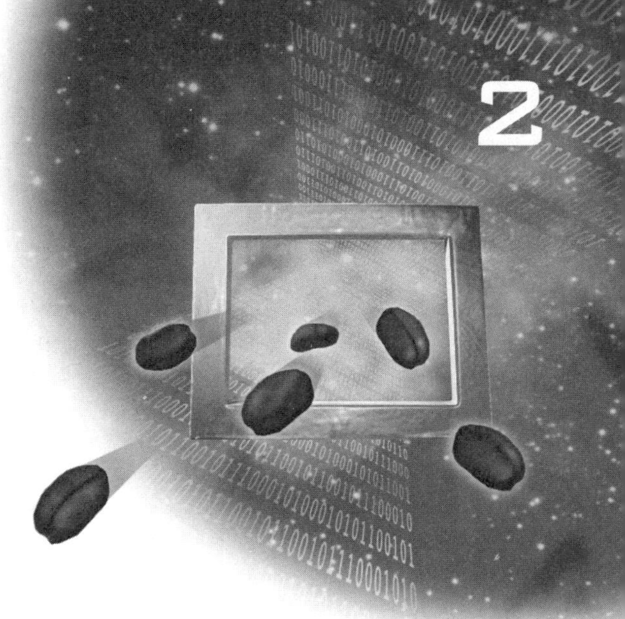

Chapter 1 presented a high-level look at software components and their architectures. Now you're ready to see how these features are implemented in JavaBeans. I'll start with general information about JavaBeans, why they are useful, and why Netscape supports them. After a review of properties, methods, and events, I'll describe how JavaBeans implements these features. Chapter 2 also describes Java 1.1's new delegation event model, because the firing and responding to events is so important to JavaBeans—and to software components in general. This section contains some code examples for beans.

This chapter includes a fair level of detail but can't include everything. For example, the JavaBeans extended support for properties (such as bound and constrained properties, and a more comprehensive view of events) will be given more detailed treatment in later chapters.

What Is JavaBeans?

JavaBeans is a component architecture from Sun Microsystems that is written in and works with Java. (See Chapter 1 for a quick overview of JavaBeans software components and component architectures.) JavaBeans is really a component architecture for the Internet. Java already has wide applicability to the Internet (as well as being a stand-alone programming language). It was a natural extension to the language to add the ability to use Java classes as building blocks for application development that could be designed, developed, and packaged as individual components.

The JavaBeans specification was written in 1996 and released in early 1997. Its release was concurrent with the release of the new version of Java—Java 1.1 (or JDK 1.1). JavaBeans is intimately connected with certain new features of Java 1.1; among these are the *core reflection mechanism* and the new 1.1 event model, which I'll describe later in this chapter.

TIP

The JavaBeans API is contained in a new package, introduced in Java 1.1, called java.beans.

Why Use JavaBeans?

You might want to use JavaBeans for these reasons:

- To develop a client-side Java application rapidly from interchangeable building blocks.
- To link up various features in a Web page that are difficult to link up with applets.
- To use application services made available as JavaBeans, such as CORBA IIOP services, directory, or mail services.
- To leverage your knowledge of Java and Java applets to develop crossware applications.

JavaBeans integrates well with existing Internet standards such as HTML, HTTP, and many client-side Web browsers. Another category of JavaBeans called Enterprise JavaBeans works on the server side or in three-tier applications (where a Web server needs to access a back-end database). And JavaBeans has the support of a tool vendor that is dedicated to open systems, Netscape.

TIP

Sun's Web page at java.sun.com is a good resource for all kinds of information about Java and JavaBeans. One general URL that has information about JavaBeans is http://java.sun.com/beans. As well as JavaBeans information, this URL has links to topics such as JDBC, AWT name changes, how to upgrade from JDK 1.0, Java serialization support, and the Jar compiler specification.

Netscape & JavaBeans

Netscape's vision of crossware applications meshes well with a cross-platform component model. After all, components are cross-platform building blocks, and Netscape's goals are strongly related to creating applications that can cooperate over intranets and the Internet without regard to the operating systems the clients and servers are using.

Netscape's existing solution for developers of intranet/Internet crossware applications is called Netscape Open Network Environment (Netscape ONE). Java has been an important component of Netscape ONE from its beginning (the IFC is written in Java, for example).

Some of the features of Netscape ONE include:

- HTML
- Java
- JavaScript
- CORBA support
- Netscape plug-ins

JavaBeans support is a natural addition to Netscape ONE. JavaBeans fits in well with the HTML, Java, JavaScript model. JavaBeans is supported in Netscape Communicator, and Communicator support such as the mail service will be available for use as a JavaBean. Visual JavaScript and Netscape's Component Development Kit (CDK)—described later in the book—will allow easy integration of HTML, Java, Java applets, JavaScript objects and components, and JavaBeans.

Component Architecture Features

The JavaBean architecture lets you base your component development upon a Java class. In fact, if you give a Java class some public methods, it already meets the minimal requirements of a bean. A bean is first and foremost a Java class. Now, let's reiterate the features of component architectures discussed in Chapter 1.

- **Properties.** These are attributes that you can use to affect the color or icon of a button component, for example.
- **Methods.** These provide an interface, sometimes standard or 'expected,' to properties and other features.
- **Events.** These are the means of linking components together.

- **Publishing.** This is the method by which component properties, methods, and events are readable by a containing application.
- **Graphical Editing.** These are the capabilities that affect the appearance of a component in a graphical user interface.
- **Customization.** In addition to graphical editing, there may be a way to affect the properties or events of a component via a programming language.
- **Persistence.** This is the ability to save a component, possibly with some of its surrounding *context*.

Components & Code Libraries

Conceptually, using a component is similar in some ways to using a function from a library—whether in a procedural or object-oriented language. Libraries can be used in many different programs, are often written by someone else, have an interface for you to learn, and don't require you to learn their internals. Ideally, components can be used more easily and mixed-and-matched better than libraries because they aren't tightly bound, may be graphically edited, and can be linked up at 'design-time' with other components.

JavaBeans, being a respectable model for building components, supplies classes, interfaces, and conventions that provide all of the features just mentioned. Let's get better acquainted with JavaBeans by looking at how it implements all the typical component features.

How JavaBeans Supports Properties

Properties are implemented by defining member variables. To conform with the conventions of JavaBeans, though, it isn't enough to just define a member variable. A builder tool like Visual JavaScript (or a container like the BeanBox in Chapter 3) must have a way to discover this member variable to find out about it. You must publish the property. The easiest way to do this is to follow what JavaBeans calls *design patterns*. These are really a naming convention that parts of the JavaBeans specification follow.

Design Patterns: the Concept

There is a topic called 'design patterns' that has been making the rounds of the software development community for the past few years. Design patterns is an attempt to understand and document the design of object-oriented systems by cataloging a series of patterns that often occur. JavaBeans's design patterns are a convention for naming methods. Perhaps a better name would have been 'naming conventions.'

For example, you're building a simple component, and you want to let a builder tool access its color. You create a Java class, and you define a member variable in this class named "color." You then provide two methods: getColor( ) to access the color property, and setColor( ) to set the color property. If the builder tool has been designed correctly, it will have no trouble discovering that your component has a property called color. Listing 2-1 defines a class called aSimpleBean with one property named color.

Listing 2-1: aSimpleBean with one property named color.

```
class aSimpleBean extends Canvas {
    private Color color;
    public Color getColor()
    {
        return color;
    }
    public void setColor(Color aColor)
    {
        Color = aColor;
    }
}
```

The preceding class fits the definition of a bean. It also would be a visible bean—will have a screen representation in a GUI—since it has been derived from the AWT class Canvas.

Reflection Versus Introspection

The JavaBeans specification often refers to the reflection API and the introspection API. These are both ways of discovering the properties and events a bean supports. Reflection usually refers to the design pattern approach. Introspection usually refers to the overall process of analysis, or sometimes the analysis using the BeanInfo interface (which I'll discuss later).

Now that you've gotten an idea of how the JavaBeans architecture supports properties, let's look at how it supports events.

How JavaBeans Supports Events

In Java 1.1, Java's handling of events has been rewritten from a new point of view. This new way of dealing with events is called a *delegation* model, since the handling of events is delegated to certain objects called event *listeners*.

Why did the creators of Java want to change the way events behaved? Well, in their wisdom, they examined how events were implemented in 1.0, and there they saw imperfection. So first let's talk about how you 'did events' the old way and examine previous problems.

Java 1.0 Event Model

The old event model was based upon inheritance. That is, you were required to override certain methods in order to manage events. The methods you overrode most often were one of the following:

```
boolean action (Event evt, Object what);
boolean handleEvent(Event evt);
```

Also, there were other specialized methods in class component that broke out some of the event functionality into separate methods. (These are sometimes called convenience methods.) For example, the following methods handled mouse events:

```
boolean mouseUp()
boolean mouseDown()
boolean mouseMove()
boolean mouseDrag()
```

Return values could be a source of confusion in Java 1.0. All of action( ), handleEvent( ), and the convenience methods for the mouse and key strokes return Boolean values. These Boolean return values have a special meaning to event processing.

In this model, when you are finished processing an event in your event method, you return 'true' to say you're done with that event. If the event is not handled at all (or is only partially handled), you return 'false' to let the event propagate to the superclass (often the container holding your GUI elements).

For Windows SDK Programmers

Processing events with handleEvent( ) under Java 1.0 will be familiar to anyone who has programmed using the Windows Software Development Kit (SDK). Checking event Ids with a large switch statement and the returning of Boolean values are similar to code required with the SDK. (In Windows one usually returned false to say an event had been handled and called a function (DefWindowProc( )) otherwise.)

Another peculiarity of the inheritance-based model was that only components could respond to events (the code to respond was firmly in the class of some component); the new approach has no such restriction.

The inheritance approach led to two modes of dealing with the events in your program. You could:

1. Handle events by declaring your own subclasses of a component, such as a subclass of Button which handles its own events by overriding an action( ) method.
2. Override Component.handleEvent( ) and process all events in there with a switch statement.

Listing 2-2 is an example of handling events by declaring a subclass (approach 1 above). The example is an applet that adds two buttons to itself and responds to events from the buttons by overriding the action( ) method.

Listing 2-2: Handling events by declaring a subclass.

```
import java.awt.*;
import java.applet.*;
class RedButton extends Button
{
       RedButton()
       {
        this.setLabel("Red");
        this.setBackground(new Color(255,0,0 ));
        }
} // RedButton
class YellowButton extends Button
{
        YellowButton()
        {
        this.setLabel("Yellow");
        this.setBackground(Color.yellow);
        }
```

```
} // YellowButton
public class BigApplet extends Applet
{
    public void init()
    {
        RedButton aRedButton = new RedButton();
        YellowButton aYellowButton = new YellowButton();
        add(aRedButton);
        add(aYellowButton);
    } // init

    public boolean action(Event evt, Object what)
   {
        if (what == "Red"){
        System.out.println("Red button pressed.");
        return true;
        }
        else if (what == "Yellow"){
        System.out.println("Yellow button pressed.");
        return true;
        }
        return false;
        }
} // BigApplet
```

Note that once you've received the action event, you still must compare the button label to a string to identify the button with which you're dealing.

Now that you've seen how action events were handled, let's see an example of handling events by overriding handleEvent( ). The following example creates a frame, then adds a button to it. It uses handleEvent( ) to do all its event handling, including the processing of the button click. See Listing 2-3.

Listing 2-3: An example of handling events by overriding handleEvent( ).

```
import java.awt.*;
class MyButton extends Button
{
    MyButton()
    {
     setLabel("FooBar");
    }
}
public class EventFrame extends Frame
{
    EventFrame()
    {
```

```
 setSize(250, 345);
 setVisible(true);
}
public static void main (String argv[])
{
    EventFrame app = new EventFrame();

    MyButton aButton = new MyButton();

    app.add(aButton);
    aButton.move(100, 50);
    aButton.setSize(75, 40);
}

public boolean handleEvent(Event evt)
{
    if (evt.id == Event.ACTION_EVENT)
    {
     System.out.println("Received an action \Event from a button!");
     return true;
    }
    else if (evt.id == Event.MOUSE_DOWN)
    {
     System.out.println("was a mouse down Event!");
         return true;
    }
    else if (evt.id == Event.WINDOW_DESTROY)
    {
            System.out.println("Window destroy event!");
        return true;
    }
    return false; // let superclasses process
 }
 } // EventFrame
```

So these were the ways to handle events in Java 1.0. Let's try to summarize the problems with the old approach:

- Having to return true and false is difficult and a possible source of errors. Maintaining large switch statements is error prone.
- Events are broadcast to all components or containers, not just those who are interested.
- Bugs could be introduced if you forgot to return true or false at the right time.

Let's look at Java 1.1's delegation event handling in more detail to see how it works and how it solves these problems.

Java 1.1 Event Model

In Java 1.1 events, an object is either a source or a listener. Events are implemented by the event source calling a target method on the event listener. The event object becomes a parameter to the method in the event listener. Now other objects besides subclasses of Component can be listeners. Also, events are no longer broadcast everywhere to every component in the hierarchy. Figure 2-1 shows an event source.

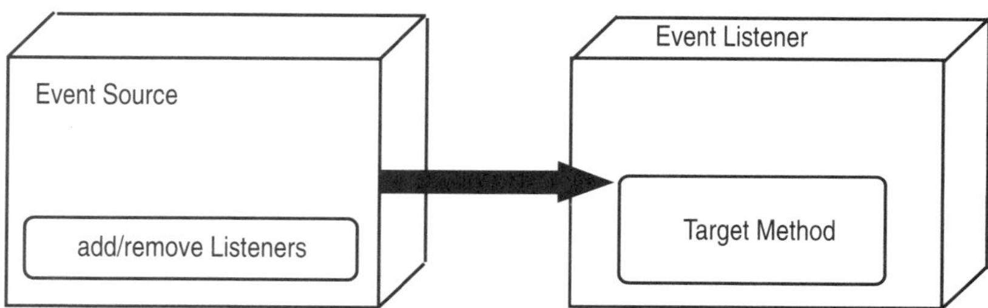

Figure 2-1: This drawing shows an event source (the box at left) and an event listener. The line between them shows the event being fired.

How does the event source get hooked up with the event listener? The event listener advertises its intention to listen for events of a particular type. This is done by registration. First, the listener object implements an EventListener interface. The EventListener interfaces define methods with certain signatures. There are a number of EventListener interfaces in the Java library.

For example, if Class A wishes to respond to an action event, it implements the ActionListener interface. ActionListener contains a method with a *signature*: actionPerformed( ). The programmer then overrides the actionPerformed( ) method and codes what he 'wants to do' in response to the action event. To link up Class A to a source of action events (say, a button), the programmer passes the event listener to the button's addActionListener( ) method.

TIP

A method signature is a method with an expected or specified number and type of parameters, a specified return type, and possibly a name that conforms to a naming scheme.

New Event Classes

In JDK 1.0 event objects were represented by the java.awt.Event class. Now there are all sorts of classes to represent events. Before, you had to check the Event.id field in the event class (to get the type of event), then perhaps check another argument to see which object had sent the event. (Recall our example where we checked the label string for a button.) Having a bunch of event classes available makes checking Ids unnecessary in most cases.

Having Your Id Checked May Be OK

Sun has tried to provide a balance between defining a class for every type of event on the one hand, and having one big Event class on the other. Thus some of the events have been aggregated in a single event class. The class mouseEvent handles mouseUp and mouseDown, for example. How does one distinguish between mouseUp and mouseDown? By checking Ids.

Let's summarize some concrete steps to hook up an event source to an event listener:

1. Subclass (using the 'implements clause') the EventListener interface for the type of event you're interested in. The EventListener interfaces define empty methods with predefined signatures to handle events.
2. Implement the appropriate empty method. Stick the code to respond to the event into this method.
3. Pass an instance of your interface to the addABCListener( ) method for the component with which you are interested in registering. Many 1.1 components already have addABCListener( ) methods declared. For example, class Button has an addActionListener( ) method defined.

Listing 2-4 is an example of hooking up a source and a listener; it links a button with an ActionListener.

Listing 2-4: An example of hooking up a source and a listener.

```
import java.awt.event.*;
import java.awt.*;
import java.applet.*;
class AButtonListener implements ActionListener {
    public "void" actionPerformed(ActionEvent evt)
    {
        System.out.println("Button pressed!");
    }
} // class

public class ButtonApplet extends Applet
{
    public void init()
     {
        Button aButton = new Button("Press");
        add(aButton);
        aButton.addActionListener(new AButtonListener());
    } // init

} // ButtonApplet
```

Here I've declared a class AButtonListener that implements the ActionListener interface. The listener is associated with the button by the statement:

```
aButton.addActionListener(new AButtonListener());
```

It would have been possible to have the applet class, "ButtonApplet," implement the ActionListener interface directly. In that case, the statement to add the listener to the button would be:

```
aButton.addActionListener(this);
```

The keyword "this" would refer to an object of the ButtonApplet class, which would be a listener (and also an applet).

Publishing

In JavaBeans, there are two ways for beans to publish their properties and events. The first, in JavaBeans lingo, uses something called the reflection API. Basically, a builder tool or container application needs to be able to present a list of properties and events to the user. Then the builder can interact with these properties and events in order to customize the component, for example. So the properties and events of the bean need to be discovered. The low-level reflection API makes this discovery possible.

Reflection makes use of the design patterns for properties and events already discussed. If you've followed the getABC( ), setABC( ) convention, Java's low-level analysis can discover that your bean has a property called ABC. It's important to mention that the internal name of ABC doesn't matter. That is, the internal name of the ABC could be m_ABC, for example, and the reflection process would still see the name as ABC.

More About Interfaces

Java *interfaces* are used quite a bit when developing JavaBeans. An interface is a class with empty methods that acts as a specification for classes that 'implement' it. The methods of the interface have no implementation, and the implementation must be provided in any class that subclasses or implements the interface.

I mentioned a second way to publish properties and events; that is, to create a class that implements the BeanInfo interface. The BeanInfo interface lets you supply information about properties, methods, and events. It has methods that return information in array-like form for properties, methods, and events. A builder application that uses JavaBeans, like Visual JavaScript, can use the BeanInfo object to discover this information about a bean.

In fact, the Beans specification specifies that a routine introspection process first begins by asking for a BeanInfo object named XYZBeanInfo (for class named XYZ), and if found, the information about properties, methods, and events is used. The introspection process continues with the low-level reflection method if the search for a BeanInfo fails or if one of the BeanInfo methods returns null (null means no information available). BeanInfos can also be used to supply locale-dependent information.

BeanInfo & JavaScript

The BeanInfo interface will be of particular interest to users of Visual JavaScript (Visual JavaScript is discussed in Chapter 7). Visual JavaScript requires that you supply a BeanInfo class for your beans; in other words, its low-level reflection ability is limited (as of this writing).

Graphical Editing

JavaBeans can be viewed graphically. Not all JavaBeans need to be visible, but many of them are. In Visual JavaScript, beans are displayed as icons in the palette window; when you drag a visible bean from the palette to an HTML document, you will see a visual representation.

Why would you want to develop an invisible component? Invisible beans would be particularly suited for performing a computational function or sending queries to a database in the background, for example.

Customization

JavaBeans provides support for customizers that can be used at design-time to provide an automated ability to design beans. The PropertyEditor interface in the java.beans package provides a type of customization by letting a builder environment customize a bean during design time. You'll see examples of a property editor in Chapter 3, when we talk about the BeanBox.Persistence.

Chief among the goals of the JavaBeans designers has been to let individual JavaBeans be saved, or to persist in an easy, straightforward way. The key to the notion of persistence is that a component is saved, or stored away, with some of its context. The context includes any modifications, such as changes in color or size, that may have been done by a developer while designing in a builder environment. Persistence will be covered in better detail in Chapter 11.

Simple Beans

Let's use what we've learned, especially the knowledge about properties and events, to code some simple beans. Listing 2-5 is the first example bean. You might call it the simplest bean. It has one property.

Listing 2-5: The first example bean.

```
import java.awt.*;
import java.beans.*;
import java.awt.event.*;

public class MyFirstBean extends Canvas
{

        private Color color;
        public MyFirstBean()
        {
```

```
        resize (60, 50); // make sure the bean is large enough
        color = new Color(255, 0,0); // instantiate a color: 'red'
        setBackground(color); // give the bean a red background
    }

public Color getColor()
{
    return color;
}

public void setColor(Color inputColor)
{
color = inputColor;
}

}
```

This example is almost the same as our Listing 2-1, class aSimpleBean. Class MyFirstBean has one property of type Color, called color. It provides a minimal interface to that property, that is by way of the setColor and getColor methods. The setSize( ) method has been called to make sure the bean is big enough to be visible. Since this bean is derived from class Canvas, it will appear as a rectangle on the screen.

This bean could be viewed as is in a container application. It could be loaded into the BeanBox—the container application described in the next chapter—right now, and it would be added to the ToolBox window. (Actually, we would have to archive this bean into a Jar file using a make file first. But we'll get into all of that in Chapter 3.)

The key thing I want you to realize is that we really have created our 'first bean.' Let's not lose sight of how easy it was. We did four things:

- Created a Java class using our previous knowledge of Java classes.
- Derived our new class from an existing class in the AWT, a class whose main use was to give us visual representation.
- Provided a constructor, which looks no different than other constructors.
- Provided two public methods, which give access to an instance variable.

And we now have a fully usable bean that could be migrated around the world via a network, used in other desktop applications far away in space and time, and appreciated by people we have never met.

Well, before we become totally overcome by our success, we have to admit that this bean doesn't do much—yet. But it meets the specifications for a bean, a reusable component, and you used only your previous knowledge of Java and a few new facts to create it.

For the next example, let's take this bean and give it the means to link up with other beans. Let's have it respond to action events and change its color by pressing a button. First, we need a listener. Let's have our class FirstBean implement the ActionListener interface directly. Then we can implement the actionPerformed( ) method. See Listing 2-6.

Listing 2-6: Taking a bean and giving it the means to link up with other beans.

```
public class MyFirstBean extends Canvas implements ActionListener
{
    private Color color;
    public MyFirstBean()
    {
        setSize (60, 50); // make sure the bean is large enough
        color = new Color(255, 0,0); // instantiate a color: 'red'
    setBackground(color); // give the bean a red background
    }


    public Color getColor()
    {
    return color;
    }

    public void setColor(Color inputColor)
    {
     color = inputColor;
    }
    public void actionPerformed(ActionEvent evt)
    {
        setColor(Color.green);

        repaint();
    }

}
```

Now that the preceding bean implements the ActionListener interface, it can easily be connected to a source of action events, such as a button. A code fragment that creates a button and adds MyFirstBean as an action listener is as follows:

```
Button button = new Button("Change Color");
button.addActionListener(MyFirstBean);
```

Let's move on to the similarities between applets and beans.

Applets & Beans: The Similarities

It's one of the interesting features of the JavaBeans specification that applets and beans aren't too far apart. In the next chapter we'll see the Juggler Bean, which is actually an animation applet. Also, applets can load beans. The Beans Development Kit provides a wrapper class—an applet that loads a bean and displays it. So an applet can act as a simple bean *container*. (We'll talk about containers in the next chapter.) To create an applet that loads a bean, we need to make use of a class loader. We can write such an applet ourselves as follows (see Listing 2-7 and Figure 2-2):

Listing 2-7: Creating an applet that loads a bean.

```
import java.applet.*;
import java.awt.*;
import java.beans.*;

public class BeanLoaderApplet extends Applet
{
    private String beanName;
    private Component aBean;

    public void init()
    {
        //get the bean name from an HTML file
        beanName = getParameter("BEANNAME");
        try
        {
            ClassLoader cLoader = this.getClass().getClassLoader();
            aBean = (Component)Beans.instantiate(cLoader, beanName);
        }
        catch (Exception e)
        {
            System.out.println("Can't load bean " + e);
        }
    }

    public void start()
    {
        removeAll();
        add(aBean);

    } // start

}
```

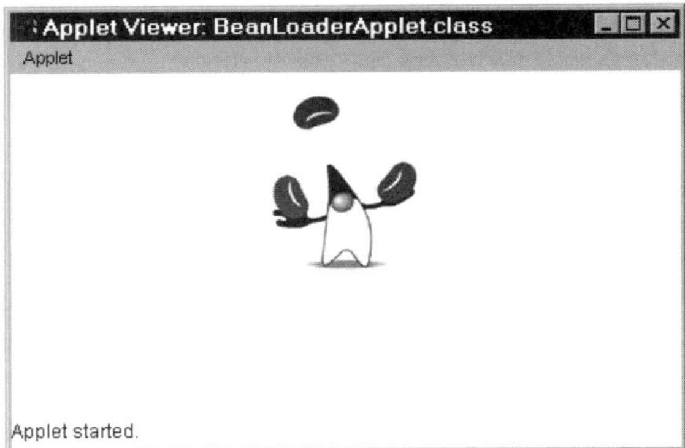

Figure 2-2: The Loader applet displaying the Juggler Bean, running in the applet viewer.

Moving On

This chapter gave you a first look at JavaBeans. I reviewed the features that are expected from a component architecture, then tied it in to how JavaBeans provides these features. It's necessary to work with the delegation event model in JavaBeans, so I explained it in some detail.

Then you saw the code for your first bean, starting simply with a bean with a color property. I added an actionPerformed( ) method that would let the bean respond to action events.

Finally I showed you the relationship between applets and beans and wrote a simple wrapper applet that would load a bean. This applet read the bean's name from a parameter in an HTML file.

In order to develop your own JavaBeans, Netscape recommends that you use Sun's Beans Development Kit (BDK). The next chapter looks at the BDK and the BeanBox, a simple container application that will let you view and work with beans.

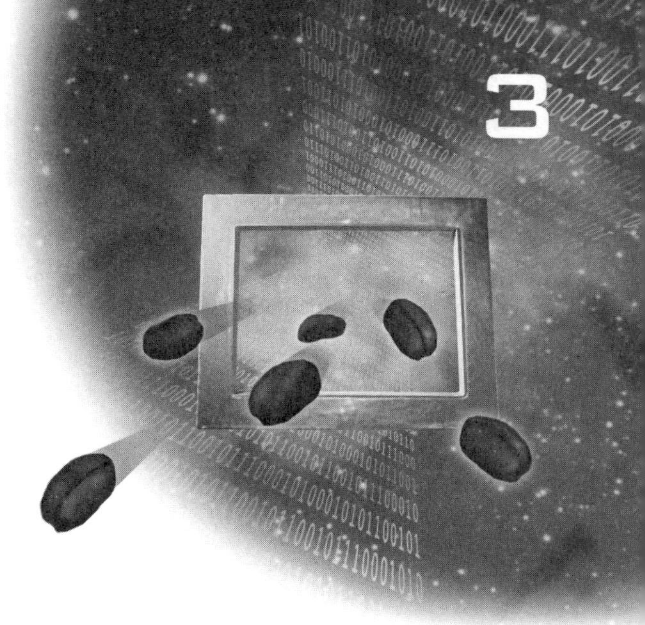

3 The Beans Development Kit

Netscape recommends that you use Sun's Beans Development Kit (BDK) to develop beans. This chapter discusses what's in the BDK and how to use it. It also demonstrates some of the example beans that come with the BDK.

What Is the BDK?

The BDK is a group of Java tools from Sun Microsystems that lets the developer create beans. The BDK contains the java.beans package and its documentation, a sample bean container called the BeanBox, example beans, and the BeanBox tutorial. To develop your own beans, you need the BDK and the Java Development Kit (JDK 1.1 or later). Netscape recommends that you use the BDK to develop beans since they have no development environment to create beans.

TIP

Visual JavaScript lets you use beans; therefore, it is a bean container. It doesn't, however, contain a Java compiler, and thus doesn't let you compile beans.

The example beans come in source file (.JAVA) and Java archive (.Jar) file format. The examples can be studied to learn how to write a bean, and they also act as a demonstration of how the various classes in the java.beans package can be used. In this chapter, I use some of the example beans to demonstrate the

BeanBox's behavior. The BeanBox can load new beans that you've written as well. I give an example of that in the section, "Loading New Beans Into the BeanBox."

TIP

Where to Find the Examples: The source code for the example beans can be found in the directory c:\bdk\demo\sunw\demo, if you've installed the BDK in the directory c:\bdk.

Compiling & Running Code With JDK 1.1

To get you up and running using the Java Development Kit (JDK 1.1), this section introduces an example Java application, BeanHello, and some notes about how to compile and run it. BeanHello is a stand-alone Java application, rather than a Java applet.

NOTE

Setting up the system (installing the javac.exe compiler and the BDK) has been covered in the introduction. This section assumes you've installed the compiler and the BDK. Additionally, you may be using JDK 1.2 by the time you read this. This section is general enough to apply to that environment, too.

Listing 3-1 is a stand-alone Java program that uses the Abstract Window Toolkit (AWT) Frame class to display a window on the screen. After creating a new Frame (in the variable helloWindow), we make it visible and set its size using the new 1.1 setSize method. In Windows this will display a standard frame or overlapped window with the string "Hello JavaBeans!" in the title bar.

To compile Listing 3-1, use the javac.exe compiler by typing the javac command with the name of the file as a parameter. You may have to start a DOS session in Windows 95 and get to the DOS prompt if you're not already there. Type: **C:>javac BeanHello.java**

After the file has compiled with no errors, run the program with the command: java BeanHello.

This command runs java.exe, the java interpreter. Figure 3-1 is a shot of the frame window with the text, "Hello JavaBeans" in the frame's title bar.

Type in Listing 3-1 using a text editor, and save it to a file named BeanHello.java.

Listing 3-1: A stand-alone Java program that uses the AWT Frame class to display a window onscreen.

```
import java.awt.*;

public class BeanHello {

    BeanHello ()
    {
        Frame helloWindow = new Frame("Hello, JavaBeans!");
        helloWindow.setVisible(true);
        helloWindow.setSize(350, 200);
    }
    public static void main (String [] argv )
    {
        BeanHello app = new BeanHello();
    }

}
```

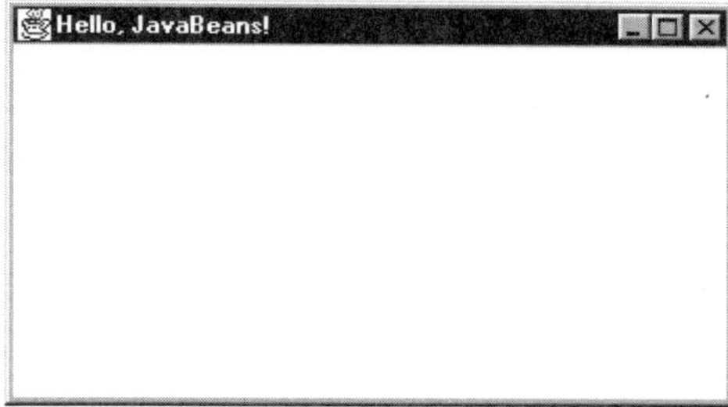

Figure 3-1: The BeanHello frame window running in the java interpreter.

NOTE

The .JAVA extension is required when compiling source files with javac. No .CLASS extension is provided on the command line when running java.exe.

Example Beans

This section describes the example beans that come with the BDK 1.0. Each bean provides an example of a feature of the JavaBeans API or shows a recommended approach to accomplishing a particular task. For example, some beans demonstrate bound properties, and some contain recommended approaches to making a bean persistent. The list I've provided is amplified with descriptions of what concepts are best demonstrated by the particular bean.

- **BeanBox.** The BeanBox container itself. It can be nested inside another parent BeanBox. The source code for this example provides a good demonstration of how to write a container.
- **Quote Monitor.** Generates Remote Method Invocation (RMI) on a remote server.
- **JellyBean.** A bean with an ICON, a bound property named "color," and a constrained property "priceInCents."
- **Juggler.** An animation. The animation can be stopped and started with an action event. This is a good example of how to call a target method.
- **ChangeReporter.** A text window that 'reports' changes to bound properties.
- **TickTock.** An invisible bean that fires a PropertyChangeEvent at intervals.
- **Voter.** Processes vetoableChange events. It can veto changes to constrained properties in another bean.
- **Molecule.** A 3-D molecule display. Molecule demonstrates a custom Property Editor.
- **OrangeButton.** An orange button. Implemented as a serialized object.
- **OurButton.** A subclass of java.awt.Canvas that acts as a button. Good example of a bean that fires an action event and targets the actionPerformed( ) method.
- **BlueButton.** A button that demonstrates serialization.
- **ExplicitButton.** A button with a BeanInfo class.
- **JDBC Select.** Runs a SQL Select statement on a remote database.
- **SorterBean.** A bean that demonstrates a few sorting algorithms, this bean is also an applet.
- **Bridge Tester.** Demonstrates how to use many different types of properties.
- **TransitionalBean.** A simple bean that only uses the features of JDK version 1.0.2.
- **EventMonitor.** Monitors all events from a source bean. This shows how one bean can analyze another.

Sun's BeanBox Tools

There are several terms to describe tools that let you view and develop with JavaBeans (as well as other components types). Containers, beanboxes, and builder tools all describe software environments that let you load, view graphically, change, link up, and save beans. Sun's BeanBox and Visual JavaScript both meet this specification. This chapter uses the Sun BeanBox to illustrate beanbox tools.

TIP

Using the terminology from Chapter 2, a beanbox tool needs to be able to perform introspection on a bean, whether with a low-level analysis or through searching for a BeanInfo class.

Sun provides the BeanBox as a simple container application in the BDK 1.0. It is not intended to be a full development environment. It doesn't implement everything that would be implemented in a full-blown application builder. Sun hopes that people will test their beans with this container to see if they meet the JavaBeans specification.

BeanBox Is a Reference Container

Sun calls the BeanBox a *reference* container. A reference application is usually most needed when a product is new and other development environments aren't yet available. It provides a 'reference' of how the technology is supposed to behave.

You can run the BeanBox, which is provided in source form as well as class file format in the BDK 1.0 by starting a DOS window in Win 95, changing to the c:\bdk\beanbox directory, and typing **run**. This command invokes run.bat, which sets up the CLASSPATH and then runs the BeanBox application. When the BeanBox application appears (it takes as long as 30 seconds on my 50 MHz PC!), the following windows will be displayed: ToolBox window, BeanBox window, and Property Sheet window. These are the windows you'll be interacting with when using the BeanBox. Let's take a closer look at each of them.

TIP

I'm assuming that you've installed the software in a directory named bdk, c:\bdk, for example. If you haven't set up your directory structure that way, make allowances in these directions for how your system is set up.

ToolBox Window

The ToolBox window contains a list of the currently available beans. These beans can be dragged from the ToolBox to the BeanBox main window. The current beans are loaded into the ToolBox from Jar files in the jar directory c:\bdk\jars. Figure 3-2 shows the ToolBox with the list of beans from the BDK.

Figure 3-2: The ToolBox with its list of example beans.

BeanBox Window

This is the main window for the BeanBox container application. The main interactions with beans—dragging them around, resizing, or hooking up with other beans—take place here. When you select a bean in this window, it will have a black border around it. The menus change to reflect the currently selected bean. Once you have dragged a bean from the ToolBox and selected it, choose Edit | Events to see what events the bean supports. It is interesting to note that the BeanBox window is itself a bean (you can see its name in the ToolBox). Therefore BeanBox windows can actually be nested inside of one another. (See Figure 3-3.)

Figure 3-3: The main BeanBox window is where you work with beans after dragging them from the ToolBox.

Property Sheet Window

This window is a type of property editor. It shows properties available in the selected bean. You are also allowed to click on properties and change them. A drop-down list lets you select from various property choices, a new color for example. (See Figure 3-4.)

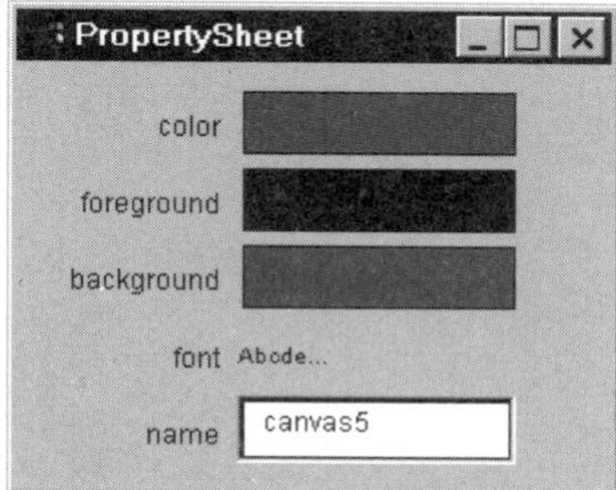

Figure 3-4: The Property Sheet window.

Using the BeanBox

You can test a bean with the BeanBox by dragging the bean from the ToolBox to the BeanBox window. You can then click on the bean to select it. Then, selecting from the Edit menu lets you see the events for the bean. Two beans can be hooked up so that one receives events from another. The container application makes this interaction possible.

You can also test new beans by loading them into the ToolBox. To do that you must create a Jar file containing the bean. Jar files and the make files used to create them are discussed in "Loading New Beans Into the BeanBox," later in this chapter.

Accessing Properties With OrangeButton

Start the BeanBox by going to the c:\bdk\beanbox directory and typing **run**. Once the windows for the BeanBox appear, pick the OrangeButton bean from the ToolBox. To do this, just click on it and drag it over the BeanBox main window; then click inside the main window. (See Figure 3-5.) The cursor will change to cross-hairs whenever you select a bean from the ToolBox.

If you have successfully dragged an OrangeButton to the BeanBox, you should see the OrangeButton with a black selection border around it. (The button appears more yellow than orange on my screen.) When this button is selected (click it again if it isn't), the Property Sheet will display the bean's properties. The properties shown are:

- **Foreground:** the foreground color.
- **Label:** the button's text.
- **Background:** the background color.
- **Font:** the font in which the label is displayed.

Clicking on either foreground or background brings up a ColorEditor window. The editor window contains a list box with color choices. Change the background color of the OrangeButton from orange to green, as a suggestion. Changes will be reflected the next time the button is repainted (which will be right away). Type a new label in the label field, or experiment with changing the font. You can also resize the button with the mouse.

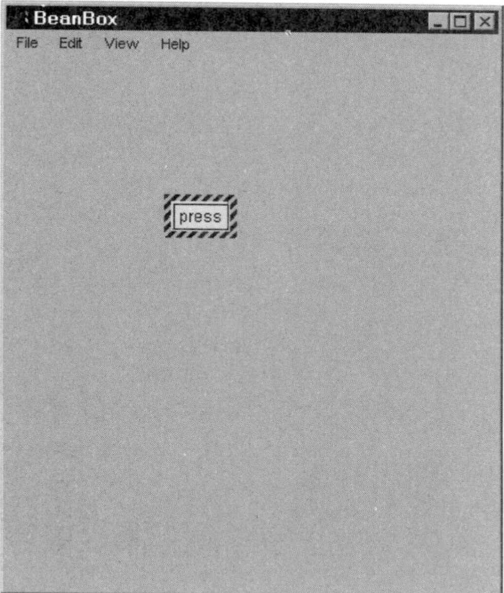

Figure 3-5: The OrangeButton running in the BeanBox.

Accessing Events With Juggler

Here is where your knowledge of events and target methods will come into play. You'll recall that events are implemented by calling a target method on an event listener. This is a good chance to see some events in action. And much of the action will be in the actionPerformed( ) method.

Drag the Juggler bean from the ToolBox as you did for the OrangeButton bean previously. It should start its animation (juggling coffee beans) as soon as it paints itself. Now, to hook up an OrangeButton via an action event to get the Juggler to stop juggling, drag an OrangeButton to the BeanBox. Click on it to select it (it should have a black border). Go to the Edit menu and select Events | action | actionPerformed (see Figure 3-6). This lets you specify what you want to happen when the OrangeButton produces an action event. In our case we will hook the OrangeButton up to the Juggler animation.

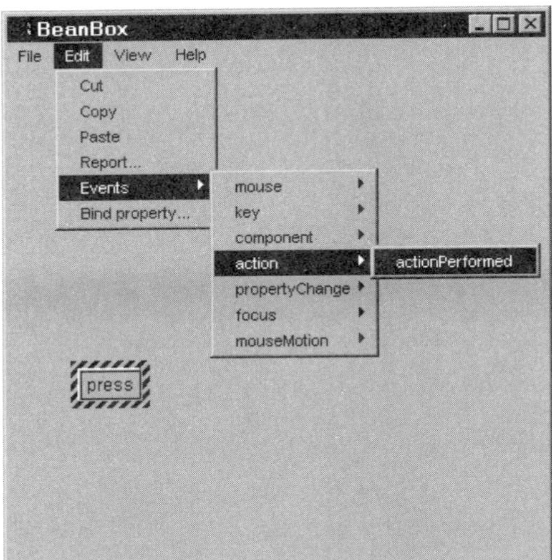

Figure 3-6: Selecting the menu item Edit | Events | action | actionPerformed for the OrangeButton.

Once you have selected actionPerformed from the Events menu, let go of the mouse. You will see a red line, which will let you connect the button to the Juggler. Extend the line to the Juggler, and click the mouse. The event target dialog will appear. This dialog contains a list of all the methods in the Juggler bean that either take an action event as a parameter or have no parameters. Select the stop( ) method (you may have to scroll down) (see Figure 3-7).

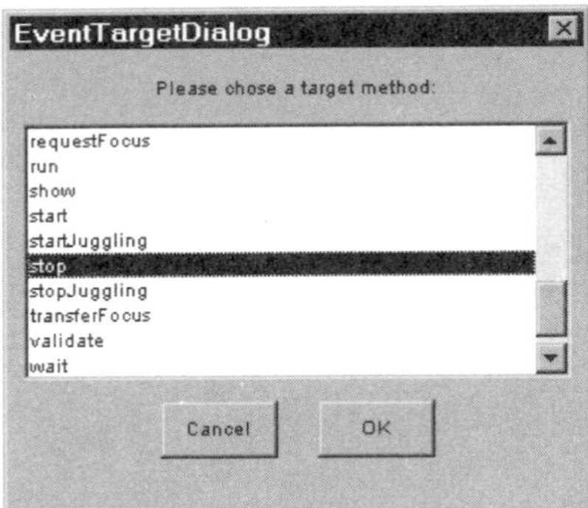

Figure 3-7: Selecting the stop( ) method from the event target dialog for the Juggler.

Now you will see a message that an adapter class is being created. The adapter class will act as a link between the OrangeButton and the Juggler bean. After the BeanBox is done generating the adapter, you will be able to click on the button and get the Juggler to stop juggling. (I'll leave the task of starting the Juggler again as an exercise for you.)

Now that you've seen some of the features of the BeanBox using the example beans, let's try to load one of our own beans.

Loading New Beans Into the BeanBox

The BeanBox is capable of loading new beans, not just the ones provided by the BDK 1.0. In this section, I'll show you how to load one of your own beans into the ToolBox. There are basically two steps to getting the BeanBox to recognize your bean. First, you must compile the class (or classes) that make up the bean. You are familiar with this step. Then you'll use the Jar compiler to create a Jar file. This is an archive file that can store Java classes and data files (such as bitmaps or GIF files). Jar files are saved with the extension .jar. But first let's look at the code for the example.

The Example Bean

For the bean we are going to load into the BeanBox, I'll use one of the simple beans from Chapter 2. This bean is a subclass of java.awt.Canvas. To get the bean into the BeanBox, the bean must be compiled and then put into a Jar file. I'll show you a make file that will do most of this for you. The Jar file also needs to be put in a certain directory: c\bdk\jars. The BeanBox loads all the Jar files in the c:\bdk\jars directory automatically when it starts up.

Listing 3-2 is the code for the example bean:

Listing 3-2: Code for the example bean.

```
import java.awt.*;
import java.beans.*;
import java.awt.event.*;

public class MyFirstBean extends Canvas
{
    private Color color; // our one private property
```

```
    // constructor
    public MyFirstBean()
    {
        setSize(60, 50); // make sure the bean is large enough
        color = new Color(255, 0,0); // instantiate a color: 'red'
        setBackground(color); // give the bean a red background
    }

    public Color getColor()
    {
        return color;
    }

    public void setColor(Color inputColor)
    {
        color = inputColor;
    }
}
```

This listing can be compiled with javac. Or, compiling the bean and adding it to a Jar file can be done all at once by using the make file in the next section.

The Make File

Make files for nmake and GNU make are provided with the BDK 1.0. (GNU is an acronym (GNU's Not UNIX!) used by the Free Software Foundation. The foundation produces well regarded products: a C/C++ compiler and the EMACS editor are examples, that can be freely distributed.) These make files are used in the examples to compile the Java class files and put the example beans into a Jar file.

Make files automate program development. They are text files that contain a number of statements; many statements consist of a target on the left-hand side and a list of files on the right-hand side. The target on the left is compared to the list of files on the right-hand side of the target. If the date of the right-hand side files is newer than the date of the target, the target is 'built.' This building may be compiling or linking, depending upon the type of target.

Make Files & IDEs

Make files have been replaced in many development products by Integrated Development Environments (IDEs). These environments automate the compiling and linking of a group of files by checking the time and date dependencies automatically. Make files are still powerful, however (if not as easy to use for the uninitiated). They excel at making command line tools work together (such as those provided with the JDK).

You'll be using Microsoft's nmake for this example, available for downloading from www.microsoft.com.

Listing 3-3: The make file for MyFirstBean.

```
CLASSFILES= \
        MyFirstBean.class

DATAFILES=
JARFILE= ..\bdk\jars\myfirst.jar

all: $(JARFILE)

# Create a JAR file with an inline manifest.
$(JARFILE): $(CLASSFILES) $(DATAFILES)
        jar cfm $(JARFILE) <<manifest.tmp .\*.class $(DATAFILES)
Name: MyFirstBean.class
Java-Bean: True
<<

.SUFFIXES: .java .class

{.}.java{.}.class :
    set CLASSPATH=.
    javac $<
```

This make file compiles the appropriate Java source files for the bean (MyFirstBean.java in this case.) It also runs the Jar compiler to store the bean (see the line that begins "jar cfm" in the listing). The Jar file format will be discussed in more detail in Chapter 14.

NOTE

Everything between the first << and the next << is called an inline file in make file terminology. In this case, manifest.tmp is a temporary inline file. All the commands between << and << will be put in this file. Manifest.tmp will be deleted when the make file is done with it.

The line "Name: MyFirstBean.class" and the line "Java-Bean: True" set the bean up in the manifest file as a bean. Since other supporting classes can be put in a Jar file also, and they don't all have to be beans, the "Java-Bean: True" or "Java-Bean:False" statement is used to distinguish them.

TIP

With nmake, you can keep the manifest.tmp file from being deleted by entering 'keep' after the last << , that is: <<keep.

The make file in Listing 3-3 can be used as is for this example. It can also be used as a generalized make file for different beans. To create a jar file for a bean contained in BeanName.class, you can change the right-hand side of the CLASSFILES target to BeanName.class. Then in the Name: section, insert BeanName.class there also. One thing to be careful of when modifying a make file like the one in Listing 3-3 is pathnames. If the locations of your Java source files or class files are different than Listing 3-3, make the needed adjustments. Make utilities like nmake seem a bit cryptic with regard to error messages; if nmake can't find your Java source file, it is likely to respond with: Don't know how to make: sourcefile.java.

The make file references the BDK jars directory, assuming that directory is c:\bdk\jars. Save the make file from a text editor into your directory. Name it myfirst.mk. Run the make file with Microsoft's nmake with the following command: nmake -fmyfirst.mk.

Running the Example

Start up the BeanBox as before. If you've successfully run the make file, the jar file for the new bean should be in the correct jars directory: c:\bdk\jars. When the BeanBox starts, you will be able to see your new bean in the ToolBox. Drag MyFirstBean to the ToolBox as with the other beans, and you will see a red rectangular bean (see Figure 3-8).

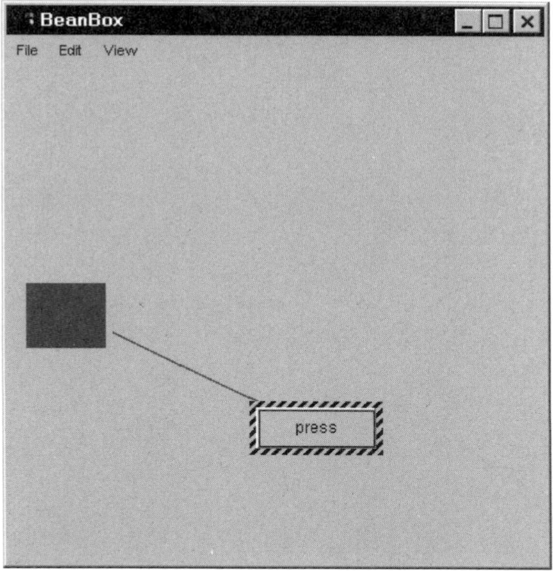

Figure 3-8: The bean: MyFirstBean running in the BeanBox.

Moving On

In this chapter you've learned about component containers (or beanbox tools) and looked at Sun's BeanBox. The BeanBox lets you load beans from Jar files to see their visual appearance. It also lets us see the properties and events a bean supports. And you set up beans as the source and receiver of events (provided their event types are compatible).

In the next chapter, you'll see how to write your own beans and create a new event type.

4

Programming a JavaBean

This chapter presents some examples of how to write a JavaBean. I take an evolutionary approach; that is, the examples will build upon what you've learned so far. The first example will build upon one of the example beans you've seen already. Later in the chapter, I show how to write two beans that are designed to cooperate by creating a custom event type and a custom event listener interface. I'll show you how to compile these beans and package them into a Java Archive (Jar) file to be run in the BeanBox. Beans can also be used from an applet; I'll demonstrate this hand-coding approach in the last section of the chapter.

Using Action Event: Class ColorSwap

The first example uses a bean similar to MyFirstBean from Chapter 2. MyFirstBean had a single color property acolor; the ColorSwap bean will add the ability to respond to action events.

Action Events

Events in the Abstract Windows Toolkit (AWT) can be grouped into two categories: *low-level* events and *semantic* events. Low-level events are events caused by actual system input like mouse clicks and keystrokes. Semantic events are at a higher level, such as pushing a button or selecting an item from a list.

AWT Class
java.awt.Button
java.awt.List
java.awt.TextField
java.awt.MenuItem
java.awt.List

Table 4-1: AWT classes generating action events.

Action events are one of the semantic events generated by the AWT. You can see from Table 4-1 that classes Button and List both generate action events. Preparing to receive an action event is the same as preparing for other event types using the delegation event model. You implement an interface, ActionListener, then register with a bean that generates action events. To register, you call the addActionListener( ) method on the bean with which you want to register. The example given here will register with class Button.

NOTE

A class that produces action events must let other objects register by providing an addActionListener method. Class Button has an addActionListener method pre-defined.

The ColorSwap Example

Let's create a bean that receives and responds to action events. In response to an action event, the ColorSwap bean will change its color from red to blue. The code for the bean is in Listing 4-1:

Listing 4-1: Code for ColorSwap bean.

```
package sunw.demo.swap;

import java.awt.*;
import java.beans.*;
import java.awt.event.*;

//File: ColorSwap.java
/** A very simple bean with a
*   single property called 'color'
*   When bean receives action events, the
* color is changed from red to blue
*/
```

```
public class ColorSwap extends Canvas implements ActionListener
{
    private Color color = Color.red;
    private Color otherColor = Color.blue;
    /** ColorSwap constructor, sets
    * size and background color
    */
    public ColorSwap()
    {
    setSize(100, 75); // make the bean large enough
    setBackground(color); // give the bean a red
background
    setVisible(true); // show the bean
    }
    /** paint -- set the background
    * to the current instance variable 'color'
    */
    public void paint(Graphics g)
    {
        setBackground(color);
    }
    /** return the color property
    * @see setColor
    */
    public Color getColor()
    {
        return color;
    }
    /** set the color property
    * and repaint
    * @see getColor
    */
    public void setColor(Color inputColor)
    {
        color = inputColor;
        repaint();
    }
    /** actionPerformed
    * implements the signature method in
    * the ActionListener interface. Here we
    * switch from red to blue and back.
    */
    public void actionPerformed(ActionEvent e)
    {
```

```
        if (color == Color.red)
            setColor(Color.blue);
        else
            setColor(Color.red); // red
    }
} // ColorSwap class
```

Let's look at the code for this bean in a little detail. The ColorSwap class extends the AWT class *Canvas* and implements the ActionListener interface. Canvas is a simple graphical item that will put a rectangle on the screen that can be subclassed to generate events.

Implementing the ActionListener interface is the key step to making this bean accept action events. The example implements the ActionListener method called actionPerformed.

Here is the declaration for the ActionListener interface:

```
public abstract interface ActionListener extends EventListener {
    public abstract void actionPerformed(ActionEvent e);
}
```

Passing Event Types as Arguments

Note that the actionPerformed( ) method gets a reference to an event object of type ActionEvent as a parameter. This is the typical pattern followed for methods that handle events in Java 1.1. The event handler takes as a parameter the type of event that it is handling. Here, we don't do anything with the event parameter except for declaring it as a parameter.

The constructor for ColorSwap sets the size of the bean and sets the background to a default color. It does this with two calls to methods in class Component as follows:

```
public ColorSwap()
{
    setSize(100, 75); // make the bean large enough
    setBackground(color); // give the bean a red background
    setVisible(true); // show the bean
}
```

TIP

A JavaBean must have at least one no argument constructor, or you will get an error (probably when trying to load the Jar file containing your bean into a beanbox tool).

The setSize( ) method has two parameters: width and height. You can adjust the size of the bean by experimenting with different values for these parameters. Class Canvas inherits the setBackground( ) method from class Component.

The paint method simply sets the background of the Canvas to the current value of the color property. The setColor and getColor methods provide access to the color property. Remember that the internal name (the variable declaration inside the class) of the color property does not have to be the same as the name used in set and get. The introspection process will return the name "color" for this property, regardless of the internal name of the instance variable.

The color swapping code is in actionPerformed( ). actionPerformed() sets a color (using a constant) by way of ColorSwap's setColor( ) method—setColor( ) will call repaint to make sure the bean is repainted with the new color.

Deprecation of Methods in Java 1.1

The javac.exe compiler gives *deprecation* warnings for methods whose names have changed in Java 1.1. I've found that resize( ) and show( ) are two very useful methods you'll run into that have been deprecated. I've used the Java 1.1 equivalent methods: setSize(width, height) and setVisible(true), in this example.

Running the ColorSwap Example

You can run this example in the BeanBox if you follow some simple steps. First of all, the ColorSwap class has been put in a named package, using the package statement. The following line in the source file declares the package:

```
package sunw.demo.swap;
```

Java will look for the class file, ColorSwap.class, in the directory sunw\demo\swap, under the current classpath directory. Therefore, to run the ColorSwap example in the BeanBox, it is important to put it under the right directory. If you follow the setup I've recommended for installing the BDK 1.0, the complete path is:

```
c:\bdk\demo\sunw\demo\swap
```

Recall that in order to load a bean into the BeanBox, you must create a Jar file containing the class file for the bean. A Jar file is similar to a ZIP file (a type of archive file) which contains Java class files. It can also contain images such as .GIF files. One unique feature of Jar files is that they contain a *manifest* file. This manifest file tells the world whether a particular class file in the Jar file is a bean or not. In Chapter 3, you saw an example make file for a bean. It ran the Java compiler to compile the bean and the Jar compiler to archive the bean.

TIP

More information about Jar files can be found in Chapter 14 and by reading the Jar file specification accessible from java.sun.com/beans/.

The make file for this example, swap.mk, is in Listing 4-2. The working directory for the swap.mk make file needs to be c:\bdk\demo. All the references to paths in this make file (swap.mk) are relative to c:\bdk\demo. (See Table 4-2 for the directory structure for the examples in this chapter( ). If you are using drive d: instead of c:, substitute your drive name in the pathnames shown in Table 4-2.)

Filename	Pathname or Location
DataSource.java	c:\bdk\demo\sunw\demo\data
DataSourceEvent.java	c:\bdk\demo\sunw\demo\data
DataSourceListener.java	c:\bdk\demo\sunw\demo\data
ColorSwap.java	c:\bdk\demo\sunw\demo\swap
DStatusBar.java	c:\bdk\demo\sunw\demo\status
all make files	c:\bdk\demo
all Jar files	c:\bdk\jars

Table 4-2: Locations of files for example code.

Listing 4-2: Make file swap.mk.

```
CLASSFILES= \
        sunw\demo\swap\ColorSwap.class

DATAFILES= \


JARFILE= ..\jars\swap.jar

all: $(JARFILE)

# Create a JAR file with a suitable manifest.

$(JARFILE): $(CLASSFILES) $(DATAFILES)
        jar cfm $(JARFILE) <<manifest.tmp sunw\demo\swap\*.class
```

```
$(DATAFILES)
Name: sunw/demo/swap/ColorSwap.class
Java-Bean: True
<<keep

.SUFFIXES: .java .class

{sunw\demo\swap}.java{sunw\demo\swap}.class :
    set CLASSPATH=.
    javac $<
```

Assuming you have installed the source in the correct directory and put the make file swap.mk in c:\bdk\demo, you can compile ColorSwap.java (See Figure 4-1) and run the Jar compiler to create a Jar file with the following steps:

1. Start a DOS session in Win95.
2. Using the DOS change directory command (CD), switch to the directory: c:\bdk\demo.
3. Type **nmake -fswap.mk**.

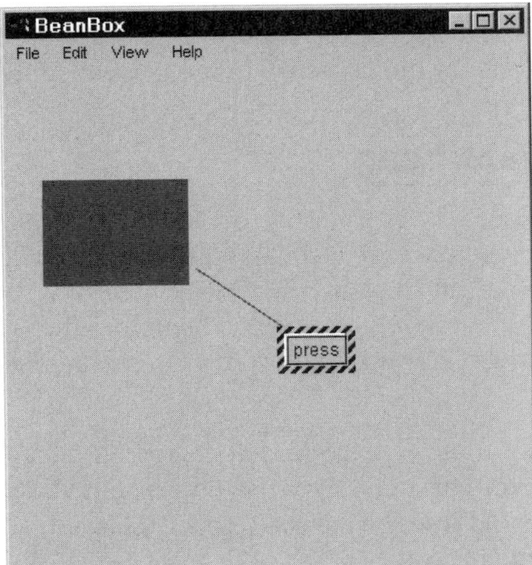

Figure 4-1: The ColorSwap bean and the OurButton bean running in the BeanBox.

A Custom Event: Class DataSource

In the previous sections you used ActionEvent, one of the built-in event types in the package java.beans. In this section I'll present an approach to creating a custom event type. The basics of this approach are as follows:

- Define an event class that is a subclass of java.util.EventObject. You may also subclass one of the other event types in the AWT, such as java.awt.event.ActionEvent.
- Create your own listener class by implementing one of the event listener interfaces in java.util.EventListener.
- Create a class that will be a source of your 'new' type of event. It must have methods to add/remove listeners for your new event type.

In this example, I'll create two beans: DataSource is a source of events of type DataSourceEvent, and DStatusBar is a receiver of events of type DataSourceEvent. DStatusBar will have to handle these events by doing some appropriate function. In this example I'll just have the DStatusBar acknowledge receipt of an event by printing out a text field in the bean itself giving the current value of the data.

First, let's look at the bean designed to be the source of events. In a following section you'll see the code for the DStatusBar bean, the event receiver.

The DataSourceEvent Bean

The DataSource bean is a source of events of type DataSourceEvent. It will keep a list of listeners for events of type DataSourceEvent. Before looking at the code for DataSource itself, let's look at how DataSourceEvent is declared.

This class inherits from or extends class EventObject from the java.util package. The java.util package has been imported with the statement:

```
import java.util.*;
```

Java.util.EventObject is used as a root type for events in Java 1.1. (There will be more on events in Chapter 6.) This event type maintains some local data. The variable dataOfEvent is passed into the constructor for the event so each event object will have its own private data.

The listing for the DataSourceEvent class is in Listing 4-3:

Listing 4-3: DataSourceEvent.java.

```
package sunw.demo.data;

import java.util.*;
```

```
//* File: DataSourceEvent.java
//* The kind of event the DataSource class
//* will emit
public class DataSourceEvent extends EventObject
{
long evtData = 0;
    // constructor
    public DataSourceEvent(DataSource source, long evtVal)
    {
        super(source); // pass to superclass
        evtData = evtVal;
    }
    public long getEventData()
    {
        return evtData;
    }
}
```

The DataSourceListener Class

Now that we've declared a new event type, a listener class is necessary to link up events at runtime. To declare a listener for events of type DataSourceEvent, you can subclass java.util.EventListener as in Listing 4-4:

Listing 4-4: File DataSourceListener.java.

```
package sunw.demo.data;

import java.beans.*;
import java.awt.event.*;
import java.util.*;


// defines the method handleData()
// listeners for DataSourceEvents implement this
public interface DataSourceListener extends EventListener
{
public void handleData(DataSourceEvent dsEvt);
}
```

This event listener interface has one method. This method has the signature:

```
public void handleData(DataSourceEvent dsEvt);
```

The handleData( ) method has one parameter of type DataSourceEvent. This method will be implemented (have its code written) by any bean listening for events of type DataSourceEvent.

The DataSource Class

Here is the source code for the DataSource bean itself. It will maintain a list of listeners for DataSourceEvents. Some things to look for when perusing the code in Listing 4-5 are the following:

- The Vector dataSourceListeners contains the list of listeners for DataSourceEvents.
- A thread is started in the constructor for DataSource.
- The run( ) method, which contains the code for the thread, creates and broadcasts DataSourceEvents to the list of listeners.
- The add/remove methods add and remove listeners using the Vector called dataSourceListeners.

The code for the DataSource bean is in Listing 4-5:

Listing 4-5: Code for DataSource bean.

```
package sunw.demo.data;

import java.awt.*;
import java.beans.*;
import java.awt.event.*;
import java.util.*;


public class DataSource extends Canvas implements Runnable {

    public DataSource()
    {
    setSize(50,50);
    setBackground(m_color);
    aFont = new Font("TimesRoman", Font.BOLD, 14);
    thread = new Thread(this);
    thread.start(); // thread start see run()
    }

    public void paint(Graphics g)
    {
    this.setBackground(m_color);
    this.setFont(aFont);
    FontMetrics fm = getFontMetrics(aFont);
    text = "  " + dataOfEvent;
    Dimension dimen = this.getSize();
    g.drawString(text,dimen.width/2-5, dimen.height/2-10);
    }
```

```
public Dimension getMinimumSize  ()
{
return (new Dimension(50, 50));
}
// return size for layout managers
public Dimension getPreferredSize  ()
{
return (new Dimension(50, 50));
}
// Java 1.0 vers. of getPreferredSize()
public Dimension preferredSize()
{
return (new Dimension(50, 50));
}

// run method called by Thread.start()
public void run ()
{
    while(true)
    {

    if (dataOfEvent == 0)
        dataOfEvent = m_max; // wrap around
    dataOfEvent--; // decrement the event 'data'
    //if there are some listeners,
    //send a datasource event to them.
    DataSourceEvent dsEvt = new DataSourceEvent(this, dataOfEvent);
    for (int i=0; i<dataSourceListeners.size(); i++)
    {
    DataSourceListener aDSListener=(DataSourceListener)
dataSourceListeners.elementAt(i);
    aDSListener.handleData(dsEvt);
    } // for
    try
    {
        thread.sleep(m_delay);
    }
    catch (Exception e)
    {
    System.out.println("Thread exception: " + e);
    }
    } // while

} // run

// add listener for DataSourceEvents
```

```
    //@see removeDataSourceListener
    public void addDataSourceListener(DataSourceListener dsl)
    {
        dataSourceListeners.addElement(dsl);
    }
    //@see addDataSourceListener
    public void removeDataSourceListener(DataSourceListener dsl)
    {
        dataSourceListeners.removeElement(dsl);
    }
    public void setAColor(Color newColor)
    {
        m_color = newColor;
        repaint();
    }
    public Color getAColor()
    {
        return m_color;
    }
    public void setDelay(long delay)
    {
        if (delay <= 0)
            delay= 1;
        m_delay = delay;
    }

    public long getDelay()
    {
    return m_delay;
    }
    // hold listeners listening for events
    // from class DataSource
    private Vector dataSourceListeners = new Vector();
    private Thread thread;
    private Color m_color = Color.yellow;
    private long dataOfEvent = 0;
    private long m_delay = 1500;
    private Font aFont;
    private String text;
    static final long m_max = 200;
}
```

The DataSource bean is in the package sunw.demo.data. The source code needs to be put in the directory c:\bdk\demo\sunw\demo\data. First, notice that DataSource bean implements the Runnable interface. The Runnable interface's one method run( ) is used by the Thread class. The constructor for DataSource sets size and background to a default size and color, creates a new font, and starts a new thread. The code for the constructor follows:

```
public DataSource()
{
setSize(50,50);
setBackground(m_color);
aFont = new Font("TimesRoman", Font.BOLD, 14);
thread = new Thread(this);
thread.start(); // thread start see run()
}
```

The paint( ) method sets the background to the value of the current instance variable m_color. This code changes the color, for example, when you pick a new color in a beanbox tool. The run method is probably the most important feature to notice about the DataSource bean. The code for run( ) is repeated here:

```
public void run ()
{
while(true)
{

    if (dataOfEvent == 0)
        dataOfEvent = m_max; // wrap around
    dataOfEvent--; // decrement the event 'data'
    //if there are some listeners,
    //send a datasource event to them.
    DataSourceEvent dsEvt = new DataSourceEvent(this, dataOfEvent);
    for (int i=0; i<dataSourceListeners.size(); i++)
    {
    DataSourceListener aDSListener=(DataSourceListener)
dataSourceListeners.elementAt(i);
    aDSListener.handleData(dsEvt);
    }
    try
    {
        thread.sleep(m_delay);
    }
    catch (Exception e)
    {
        System.out.println("Thread exception: " + e);
    }
    } // for

} // run
```

The points to notice about this run( ) method are:

- The while loop initiates an infinite loop. Effectively, our data source will generate events until we remove it from the BeanBox.
- The dataOfEvent variable is a simple decrementing variable. Each time through the loop it is decremented by one. This variable is a local to the DataSource class. It is used in the creation of an event.

The new DataSourceEvent is created with the following code:

```
DataSourceEvent dsEvt = new DataSourceEvent(this, dataOfEvent);
```

We pass the keyword this, representing the DataSource object itself, and the event data, dataOfEvent. We now have a unique DataSourceEvent object that is sent to listeners.

Sending an event to event listeners is accomplished as follows:

```
for (int i=0; i<dataSourceListeners.size(); i++)
{
    DataSourceListener aDSListener=(DataSourceListener)
dataSourceListeners.elementAt(i);
aDSListener.handleData(dsEvt);
} // for
    try
    {
        thread.sleep(m_delay);
    }
    catch (Exception e)
    {
        System.out.println("Thread exception: " + e);
    }
```

Events in Java 1.1 call target methods on an event listener. Here you can clearly see the DataSource object cycling through its list of listeners and calling the handleData( ) method on each one of them.

Multi-cast & Uni-cast Event Sources

The example demonstrates the multi-cast event approach. This means that a source of events can have one or more listeners. A source can also require that it have only one listener. This type of event is called a Uni-cast event. (If more than one event is received, an exception is thrown.)

After sending an event to the list of listeners, the thread code then sleeps for 1500 milliseconds. This delay has been made a property of the bean, so it is modifiable from the BeanBox. The internal name of the property is m_delay. The delay assures us we'll have some time between events. The initial value for the delay (1500) is arbitrary; you might experiment with 1000 or 2000 milliseconds (one or two seconds).

The other features of interest in this example are the add/remove methods declared as follows:

```
public void addDataSourceListener(DataSourceListener dsl)
{
    dataSourceListeners.addElement(dsl);
}

public void removeDataSourceListener(DataSourceListener dsl)
{
    dataSourceListeners.removeElement(dsl);
}
```

These methods use the local variable of type Vector, dataSourceListeners, to add or remove listeners. This is list management for the listeners that the source is required to do. Figure 4-2 shows the DataSource bean in the BeanBox.

Figure 4-2: The DataSource bean running in the BeanBox.

The DStatusBar Bean

This section presents the code for the DStatusBar bean. This bean receives DataSourceEvent events. Upon receiving an event and its data, it displays a simple scrolling bar. Here is the code for the DStatusBar bean, in Listing 4-6:

Listing 4-6: Source file DStatusBar.java.

```
package sunw.demo.status;

import java.awt.*;
import java.applet.*;
import sunw.demo.data.*;

//  DStatusBar
public class DStatusBar extends Canvas implements DataSourceListener
{

    // constructor
    public DStatusBar()
    {
    m_maxValue = 200;
    this.setSize(150, 100);
    this.setBackground(Color.green);
    this.setVisible(true); // show canvas
    repaint();
    }
    public Dimension getMinimumSize()
    {
        return (new Dimension(150, 100));
    }
    public Dimension getPreferredSize()
    {
    return (new Dimension(150, 100));
    }

    public void paint(Graphics g )
    {
    m_value = m_maxValue - m_value;
    if (lastValue != (m_value * 100L) / m_maxValue)
    {
    lastValue = (m_value * 100) / m_maxValue;
    g.setColor(Color.black);
    /* large box outline */
    Dimension dimension = getSize();
```

```
    g.drawRect(15, dimension.height/2-20, dimension.width-
(dimension.width/4),
dimension.height/2);

    // fill the status bar
    g.fillRect(17, dimension.height/2-20, 17+(int)lastValue,
dimension.height/2);
g.setColor(Color.green);
    }
} // end paint()
// Try to eliminate some flicker
public void update(Graphics g)
{
paint(g);
}
    // method provides a body for the
//DataSourceListener interface
    public void handleData(DataSourceEvent dde)
    {
        long data = dde.getEventData();
        setCurrentValue(data);
    }  // handleData

    // set currentValue property
    public void setCurrentValue(long inputValue)
    {
        m_value = inputValue;
    repaint(); // when value changes update
    }
    // get 'value' property--read only property
    public long getCurrentValue()
    {
        return m_value;
    }

    // set & get 'maxValue' property
    public void setMaxValue(long inMaxValue)
    {
        m_maxValue = inMaxValue;
    }

    public long getMaxValue()
    {
        return m_maxValue;
    }
```

```
    // variables
    private static  long  m_maxValue;
    private static long m_value=10;
    static long lastValue=0L;
} /* DStatusBar */
```

The main feature to notice here is that DStatusBar implements DataSourceEventListener. You'll recall that DataSourceListener was an interface with a method that needed to be implemented as:

```
handleData(DataSourceEvent dse);
```

The complete implementation of handleData for this example is as follows:

```
public void handleData(DataSourceEvent dde)
{
    long data = dde.getEventData();
    setCurrentValue(data);
}  // handleData
```

The following steps are accomplished by this code:

- It gets the data from the current event object by calling a public member function (getEventData) using the dde parameter passed to handleData( ).
- It calls the setCurrentValue to update the current value of the currentValue property. The setCurrentValue method takes care of calling repaint to repaint the status bar.

The status bar is actually drawn in the paint( ) method. First the current value is adjusted with the statement:

```
m_value = m_maxValue - m_value;
```

Then the status bar is drawn using drawRect and filled to the current value (using local variable lastValue) with the fillRect method from the Graphics class.

Notice the access methods for the two properties, currentValue and maxValue. The setter and getter methods for these two properties assure that a beanbox will discover these through introspection.

That's all for the status bar bean, so we are ready to link the status bar to the DataSource bean by way of DataSourceEvent.

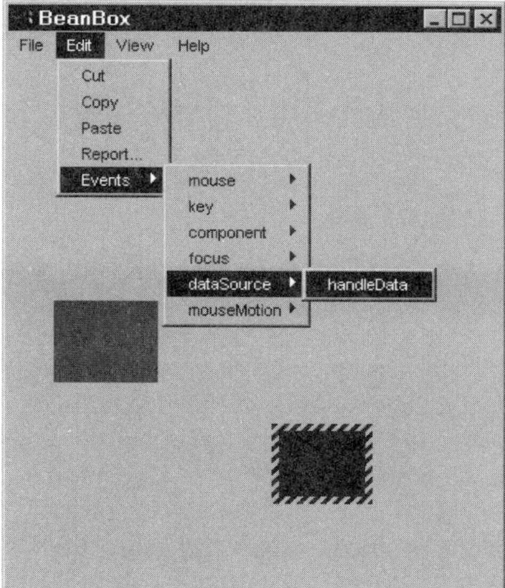

Figure 4-3: Selecting the handleData( ) target method from the DataSource Bean.

Linking DataSource With DStatusBar

To load the DataSource and DStatusBar beans into the BeanBox's ToolBox menu, (see Figure 4-3) you follow the same steps you did for ColorSwap. First, you must compile and put the status bar bean in a Jar file. Use the make file in Listing 4-7:

Listing 4-7: status.mk make file for DStatusBar bean.

```
CLASSFILES= \
         sunw\demo\status\DStatusBar.class \

DATAFILES=

JARFILE= ..\jars\StatusBar.jar

all: $(JARFILE)

# Create a JAR file with a suitable manifest.

$(JARFILE): $(CLASSFILES) $(DATAFILES)
        jar cfm $(JARFILE) <<manifest.tmp sunw\demo\status\*.class $(DATAFILES)
```

```
Name: sunw/demo/status/DStatusBar.class
Java-Bean: True
<<keep

.SUFFIXES: .java .class

{sunw\demo\status}.java{sunw\demo\status}.class :
    set CLASSPATH=.
    javac $<
```

Make File Locations

As before, you must use this make file from the c:\bdk\demo directory. All the paths for the class files are relative to that directory. And I'm putting the source for DStatusBar.java into the c:\bdk\demo\sunw\demo\status directory. Otherwise the package statement in all the files—package sunw.demo.status—won't work correctly.

Confusion About CLASSPATH?

I have occasionally found use of the CLASSPATH variable terribly confusing. If you ever get errors from the javac 1.1 compiler of the form "class sunw.demo.data.DataSource.class not found in class . . .," it has to do with Java trying to locate classes. If the JDK is set up correctly, Java should be able to find its system classes, such as those in java.io, java.lang, and so on. The CLASSPATH variable is used to help Java find your own classes. Therefore if Java is trying to find a class in package sunw.demo.data, it searches for a classfile in directory sunw\demo\data underneath one of the directories listed in CLASSPATH. For example, if you execute the statement set CLASSPATH=. , then Java starts by looking under the current directory. Also, don't forget to check that the package statements you use in your .JAVA files correspond to the directory structure; this can confuse Java's class loading procedure, too.

To compile and archive the DataSource bean, use the make file in Listing 4-8:

Listing 4-8: Make file datasrc.mkCLASSFILES= \.

```
        sunw\demo\data\DataSource.class \
        sunw\demo\data\DataSourceListener.class \
        sunw\demo\data\DataSourceEvent.class

DATAFILES=

JARFILE= ..\jars\datasource.jar

all: $(JARFILE)

# Create a JAR file with a suitable manifest.

$(JARFILE): $(CLASSFILES) $(DATAFILES)
        jar cfm $(JARFILE) <<manifest.tmp sunw\demo\data\*.class
$(DATAFILES)
Name: sunw/demo/data/DataSource.class
Java-Bean: True

Name: sunw/demo/data/DataSourceListener.class
Java-Bean: False

Name: sunw/demo/data/DataSourceEvent.class
Java-Bean: False
<<keep

.SUFFIXES: .java .class

{sunw\demo\data}.java{sunw\demo\data}.class :
    set CLASSPATH=.
    javac $<
```

This make file (Listing 4-8) assumes the source for the Datasource bean and the other support files are all in c:\bdk\demo\sunw\demo\data (see Table 4-2 for source file locations).

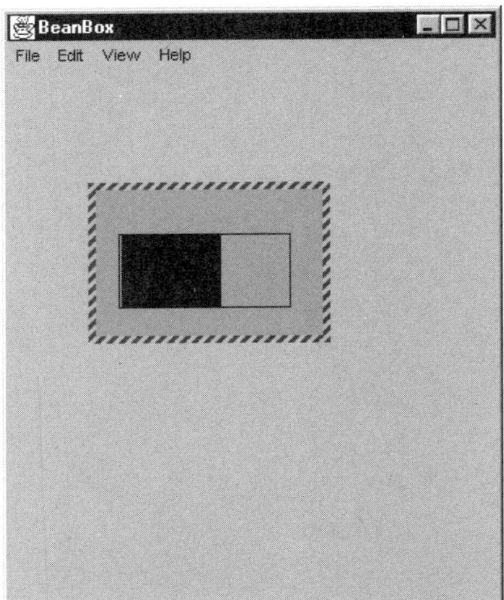

Figure 4-4: The DStatusBar in the BeanBox.

After you have the two beans in their jar files, start the BeanBox. Drag and drop a DataSource bean and a DStatusBar (see Figure 4-4) bean to the BeanBox. Select the DataSource bean and choose Events from the Edit menu. Choosing the handleData event will let you choose the DStatusBar as a target for this method. A few things you can try with this example are:

- Changing the delay value for the DataSource bean from the PropertySheet.
- Hooking up two status bars to one data source.
- Changing the value of the AColor property for the DataSource bean.
- Changing the maximum value property for the DStatusBar bean.

Hand-coding Beans From an Applet

One of the flexible features about the JavaBeans specification is that beans can be hand-coded into an applet. Although Sun envisions that most beans will find their homes in a complete application builder environment, the model for beans—based upon the Java class file format as you'll recall—is general enough to allow beans to be used without a builder environment. This section demonstrates how you would use the DStatusBar and DataSource beans from an applet. Listing 4-9 is an applet that loads the DStatusBar and DataSource beans.

Listing 4-9: App.java, applet using DStatusBar and DataSource beans. (See also Figure 4-5.)

```
import java.awt.*;
import java.applet.*;
import sunw.demo.data.*;
import sunw.demo.status.*;

public class App extends Applet
{
    public void init()
    {
    setLayout(new FlowLayout ());
    DStatusBar aStatusBar = new DStatusBar();
    DataSource dataSource = new DataSource();
    this.add(dataSource); //add Datasource to applet
    this.add(aStatusBar); // add DStatusBar
    // now link them together by adding a listener
    dataSource.addDataSourceListener(aStatusBar);
    } //init
}
```

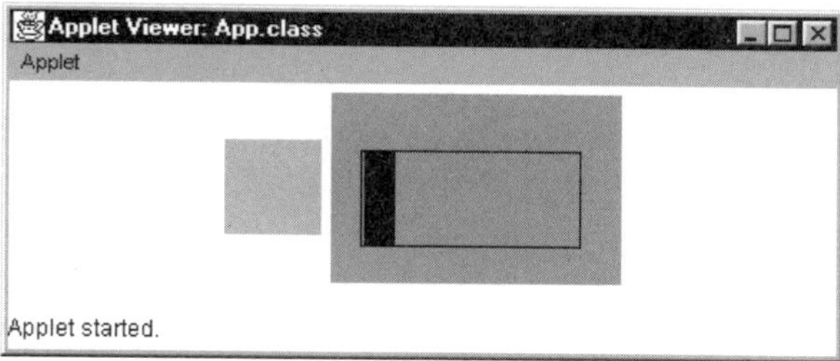

Figure 4-5: The beans DStatusBar and DataSource running in an applet inside the appletviewer.

NOTE

To make the DStatusBar and DataSource classes available, the .CLASS files for these classes must be found by the system. See the previous sidebar, "Confusion About CLASSPATH?"

Moving On

In this chapter, you've had your first look at writing some Java code to create a JavaBean. First, starting with the AWT element called Canvas, you saw how you'd create a bean with the ability to respond to action events. This gave you a general introduction to events in action.

The latter part of the chapter presented an example of two beans using a custom event type DataSourceEvent. This demonstrated custom events and showed how beans can cooperate using the new event model.

In the next chapter, I'll take you through a more detailed look at the JavaBeans specification's support for properties.

5

Programming With Properties

The programming support for properties is an important part of the JavaBeans specification. Properties, along with methods and events, are the way that beans make available their features for a beanbox tool.

In this chapter, I'll show you the various forms of property support provided by JavaBeans. In addition to the simple properties (such as color) that you've seen so far, JavaBeans has support for Boolean, indexed, bound, and constrained properties.

This chapter also includes a section on customization, which lets a developer change how a beanbox 'sees' properties, thus allowing more flexibility in designing beans. This support is provided in the form of the BeanInfo interface, the Customizer interface, and the PropertyEditor interface.

Properties & Introspection

You'll recall that one feature of a component architecture is the ability to make component features available to the surrounding software environment. This is sometimes called *publishing*. The three features of components—properties, methods, and events—all need to be discovered by a beanbox tool.

Java refers to this overall process of discovering properties, methods, and events as *introspection*. When a bean is inside a container application like the BeanBox, the introspection process proceeds as follows:

1. The environment first looks for an object that implements the interface BeanInfo. This object will have the name or signature MyBeanNameBeanInfo, where the "MyBeanInfo" part is the name of your bean class. If the BeanInfo object is found, the introspection process uses what it can find out from the contents of the BeanInfo. The programmer or developer of the bean can even use the BeanInfo object as a form of customization or locale independent information (properties can have different names than are used in their set and get accessor methods, for example).
2. If no information is found from the BeanInfo for any of the properties, events, or methods (or the BeanInfo object is not found), introspection continues by a lower level process; this is sometimes referred to as *reflection*.

High-level Introspection Versus Low-level Reflection

Why is providing a BeanInfo object high-level and searching through method names low-level? High-level in this case implies that the JavaBeans developer has more to do with the process. If he or she doesn't provide the BeanInfo object, the beanbox tool takes over. The API used for this low-level search is called the *reflection API* or sometimes *the core reflection API*. See Sun's Java page at http://java.sun.com/beans for more information about reflection API.

Therefore, you can either provide a BeanInfo object to describe your bean or let the system's low-level reflection process discover your properties for you. The system's reflection process makes use of the naming convention we briefly mentioned in Chapter 2, design patterns. Next, let's look at these design patterns in more detail.

Design Patterns for Properties

What Sun calls design patterns are naming conventions for methods, event classes, event listeners, property listeners, and BeanInfo classes. In this section, I'll focus on the design patterns for properties and the classes that support properties. First, there are two rationales behind these design patterns:

1. Naming conventions (sticking to consistent methods of forming names of methods and classes) document code well for developers. They make it easy for the user of an API to see what features are available and how they behave.
2. Consistent naming makes it possible to develop automated tools to inspect (or introspect) beans and discover which properties and events they support.

TIP

Class Introspector knows about design patterns. The Introspector class is in: java.beans.Introspector. Perusing it can be educational for what kind of introspection support JavaBeans provides.

You've seen design patterns at work in naming accessor methods for properties. For example, when we had a property called color, we used these method names:

```
public Color getColor();
public void setColor(Color newColor);
```

In using these method names that match the design patterns for naming a property, the examples so far have relied exclusively on the low-level reflection mechanism. We didn't design our own beans to use the BeanInfo interface. You see some examples of how to create a BeanInfo class later in this chapter in the section entitled "Customization Support."

Keep in mind the idea of design patterns and for what they're used as we next look at the different types of properties that JavaBeans supports.

Following the Design Pattern Convention

Strictly speaking, you aren't required to name your methods by following the design pattern convention. If you use a BeanInfo object, it will let you supersede the patterns. I recommend that you do, however, use the patterns, since your beans will be more easily understood by end users and by you!

Simple Properties

The properties we've seen so far in the examples are simple properties. They represent a single attribute of a bean, such as a color or a boundary value. Simple properties can be of the primitive types or a class type (user-defined or one of the library types such as java.awt.Component). Simple properties may be Boolean too. The design pattern for simple (non-Boolean) properties is:

```
public void setPropertyName(PropertyType newProperty);
public PropertyType getPropertyName(PropertyType newPropValue);
```

The reflection mechanism will get a property called PropertyName when examining the previous methods. Note that the first letter is lowercase. Recall also that the internal name (the actual name of your property variable declared inside your bean class) need not have the same name as "PropertyName."

The preceding pair of set and get methods defines a property that can be both read from and written to—this is called a *read/write property*. If a property has a get method without a set method, the beanbox tool will see it as a read-only property. You can also create a write-only property by providing a set method without a get method.

Boolean Properties

Boolean properties are simple properties that have type Boolean. The design pattern lets you replace the get method with this:

```
public boolean isPropertyName();
```

You can also have a set method as for non-Boolean simple properties (you can even provide both a get PropertyName and is PropertyName method in the same bean). Java's Introspector will use the isPropertyName method by default to read the property value (if you have provided it).

Indexed Properties

In contrast to the simple properties described above, *indexed properties* let the bean developer provide an array of values. The accessor methods for indexed properties are similar to those for simple properties, with the difference that one may access single elements of the array or the array in its entirety. The set and get methods for accessing single elements from the array are declared as follows:

```
public void setPropertyName(int index, PropertyType value);
public Element getProperty(int index);
```

You can also set or get the entire array of properties at one time:

```
public void setPropertyName(PropertyArrayType x[])
public PropertyArrayType[] getPropertyName();
```

TIP

The BeanBox in the BDK 1.0 does not support indexed properties, but it may by the time you read this. You can keep a lookout for improvements to Java and JavaBeans at http://java.sun.com/beans. You should note that methods accessing indexed properties might throw an array out of bounds exception, just as for regular Java arrays.

Bound Properties

Since beans are designed to be components that can interact at design time and at run time, additional property support may be needed. In addition to simple properties and indexed ones, properties in JavaBeans can be *bound*. Binding a property lets other beans know when the value of the bound property changes. As is the case for events, beans need to register as listeners to be notified of these changes in a property. Basically, a bean that supports a bound property will do the following:

- Implement add/remove methods for interface PropertyChangeListener.
- Fire an event of type PropertyChangeEvent when the bound property changes. This will usually be in the set method for the property that has changed.

This is the same as the approach to other events types; that is, events are only sent to other objects that have registered to receive such an event. Here, the event says simply that 'a property has changed.'

JavaBeans has provided the class PropertyChangeSupport to make bound properties easier to use. A variable of type PropertyChangeSupport can be created within your bean class. When the value of a bound property changes you will call firePropertyChange( ) by way of this support class. A PropertyChangeSupport object can be created as follows:

```
PropertyChangeSupport support = new PropertyChangeSupport(this);
```

The following code fragment shows how a bean would handle a bound property. The bean has a bound property named accountBalance. At run time, other beans might want to be notified whenever the accountBalance changes. (This bean may be connected to a charting component, for example, and the chart will need to redraw itself.) When the property accountBalance is changed, all beans that have registered will be notified of the change.

```
class BoundPropertyBean extends java.awt.Canvas
{
private long accountBalance = 0;
support = new PropertyChangeSupport(this);

// set the property 'accountBalance'
public void setAccountBalance(long newBalance)
{
    long oldBalance = accountBalance; // save old value
    accountBalance = newBalance;
    support.firePropertyChange("accountBalance", new
long(oldBalance), new long (newBalance));
}
```

This code creates a PropertyChangeSupport object as an instance variable. PropertyChangeSupport contains useful methods to make the use of bound and constrained properties easier. The property accountBalance is first set to the new value (the parameter newBalance). Then, the PropertyChangeSupport object is used to fire the property change notification. Notice that the parameters of the property change notification include the property name, along with the old and the new values.

NOTE

With bound properties you first set the new value of the property, then fire the event to notify listeners of the change. (With constrained properties, which I'll explain next, the order of change and firing of the event is reversed.)

Name	Description
class PropertyChangeSupport	General support class for bound properties.
class PropertyChangeEvent	Event type used for state information for a property change.
class PropertyVetoException	An exception possibly thrown by a method trying to set a constrained property.
class VetoableChangeSupport	Support class for constrained properties.
interface PropertyChangeListener	Listener class for classes interested in listening for changes in a bound property.
interface VetoableChangeListener	Listener class for classes interested in listening for changes in a constrained property.

Table 5-1: Classes and interfaces in the package java.beans supporting bound and constrained properties.

Constrained Properties

Constrained properties, like bound properties, notify listeners when their values change; they also let a listener reject or veto such a change. JavaBeans calls these constrained properties because they take on values that may be limited by other beans. You may want to use constrained properties when a change to a property might affect the behavior of another bean. By doing so, you can let other beans reject the changes if they desire.

The steps to remember when using constrained properties are:

1. Decide which property you would like to make constrained.
2. Declare a method to set the constrained property, and declare it to throw a PropertyVetoException.
3. In your set method for the property, let listeners know when the property is about to change by firing a fireVetoableChange method.
4. Do something appropriate if a listener vetoed the property change.
5. Implement add/remove methods in your bean class for VetoableChangeListeners.

A fragment of code demonstrating a bean that supports a constrained property called limitedAmount is as follows:

```
class ConstrainedBean extends java.awt.Canvas
{
    private int limitedAmount = 0;
    private VetoableChangeSupport support = new VetoableChangeSupport(this);

    public void setAmount(int newAmount) throws PropertyVetoException
    {
        // use the veto support class
        // to fire the 'vetoable event'
        support.fireVetoableChange("limitedAmount", new
Integer(oldAmount), new Integer(newAmount));
        // now set the new value
        limitedAmount = newAmount;
    }
    public void removeVetoableChangeListener(VetoableChangeListener l)
    {
        support.addVetoableChangeListener(l);
    }

    public void addVetoableChangeListener(VetoableChangeListener l)
    {
    support.removeVetoableChangeListener(l);
    }
}
```

Customization Support

There are a few features in JavaBeans that come under the umbrella of customization. *Customization* is support that is given by the component architecture for modifying the presentation of properties, methods, and events in a container environment. I'll discuss the following three customization features of JavaBeans:

- The BeanInfo interface
- The Customizer interface
- The PropertyEditor interface

The BeanInfo Interface

BeanInfo classes are a good method for providing a custom interface to a bean. The BeanInfo class you supply lets you specify information about properties, methods, and events; I'll focus upon properties in this section.

What you are doing when you provide BeanInfo support for your bean is telling the beanbox tool directly how you want your bean to be analyzed. You can also vary the information in the BeanInfo object from what is actually contained in your bean, as a form of customization or for locale dependent code. (You can call properties by different names than those that would be obtained by the low-level reflection process.) Also, with a BeanInfo object, you don't need to provide information for every property or event declared by your bean. (If you don't provide information for some features, the introspection process will discover these features during a low-level analysis.)

How do you set up a BeanInfo class—a class that implements the BeanInfo interface? Let's see a fragment of code that would declare a BeanInfo object for a bean named MyBean.

```
import java.awt.*;

class MyBeanBeanInfo extends SimpleBeanInfo
{
    public Image getIcon(int iconType)
    {
        if (type == BeanInfo.ICON_COLOR_16x16) {
            Image anImage = loadImage("AnImage.GIF");
            return anImage;
        }
        return null;
    }
} // MyBeanBeanInfo
```

This class does not implement the BeanInfo interface directly, but rather extends a class called SimpleBeanInfo. The one method getIcon( ) is overridden to return an image object. It is a typical use of a BeanInfo class to return an icon that can be used by a beanbox tool in toolbars or menus.

The class that MyBeanBeanInfo extends, SimpleBeanInfo, is a utility class provided by the java.beans package to make declaring BeanInfo classes easier. SimpleBeanInfo provides what are called *no-ops* (methods with 'no operations') for all of the methods in the BeanInfo interface.

When you implement a Java interface, you need to provide an implementation for each of its methods. Therefore, when declaring a BeanInfo class, you'd normally be required to provide an implementation (even if it were an empty method) for each of the BeanInfo methods. The SimpleBeanInfo class actually does this for you. It provides an implementation that says 'no value' for all the BeanInfo methods that return values. So, when you derive a BeanInfo class from SimpleBeanInfo, you only need to override those methods in SimpleBeanInfo that you are going to use. Table 5-2 shows the methods of the BeanInfo interface with their descriptions.

Name	Description
getAdditionalBeanInfo	Finds and returns collection of BeanInfo objects if present.
getBeanDescriptor	Returns a BeanDescriptor object with overall information about a Bean.
getDefaultEventIndex	Returns the index of the most used Event; the index is in an EventSetDescriptor array.
getDefaultPropertyIndex	Returns the index of the most used property. The index is the PropertyDescription array returned by getPropertyDescriptors.
getEventSetDescriptors	Returns an array of EventSetDescriptor objects detailing events.
getIcon	Loads and returns an Image object when an icon is present.
getMethodDescriptors	Returns an array of objects of type MethodDescriptor.
getPropertyDescriptors	Returns an array of objects of type PropertyDescriptor.

Table 5-2: Methods in the BeanInfo interface.

Class Introspector

Class java.beans.Introspector does much of its introspection using the method that has a signature as follows: `public static BeanInfo getBeanInfo (Class beanClass)`. This method returns a BeanInfo object containing information about properties, methods, and events on the target bean if it's successful. This method throws an IntrospectionException if it fails.

Now let's see a declaration for a BeanInfo class that does more than just provide support for an icon. Listing 5-1 is the code for the ExplicitButtonBeanInfo class from the BDK. ExplicitButtonBeanInfo is a BeanInfo object that sets both property and icon information for the ExplicitButton bean.

Listing 5-1: Code for ExplicitButtonBeanInfo class from the BDK.

```
/**
* @see sunw.demo.buttons.ExplicitButton
 */
public class ExplicitButtonBeanInfo extends SimpleBeanInfo {

    public PropertyDescriptor[] getPropertyDescriptors() {
        try {
            PropertyDescriptor background =
            new PropertyDescriptor("background", beanClass);
        PropertyDescriptor foreground =
            new PropertyDescriptor("foreground", beanClass);
        PropertyDescriptor font =
            new PropertyDescriptor("font", beanClass);
            PropertyDescriptor label =
            new PropertyDescriptor("label", beanClass);

            background.setBound(true);
            foreground.setBound(true);
            font.setBound(true);
            label.setBound(true);

            PropertyDescriptor rv[] = {background, foreground, font, label};
            return rv;
        } catch (IntrospectionException e) {
            throw new Error(e.toString());
        }
    }
```

```
    public int getDefaultPropertyIndex()
    {
        // the index for the "label" property
        return 3;
    }


      public BeanDescriptor getBeanDescriptor() {
        return new BeanDescriptor(beanClass, customizerClass);
    }

    public java.awt.Image getIcon(int iconKind) {
    if (iconKind == BeanInfo.ICON_MONO_16x16 ||
        iconKind == BeanInfo.ICON_COLOR_16x16 ) {
        java.awt.Image img = loadImage("ExplicitButtonIcon16.gif");
        return img;
    }
    if (iconKind == BeanInfo.ICON_MONO_32x32 ||
        iconKind == BeanInfo.ICON_COLOR_32x32 ) {
        java.awt.Image img = loadImage("ExplicitButtonIcon32.gif");
        return img;
    }
    return null;
    }

    private final static Class beanClass = ExplicitButton.class;
    private final static Class customizerClass = OurButtonCustomizer.class;
}
```

Notice that the method getPropertyDescriptors returns a number of PropertyDescriptor objects for the properties named foreground, background, font, and label. This code also has support for a BeanDescriptor object. We haven't talked about BeanDescriptors before except to say that getBeanDescriptor( ) is one of the methods in the BeanInfo interface (see Table 5-2). The important feature of a BeanDescriptor is that it can take a customizer class as a parameter. Here, a BeanDescriptor object is created that has a customizer called customizerClass, which is initialized to be an OurButtonCustomizer. (Customizers are discussed in the next section.)

The class PropertyDescriptor is a subclass of the more general class FeatureDescriptor. See Table 5-3 for a list of the subclasses of FeatureDescriptor and what they do.

Name	Description
FeatureDescriptor	Superclass of other more specific descriptor classes.
MethodDescriptor	Class used in BeanInfo objects to provide information on the methods a bean supports.
PropertyDescriptor	Class used in BeanInfo objects to provide information on the properties a bean supports.
EventSetDescriptor	Class used in BeanInfo objects to provide information on the event sets a bean supports.
BeanDescriptor	Class used to provide information about a JavaBean; it can also associate a Customizer with a bean.
ParameterDescriptor	Class used in BeanInfo objects to provide information about the parameters of the public methods of a bean.

Table 5-3: FeatureDescriptor and some of its important subclasses.

Class PropertyDescriptor also has a subclass called IndexedPropertyDescriptor.

The other thing to notice about the code in Listing 5-1 is the getIcon( ) method, which looks similar to the getIcon( ) method you saw before. It returns an Image object based upon some constant identifiers that are part of the BeanInfo class:

- BeanInfo.ICON_COLOR_16x16
- BeanInfo.ICON_COLOR_32x32
- BeanInfo.ICON_MONO_16x16
- BeanInfo.ICON_MONO_32x32

These constants specify whether an icon is 16 by 16 or 32 by 32, and whether it is color or monochrome.

The Customizer Interface

The Customizer interface provides support for customizing properties by letting you create a custom graphical interface to affect the properties of a bean. To create a customizer class, you first declare a class that implements java.beans.Customizer.

Since a customizer is designed to be used in a GUI environment, the customizer class also usually extends one of the subclasses of Component. The class java.awt.Panel is often used for this purpose. Since your customizer class is a subclass of Component, it can easily be added to an AWT dialog or frame.

Once you've declared your customizer class, the object to be customized is associated with the customizer by calling the Customizer.setObject( ) method:

```
public abstract void setObject(Object bean);
```

This method is abstract; it needs to be overridden in any customizer class you may create. The design pattern for customizer classes is to name your customizer class by appending the word Customizer to the bean class name. For example, a bean named ColorSwap would have a customizer class named ColorSwapCustomizer.

```
public class ColorSwapCustomizer extends Panel implements Customizer
{

}
```

The other two methods in the Customizer interface are:

```
public abstract void addPropertyChangeListener(PropertyChangeListener l);
removePropertyChangeListener(PropertyChangeListener l);
```

You will be familiar with these methods for adding PropertyChangeListeners. They let you link up with objects that might be interested when your properties change. But what does the setObject( ) method do?

At run time, while running in the BeanBox, the setObject( ) method of your customizer is called with your bean as an argument. Then you can provide customization support for your properties. One approach is to add textFields to your Panel that let the user of your bean enter values. Look at the overridden setObject( ) method from the OurButton example from the BDK:

```
public void setObject(Object obj)
{
    target = (OurButton) obj;

    Label t1 = new Label("Caption:", Label.RIGHT);
    add(t1); // adds Label to Panel
    t1.setBounds(10, 5, 60, 30);

    labelField = new TextField(target.getLabel(), 20);
    add(labelField); // adds text field to Panel
    labelField.setBounds(80, 5, 100, 30);

    labelField.addKeyListener(this);
}
```

When the OurButton example is running, the preceding setObject method is passed an object of type OurButton. The code for the setObject method creates a TextField and a label containing the text "Caption:". The TextField is called labelField.

The customizer class containing this setObject method implements the keyListener interface. When a key is typed in the field labelField, a PropertyChangeEvent is fired and caught by any listeners. Then, the text can be removed from the text field and passed to the target bean, in this case setting the label of a button of type OurButton. That is, when a new label is typed into the text field, the following code will be executed:

```
txt = labelField.getText; // get text from field
target.setLabel(txt); // pass text to an OurButton
```

How does one specify a customizer for a bean? Once the customizer is created by implementing the Customizer interface as in the preceding ColorSwapCustomizer declaration, you can associate this customizer with the bean you are interested in by creating a BeanDescriptor object and passing your customizer to the constructor. The declaration of the BeanDescriptor constructor is as follows:

```
BeanDescriptor (Class aBeanClass, Class aCustomizerClass);
```

For the OurButtonCustomizer, the code to associate the customizer would be:

```
BeanDescriptor aBeanDescriptor = new BeanDescriptor (OurButton,
OurButtonCustomizer);
```

Using the BeanDescriptor object as shown is the usual way to associate a customizer with a bean. But, since beans and the bean support classes are just Java classes, we can, for demonstration purposes, link up a customizer with a bean in a stand-alone program.

As an example of what the a customizer looks like and how it can be used, I've written the following code. It uses the OurButtonCustomizer from the BDK that you've seen previously. The following Java stand-alone program adds an OurButtonCustomizer and an OurButton to a Frame object and displays both of them. You can type the following code in and see the customizer interact with the button (see Figure 5-1). Just create a new directory under the directory c:\bdk\demo\sunw\demo and type in the following code (see Listing 5-2).

Listing 5-2: CustApp.java.

```
import java.awt.*;
import sunw.demo.buttons.*;

/** CustApp is a class that
* exercises the OurButtonCustomizer class
```

```
*
*/
public class CustApp extends Frame {
    private OurButton ourButton;
    private OurButtonCustomizer aButtonCustomizer;

    public CustApp()
    {
    setLayout(new FlowLayout());
    this.setSize(300, 200);
    this.setTitle("A Customizer Frame");

    // now create an OurButton
    ourButton = new OurButton();

    // now create an OurButtonCustomizer and
    // set its 'object' as the OurButton
    aButtonCustomizer = new OurButtonCustomizer();
    aButtonCustomizer.setObject(ourButton);

    // now add customizer and the OurButton to CustApp's Frame
    aButtonCustomizer.setVisible(true);
    this.add(aButtonCustomizer);
    ourButton.setVisible(true);
    this.add(ourButton);
    this.show();
    }

    public static void main(String [] args)
    {
    CustApp anApp = new CustApp();
    }

    public void paint(Graphics g)
    {
    // make sure ourButton updates
    ourButton.repaint();
    }
}
```

As always, you can compile and run the CustApp example, by typing: **javac CustApp.java**. And then, after receiving no errors: **java CustApp**.

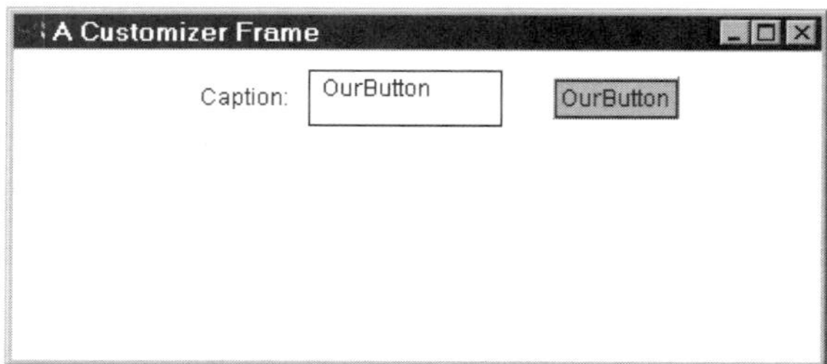

Figure 5-1: The CustApp class displaying an OurButton and an OurButtonCustomizer in a Frame.

The PropertyEditor Interface

You've noted from running the BeanBox that the property sheet provided property editors for properties with simple values. When choosing a new color, for example, you saw a color editor displaying a drop-down list with various colors to select from.

Many of the properties we've dealt with have been simple types like integers or colors. A property whose range of values doesn't fit into one of these simple types may need a special property editor that will let you customize how the choices are presented. For example, an *enumerated* type (a type that only takes on certain values) may need such an editor. An enumerated type might be interpreted by the default BeanBox property sheet as an integer. Therefore, the default property editor would let end users type in any valid integer value. For an enumerated type, this is not what you'd want.

The MoleculeName bean in the BDK displays graphical representations of various *molecules*. These molecules need to be presented to the end user in a property editor as strings. Since there is a finite number of molecules that the MoleculeName bean can handle, MoleculeName uses a custom property editor. When an end user selects a string from the property editor, the property editor uses the getTags( ) method to return the particular string the end user has selected. Here's the code for MoleculeNameEditor from the BDK (see Listing 5-3):

Listing 5-3: MoleculeNameEditor.java.

```
package sunw.demo.molecule;

/**
 * Special case property editor for molecule names.
 */

public class MoleculeNameEditor
        extends java.beans.PropertyEditorSupport {
```

```
    public String[] getTags() {
    String result[] = {
        "HyaluronicAcid",
        "benzene",
        "buckminsterfullerine",
        "cyclohexane",
        "ethane",
        "water"};
    return result;
    }

}
```

A property editor can be created by implementing the PropertyEditor interface directly. There is also a support class, PropertyEditorSupport, to help you with creating a PropertyEditor. You can see that the MoleculeNameEditor overrides PropertyEditorSupport. PropertyEditorSupport implements most of the methods in the PropertyEditor interface. The implementations of the overridden methods return no-ops (no operations) that give default values. So, by extending PropertyEditorSupport, you can simply provide those methods that you absolutely need. As mentioned above, getTags and setAsText are still two important methods if your property type requires them. The preceding MoleculeNameEditor is a good example of this: it has a property whose only values are certain strings; therefore it only overrode the getTags method in class PropertyEditorSupport.

Property editors link up with beanbox tools by firing a PropertyChangeEvent. Their main function is to let developers modify properties at design time, so it's necessary for them to fire events. They also provide interfaces to properties that aren't easily handled otherwise, like the enumerated type example.

Moving On

You've learned a lot about the property support provided by JavaBeans in this chapter. You learned about various types of properties, for example: simple, Boolean, bound, constrained, and indexed. Then you learned about the JavaBeans concept of customization, which lets a developer tailor information about a bean and the way it will be accessed by a software environment.

In the next chapter, I'll take a similarly detailed look at events, including a look at the different event classes that are new with Java 1.1.

Programming With Events

6

In modern Graphical User Interface (GUI) environments, an application is typically event driven. That is, the application spends much of its time waiting for user input in the form of mouse clicks or key strokes. These mouse clicks and keystrokes are packaged into an entity called an *event*. Since programming with events is one of the key features of working with a component architecture like JavaBeans, this chapter takes an in-depth view of the behavior and types of events available in Java 1.1.

You may recall from Chapter 2 that Java 1.1 has a new way of handling events: the delegation event model. Also, in Chapter 4 you created beans that used a custom event type. So far, we haven't looked at how events are produced. For example, which of Java's AWT objects produce which events? What event is produced when you click the mouse or click on a button? And how does the Java 1.1 event model handle a mouse click differently than Java 1.0? This chapter will answer these questions for you.

Java 1.0 Event Model

Two important areas of the Java 1.0 event model involve how events were represented and how they were responded to in your program. This section describes the java.awt.Event class and the inheritance method of responding to events that was required in 1.0.

Java 1.0 Event Class

In Java 1.0, events in the AWT are represented by the class java.awt.Event. Two fields that are important for using class Event are:

```
public int id;
public Object arg;
```

The field id is the identifier of the event. Check this identifier to see what event has occurred. The arg field contains extra information about the event; it does not have a value for all event types. The Event class also declares a number of constants that are possible values of the id field:

```
ACTION_EVENT
GOT_FOCUS
LOST_FOCUS
LIST_SELECT
LIST_DESELECT
MOUSE_DOWN
MOUSE_UP
WINDOW_DESTROY
WINDOW_MOVED
```

These constants are used in the id field to specify the type of event. Two other fields, target and when, are also important to the developer. For example, the when field contained the time of the event, and target was always the object receiving the event.

Rumors of 1.0's Death Greatly Exaggerated

The java.awt.Event class is still available in Java 1.1; it's just been superseded by the newer event model. At the time of writing, many browsers and Java development tools still don't fully support Java 1.1, so it's useful to know about the 1.0 model, too. You can learn much about events in the AWT by looking at the documentation of the java.awt.Event class to see what kinds of fields and methods it provides. Sun's Web site at http://java.sun.com provides all sorts of links to Java documentation.

Java 1.0 Events & Components

The Java 1.0 event model is based upon inheritance. That is, the way events function is heavily dependent upon the relationships between the classes in the AWT. The class Component contains a method called handleEvent to dispatch events. All of the AWT components, such as buttons, check boxes, and the like, inherit from Component. handleEvent, by default, is responsible for default handling of events routed to it and dispatching events to the convenience methods such as mouseUp, mouseDown, and action. When programming with this model, you either override handleEvent in your component subclass, or override some of the convenience methods. Inside handleEvent you decide among events using a large switch statement that checks the id field of the Event class and often other Event fields such as arg, what, x, and y.

The convenience methods such as mouseUp, mouseDown, and action break off some of the event functionality by handling specific events. It's important to remember that handleEvent is the dispatcher of events; it really dispatches events to the convenience methods. In the case of programming Java applets, the handleEvent method is in the java.applet. Applet class is often overridden; then all events coming to the applet are handled using the switch statement approach.

Problems With Java 1.0 Events

The Java 1.0 event model is fine for smaller applications, but does not scale well for larger applications. It also has a number of features that make it inefficient or difficult for the developer to work with. The new event model was implemented to fix some of these deficiencies. The new model also was necessary to support JavaBeans.

Here is a summary of the problems with the Java 1.0 event model:

- Events are broadcast to every object in the system whether that object is interested in the event or not.
- Remembering to return true or false to signal (whether you've finished with an event) is error-prone for the developer and difficult to maintain.
- Subtle bugs can be introduced if you forget to call the handleEvent method of the superclass after using one of the convenience methods.

Subtle Bugs With handleEvent( )

Forgetting to call the superclass's handleEvent when using the convenience methods can be dangerous to your health. handleEvent in class Component by default is the dispatcher of all messages. If you override mouseDown, for example, and don't override any other mouse events, the superclass's handleEvent needs to trap it. If you don't call super.handleEvent, these mouse events may be lost.

Java 1.1 Event Model

Java 1.1 introduces the delegation event model. In this model, the event space is divided up into event sources and event listeners. A summary of the ideas important to handling events in Java 1.1 is as follows:

- The event state is stored in an event object. Every event object is a subclass of java.util.EventObject.
- An object producing an event is called an *event source*. An object interested in receiving a certain type of event is called an *event listener*.
- An object that wants to receive events registers with a source for those events. The source implements add/remove methods for event listeners.
- A special *listener interface* is implemented by objects listening for certain events. If the event is called ABC, the listener interface has the name: ABCListener.
- Event listeners implement code of an actual event handling method by overriding methods (possibly more than one) in the listener interface.

Many New Event Classes

There are many different types of events generated in a GUI system. Any time the user moves or clicks the mouse or presses a key, a new type of event is generated. Whereas Java 1.0 uses the Event class in conjunction with Event.id to represent events, Java 1.1 uses many different event classes to represent events. One convenient way to categorize the various events is as high-level (or semantic) events and low-level events.

High-Level or Semantic Events

Semantic events encapsulate meaning from a low-level event. A command to close a dialog box frequently starts out in life as a single mouse click. The mouse click itself doesn't yet have a lot of meaning until we get the location of the click, decide that its location is inside the OK button of a particular dialog box, then translate it to an action event. Table 6-1 gives a list of semantic event types in Java 1.1.

Event type	Meaning
ActionEvent	Indicates an 'action.' Produced when an end user clicks a Button or selects an item in a List.
AdjustmentEvent	Produced by moving a Scrollbar.
ItemEvent	Selection or deselection of a CheckBox, CheckboxMenuItem, Choice, or List.
Text Event	Produced when an end user changes a value in a text field.

Table 6-1: High-level semantic events.

Semantics VS. Syntax

The word semantic is used in programming languages much the same way as it is used in natural languages. I think of semantics as the meaning of language, rather than grammar and syntax. In programming languages, semantic usually refers to 'what a computer statement does,' as opposed to: 'how do you write the code for it.' (The latter would be called syntax.)

Low-Level Events

Low-level events are units like mouse clicks and key strokes. MouseEvent is one of the Java 1.1 event types, and it deals with mouse clicks and mouse motion. Table 6-2 lists types of low-level events.

Event	When generated
ComponentEvent	A component is moved or hidden or resized.
ContainerEvent	A component is added to a container.
FocusEvent	A component gains or loses the focus.
KeyEvent	The user presses a key.
MouseEvent	The mouse moves, or a mouse click is received.
WindowEvent	A window is opened or destroyed.

Table 6-2: Low-level event classes.

Java 1.1 Event Class Hierarchy

Java 1.1 represents events with event classes for many types of events. Two very important classes at the base of the class hierarchy in Java 1.1 are EventObject and AWTEvent. The relationship between EventObject, AWTEvent, and the AWT event subclasses is shown in Figure 6-1. This section looks at EventObject and AWTEvent to see what role they play in the handling of events.

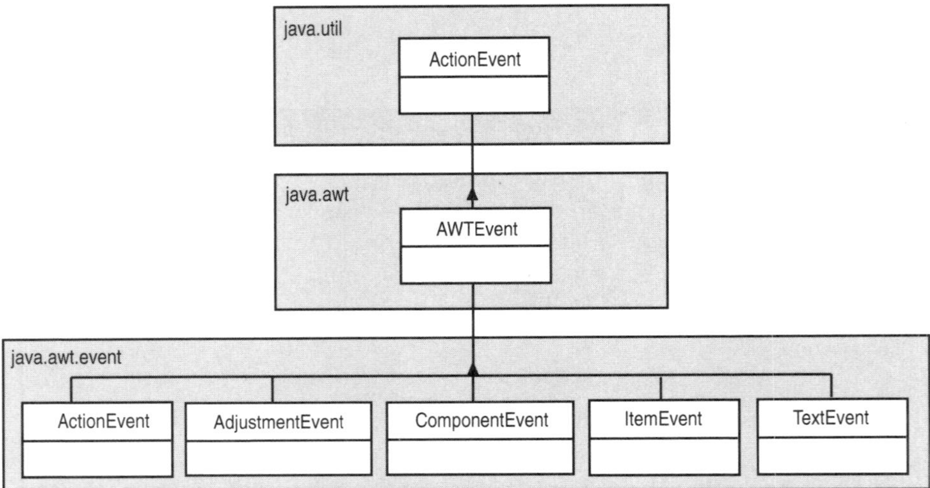

Figure 6-1: EventObject, AWTEvent, and some of their Event subclasses.

Class EventObject

EventObject, in the package java.util, is the superclass of event classes in the AWT and JavaBeans. It is the superclass of AWTEvent in the package java.awt. AWTEvent is, in turn, the superclass of the other event classes in the AWT. Java 1.1 has introduced a special package for AWT events called java.awt.event.

EventObject, as the "mother of all events," has some variables and methods universally applicable to all other event types. It has one protected instance variable, a public constructor, and two public methods. Its instance variable is declared as follows:

```
protected transient Object source;
```

The variable *source*, at run time, is the object that produced the event. The keyword transient means that this field will not be written out or serialized when the event object is saved. (Interestingly, transient was a legal keyword in Java 1.0 but had no effect—it was not implemented.) The public methods in EventObject are:

```
public EventObject(Object source);
public Object getSource();
public String toString(); //overrides class Object's
```

The constructor for EventObject takes one parameter, the source of the event. getSource( ) lets you retrieve the source of the event. This method is also inherited by AWTEvent and can be used there as well. The toString( ) method produces the result of the object as a string. All classes throughout Java have a toString( ) method since it is also implemented by class Object. (Many of the event classes use the AWTEvent version of toString( ) rather than provide their own implementation.)

Class AWTEvent

AWTEvent is the parent of all AWT event classes. AWTEvent, in the package java.awt, inherits its source object from EventObject. It uses the inherited getSource method to retrieve the source of the event. It contains an id, declared protected int, that can be used to identify the type of AWT event (the subclass representing the particular AWT event usually defines constants for its own event type).

Some important public methods in AWTEvent are:

```
public int getID();
String toString();
```

The getID( ) method is used to retrieve the id of an AWT event subclass. This lets the developer determine the actual type of the AWT event at run time. toString( ) is inherited and used by event subclasses since they usually don't override this method.

The other interesting feature of AWTEvent is its list of event masks such as:

```
public static final long ACTION_EVENT_MASK;
public static final long ADJUSTMENT_EVENT_MASK;
public static final long COMPONENT_EVENT_MASK;
public static final long CONTAINER_EVENT_MASK;
```

These constants are used by applets or programs that use events without using the event listener approach. This uses a method called enableEvents and is described later in this chapter in the section, "Java Events Without Listener Interfaces."

Event Objects Must Call Their Super

You saw that EventObject has a constructor and a method to get the source of the event. If you look at the code for an event class, (either an existing event type or an event type you've created yourself), you'll see a statement in the constructor such as:

```
super(source);
```

This statement passes the source of the event up to the superclass; it will finally get to the EventObject class, where it will be assigned to the source instance variable.

Introspection & Events

Just as for properties, there are design patterns and BeanInfo classes to help with the introspection of a bean's events in a beanbox tool. This section focuses on the design patterns for event listeners and the event support you can provide by declaring your own BeanInfo class.

Design Patterns

With Java 1.1, you may name your event classes whatever you like. However, there are design patterns for event listeners and their add/remove methods. For an event called TemperatureEvent, for example, the conventional listener name is TemperatureEventListener. Your listener will be derived from java.util.EventListener, and the add/remove methods have the following names below:

```
public void addTemperatureEventListener (TemperatureEventListener l);
public void removeTemperatureEventListener(TemperatureEventListener l);
```

Events & BeanInfo

The java.beans package has added a number of classes to the Java API that represent the features of a bean. Features such as methods, properties, events, and parameters are all features that have their own feature descriptor classes. These feature descriptor classes are used with introspection and are all subclasses of java.beans.FeatureDescriptor. Table 6-3 lists the feature descriptor classes that are used in conjunction with a BeanInfo class.

Class	Use
FeatureDescriptor	The superclass of all feature descriptor classes.
BeanDescriptor	Describes bean class and Customizer class.
EventSetDescriptor	Provides information about a bean's events.
MethodDescriptor	Provides name and information about a method.
ParameterDescriptor	Describes parameters; used with MethodDescriptors.
PropertyDescriptor	Describes the properties of a bean.
IndexedPropertyDescriptor	Describes indexed properties of a bean.

Table 6-3: Feature descriptor classes.

Using the EventSetDescriptor class, a BeanInfo can specify information about events. The BeanInfo method getEventSetDescriptor returns an array of EventSetDescriptor objects. A set of events is the methods of a single event listener. (A listener interface may declare more than one method for a single Event type.) The constructor for an EventSetDescriptor has parameters including the class of the bean, the name of the event class you're describing, the name of the event listener interface, and method names for the event handling methods. There is also a constructor that lets you specify the names of the add/remove methods for event listeners.

Event Adapter Classes

The classes called adapter classes in Java 1.1 are used as intermediaries between sources and listeners. You may recall hooking up a button with an event listener using the BeanBox. The message "Creating adapter class" displays. To explain what adapters do, consider that if you want to listen for mouse events, MouseListener requires you to implement all of the following methods—even if they are implemented as empty methods:

```
mouseClicked
mouseEntered
mouseExited
mousePressed
mouseReleased
```

The class MouseAdapter implements this interface and provides empty implementations of each of the methods. To catch mouse events, you can just subclass MouseAdapter rather than implement all the MouseListener methods. There are adapter classes in the Java 1.1 API for those event listeners that have more than one method in them. ActionListener, for example, with its one method actionPerformed, does not have an adapter class.

The idea of adapter classes can be extended to the more general case of needing two or more different actions for one event. A Button produces an action event. Usually in a program you set it up to perform one action only. If you want one Button to perform two different actions (call two different methods), you can create an adapter class to do the switching. See the following code:

```
import java.awt.event.*;

public class ButtonAdapter implements ActionListener
{
static final int FIRST = 0;
static final int SECOND = 1;
int ident;
App target;

public ButtonAdapter(int id, App target)
{
    this.ident= id;
    this.target = target;
}
public void actionPerformed(ActionEvent e)
{
    switch (ident)
    {
    case FIRST:
        target.firstMethod(); break;

    case SECOND:
        target.secondMethod(); break;
    } // switch
} // actionPerformed
} // class
```

The class ButtonAdapter sits between a main application (called target here) and another class containing the interface. This other class might be the GUI of the application. The following code, for the graphical part of the application, shows the creation of two buttons and two ButtonAdapters. It then associates the two buttons with the ButtonAdapters:

```
class Graphical extends Frame
{
    public Graphical(AppType target)
    {
    // create two buttons
    button1 = new Button("First");
    button2 = new Button("Second");

    // create two adapters
    Adapter1=new ButtonAdapter(ButtonAdapter.FIRST, target);
    adapter2=new ButtonAdapter(ButtonAdapter.SECOND, target);

    // add the adapters as listeners for the buttons
    button1.addActionListener(adapter1);
    button2.addActionListener(adapter2);

    setVisible(true);
}
```

Of course, I haven't shown the main application (called target in the code example). The target application would be created in another part of the code and passed to the constructor for the class Graphical. The target application could contain only application-specific code, since the code for the interface has been placed in the class Graphical. The main idea is that when you click a button, it sends an action event to the adapter class, which calls (via the switch statement) different methods, depending upon the internal constant that has been set. Adapter classes are used heavily in Sun's BeanBox when you connect one component to another.

Samples of Handling AWT Events

This section catalogs some AWT event classes and their listeners that you will frequently encounter. Each section contains the same parallel form; that is, the event class is described, along with its listeners, adapters, and type of AWT element that produce the event. Example code follows each section to demonstrate how to use the event listener of the appropriate type.

Class ActionEvent

Action events represent a high-level action of some sort from the GUI. The ActionEvent has a listener class called ActionListener. ActionListener has one method, actionPerformed. The AWT classes that produce action events are

Button, List, MenuItem, and TextField. Since ActionListener has one method only, there are no adapters. A code example using an ActionListener is as follows:

```
import java.awt.event.*;
public class MyApplet extends java.applet.Applet
implements ActionListener
{
    public void init()
    {
        setLayout(new FlowLayout());
        Button button = new Button("press");
        button.addActionListener(this);
        this.add(button);
    }
    public void actionPerformed(ActionEvent e)
    {
        System.out.println("a button was pressed.");
    }
}
```

Class AdjustmentEvent

AdjustmentEvent represents the action when an end user moves a scrollbar. AdjustmentEvent's listener class is called AdjustmentListener. The AdjustmentListener interface has one method, AdjustmentValueChanged. An AdjustmentEvent is produced by a scrollbar and by no other AWT elements. As for other events with only one method, there is no adapter class. A code example is as follows:

```
import java.awt.event.*;

public class Applet2 extends java.applet.Applet
implements AdjustmentListener
{
    public void init()
    {
    setLayout(new FlowLayout());
    Scrollbar s =
    new Scrollbar (Scrollbar.Horizontal);
    s.addAdjustmentListener(this);
    this.add(s);
    } // init
```

```
    public void adjustmentValueChanged(AdjustmentEvent e)
    {
    System.out.println("Scroll moved.");
    }
} // class
```

Class ItemEvent

ItemEvent represents what happens when an end user selects or deselects an item. ItemEvent's listener interface is ItemListener. ItemListener defines one method, itemStateChanged. Item events are generated when an end user selects or deselects (changes the selection state) of an item in a List. Also it is generated when a selection or deselection occurs on a Checkbox, CheckboxMenuItem, or Choice (a drop-down list). There is no adapter class for ItemEvent. A code example using a Checkbox is as follows:

```
import java.awt.event.*;

public class Applet3 extends java.applet.Applet
implements ItemListener
{
    public void init()
    {
    setLayout(new FlowLayout());
    Checkbox cb = new Checkbox();
    cb.addItemListener(this);
    this.add(cb);
    }
    public void itemStateChanged(ItemEvent ie)
    {
        System.out.println("item state changed.");
    }
} // class
```

Class TextEvent

TextEvent represents what happens when an end user changes the text in a TextComponent. A TextComponent is a graphical item holding text. A TextEvent uses the TextListener interface. TextListener has one method, textValueChanged. Text events are generated when the end user changes the text in a TextComponent. This happens when typing new text into a TextField class object. TextComponent is the superclass of TextArea and TextField. You do not create an instance of TextComponent in your program, only one of its subclasses. There is no adapter class for TextEvent. A code example using a TextField is as follows:

```
import java.awt.event.*;

public class Applet4 extends java.applet.Applet
implements TextListener
{
    public void init()
    {
    setLayout(new FlowLayout());
    TextField t = new TextField();
    t.addTextListener(this);
    this.add(t);
    }
    public void textValueChanged(TextEvent te)
    {
        System.out.println("text value changed.");
    }
} // class
```

Class MouseEvent

MouseEvent handles mouse motion and events that are generated when the mouse is clicked. MouseEvent has two listeners, MouseListener and MouseMotionListener. The methods in MouseListener are mouseClicked, mouseEntered, mouseExited, mousePressed, and mouseReleased. The methods in MouseMotionListener are mouseDragged and mouseMoved. MouseEvent has one adapter class called MouseAdapter. The following example uses three of the mouse methods, mouseClicked, mouseReleased, and mousePressed. It prints a message to the standard output when the mouse is pressed, clicked, or released. I've implemented the MouseListener interface directly. Note that we must provide empty implementations for the MouseListener methods we are not using.

```
import java.awt.event.*;

public class Applet5 extends java.applet.Applet implements MouseListener
{
    public void init()
    {
        addMouseListener(this);
    }
```

```
    // override the mouse pressed method
    public void mousePressed(MouseEvent mEvt)
    {
        int x = mEvt.getX();
        int y = mEvt.getX();
        System.out.println("Mouse pressed at " + x + " " + y);
    }

    // called when mouse clicked
    public void mouseClicked(MouseEvent mEvt)
    {
        int x,y;
        x = mEvt.getX();
        y = mEvt.getX();
        System.out.println("Mouse clicked at " + x + " " + y);
    }
    // called when mouse button released
    public void mouseReleased(MouseEvent mEvt)
    {
        int x,y;
        x = mEvt.getX();
        y = mEvt.getX();
        System.out.println("Mouse released at " + x + " " + y);
    }
    // empty methods follow
    public void mouseEntered
    {
    ;
    }
    public void mouseExited
    {
    ;
    }

}
```

Class KeyEvent

KeyEvent handles key strokes. KeyEvent has one listener, KeyListener. The methods in KeyListener are keyPressed, keyReleased, and keyTyped. KeyEvent has one adapter class called KeyAdapter. The following example simply traps the three key events. The applet implements the KeyListener interface directly.

```
import java.awt.event.*;

public class Applet6 extends java.applet.Applet implements KeyListener
{
    public void init()
    {
        addKeyListener(this);
    }
    // override the key pressed method
    public void keyPressed(KeyEvent k)
    {
        System.out.println("Key pressed");
    }

    public void keyReleased(KeyEvent k)
    {
        System.out.println("Key released");
    }
    public void keyTyped(KeyEvent k)
    {
        System.out.println("Key typed");
    }

}
```

Java Events Without Listener Interfaces

Java 1.1 also has a way to handle events without using the event listener approach described in this chapter. It uses various methods whose names begin with the word, "process." A new 1.1 method called processEvents is very similar to handleEvent in class Component (in Java 1.0). processEvent is defined in a number of AWT classes including Component, Button, TextField, and Window. There are also specialty methods analogous to the convenience methods (such as mouseUp and mouseDown). Some of these methods include processMouseEvents and processKeyEvents.

To use this way of handling events, you must first enable events by calling enableEvents. enableEvents is passed to a parameter: a mask representing the type of events you are interested in receiving. The event masks that are declared in class AWTEvent are used for this purpose. The following code only enables one type of event with enableEvents: a mouse press event. It then overrides the processMouseEvent method to print out a message when the mouse is pressed.

```
import java.awt.event.*;
import java.awt.*;
public class MouseApplet extends java.applet.Applet
{
public void init()
{
    this.enableEvents(AWTEvent.MOUSE_EVENT_MASK);

}
public void processMouseEvent(MouseEvent mEvt)
{
    if (mEvt.getID() == MouseEvent.MOUSE_PRESSED)
    {
        System.out.println("MousePressed");
    }
    else super.processMouseEvent(mEvt);
}
} // applet class
```

Moving On

You've learned a lot about event support in Java 1.1 in this chapter. In the next chapter, we'll get into Netscape's support for JavaBeans when we talk about Netscape's Visual JavaScript.

7

Visual JavaScript

This chapter begins a discussion of Netscape's support for integrating components into your applications. You may be familiar with the language JavaScript. Although it inherits part of Java's name, Java and JavaScript are different. Java is a general purpose language with some similarities to C and C++. JavaScript is a scripting language that enhances Web pages and gives you some capabilities not found with HyperText Markup Language (HTML) alone. Netscape's Visual JavaScript provides a visual interface to garden-variety JavaScript while letting you build on the power of components with your HTML pages. Your applications can be previewed and deployed using Navigator 4.0. Visual JavaScript also cooperates with Netscape's Composer, the Web page editor component of Netscape Communicator. JavaBeans, HTML components such as forms and tables, and the new JavaScript beans are all easily used from Visual JavaScript. In this chapter, I explore Visual JavaScript, beginning with some general information about Visual JavaScript, then moving on to using components.

JavaScript & HTML

JavaScript and HTML are two languages that have grown up around the Internet. Netscape considers these two languages components of their Netscape ONE technologies: the set of technologies for creating crossware applications. HTML is of course a widely used standard; JavaScript is a scripting language invented by Netscape. A complete description of JavaScript and HTML is beyond the scope of this book, but this section provides some introductory material on these topics. If you aren't up to speed with either of these topics, some consultation of some other resources will be time well spent. (In this section I suggest some resources to get you going.)

JavaScript

JavaScript, the scripting language developed by Netscape, has various versions; the version that works with Navigator 4 is version 1.2. JavaScript code is embedded in an HTML page between <SCRIPT> and </SCRIPT> tags. Depending upon in which section of the page the <SCRIPT> tag is placed, the code might be loaded right away when the page is loaded or not. JavaScript also lets you define functions that are not executed until some event happens, such as a button click. JavaScript also has built-in events (such as onclick for button clicks) that can be linked up to functions. A book on this subject that will get you going is *Official Netscape JavaScript 1.2 Book* (Ventana 1997).

HTML

HyperText Markup Language is a method of presenting text information based upon *hypertext*. Hypertext, which has a history that predates HTML, is a method of presenting contextual information without interrupting its flow. The hypertext in HTML is the links with which every user of a Web browser is familiar. The text in Navigator (usually blue underlined) that links you to other parts of the Web is also the hypertext in HTML.

HTML is really a special form of Standard Generalized Markup Language (SGML), originally developed in the early 1960s. A book that can take you through the basics of HTML is *Official HTML Publishing for Netscape, Second Edition* (Ventana 1997). Since HTML is an open standard, there is also ample documentation for HTML available on the Web.

What Is Visual JavaScript?

Visual JavaScript is a visual development environment for JavaScript and HTML. It lets you create JavaScript code visually and add components, all centered around the Web page on which you are working. JavaScript lets you preview your Web page in the Navigator 4.0 and deploy it. It lets you easily use Composer to assist with editing your pages. This development tool includes the following important features:

- An easy-to-use page builder with three different editing views.
- A project environment with a tree-based control for ease of use and management of your projects.
- The ability to use JavaScript code and objects to enliven Web pages.
- An expandable palette of components, JavaBeans, JavaScript beans, HTML forms and tables, and CORBA compliant components.
- The ability to include LiveWire objects in your projects for communication with databases on an Enterprise server.

Visual JavaScript lets you integrate JavaScript with HTML pages in a visual way. It's also a component container that lets you integrate beans and JavaScript components into your pages.

TIP

To download Visual JavaScript, go to http://home.netscape.com | Software Download |Visual JavaScript.

About the CDK

Netscape also has a toolkit they call the Component Development Kit (CDK), which is described further in Chapter 8. It includes the source and JavaScript bean (JSB) files for sample components in JavaScript. JSBs are a new form of component for JavaScript. The CDK ships with a tool for developing JavaScript beans called Acadia Software's JavaScript Bean developer. The creation of JavaScript beans is discussed in Chapter 8, and the use of Acadia's builder tool is discussed in Appendix B.

Starting Visual JavaScript

Start Visual JavaScript by selecting it from the Start | Programs | Netscape Visual JavaScript menu item—or by going to Start | Run in Windows 95 (if you know where the program file is located). When Visual JavaScript starts up, you should see the main window (see Figure 7-1). You'll be interacting with the Visual JavaScript toolbar often while using the program. The toolbar has icons for the following functions:

- **New**. Create a new file. Usually an HTML page.
- **Import**. Import an existing file into the project.
- **Save**. Save an open file.
- **Preview**. Start Netscape Navigator 4 to preview the HTML page.
- **Compose**. Start Netscape Composer to assist with editing of your HTML pages.
- **Deploy**. Deploy your application once you are done with development.
- **Refresh**. Refresh the screen.
- **Debugger**. Start the debugger.
- **Palette**. Invoke the palette window to work with components.
- **Inspector**. Inspect an object: a component or another project object.

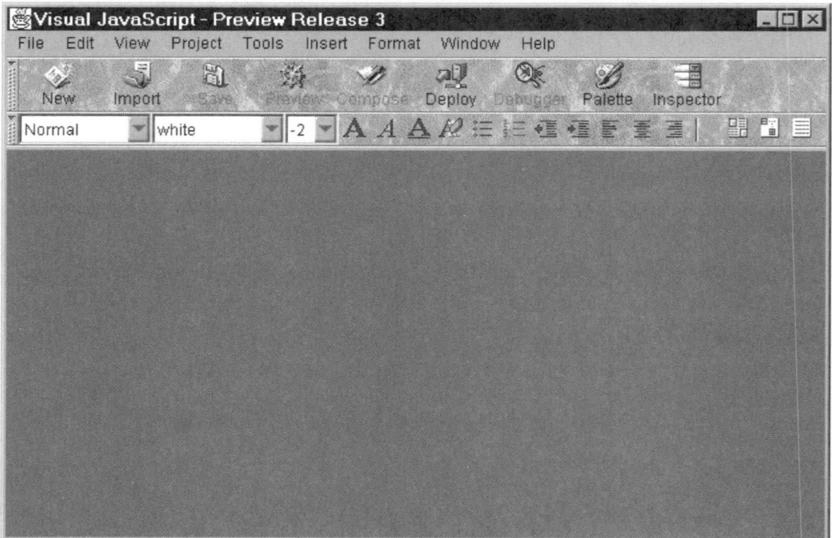

Figure 7-1: The Visual JavaScript main window with its main toolbar.

The functions chosen by these icons have equivalent items on the menu bar. For example, Tools | Palette | Load will load the palette just as clicking on the Palette button will. You can also see from Figure 7-1 that there are other icons that have to do with style functions of the page: bold, italic text, and so on. These icons are as follows:

- **Bold**. Make text bold.
- **Italic**. Italicize text.
- **Underline**. Underline text.
- **Remove all styles**. Start fresh without style codes.
- **Bulleted list**. Create a list with bullets.
- **Numbered list**. Create a numbered list.
- **Decrease indent**. Decrease the indentation of the text.
- **Increase Indent**. Increase the indentation of the text.
- **Align left, center, and right**. Adjust alignment of text.
- **Layout**. View page in layout mode.
- **Structural**. View page in structural mode.

Visual JavaScript Features

Now let's break up Visual JavaScript's support into various features. I've picked out a few important areas in which you'll be interested as a component developer and as an end user of components.

Project Feature

Visual JavaScript development is based around the concept of a *project*. If you've worked with an Integrated Development Environment (IDE) to develop code in a programming language such as C, C++, or Visual Basic, the idea of projects is familiar. See the project window in Figure 7-2. The various nodes represent the various data and source files that are part of a Web-based project: HTML pages, Java class files, data files for images like Graphics Interchange Format (.GIF) files, and so on.

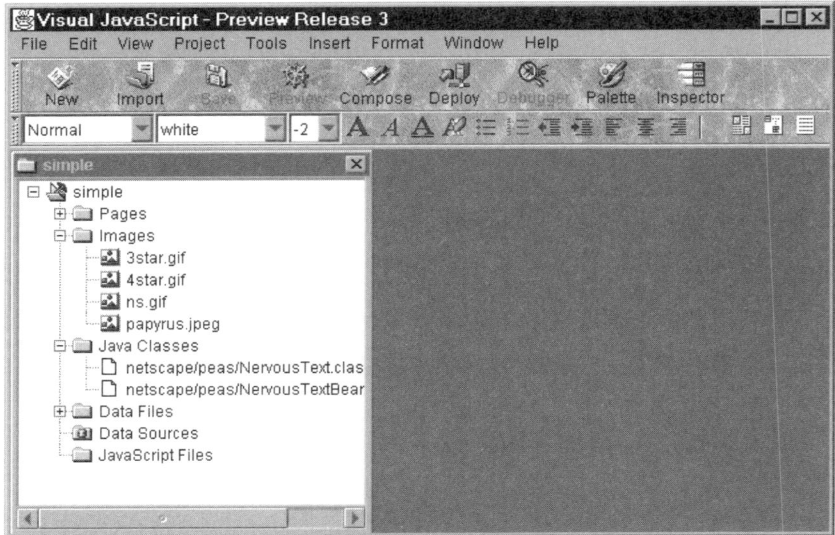

Figure 7-2: The Visual JavaScript main window with its project view window.

The project view shows your project hierarchically. The project file is stored on the disk in a file with the .PRJ extension. (The actual files making up the project are not stored in the .PRJ file, just their locations.) Double-click on a plus sign in the project window next to what you are interested in to expand it to its lower level. For example, if you click on the Pages node in the "simple" project (the simple project is one of the default projects that is loaded when Visual JavaScript starts up), you'll see the node expand to show the following files:

- **Test.html**: A test page that contains examples of HTML forms and components.
- **JSClient.html**: An example page that contains examples of JavaScript components such as buttons and the scrolling banner component.

These are the two HTML files associated with the simple project. The next feature we'll examine is at the heart of developing with Visual JavaScript, the HTML Page builder.

Page Builder Feature

The page builder is the mode in which a developer will spend most of his or her time working. It has more features than a simple HTML editor and lets you work with the page visually. With the page builder you can view a page in different modes and easily add applets, beans, HTML, or JavaScript components to the page. See Figure 7-3 for the appearance of the page builder main window.

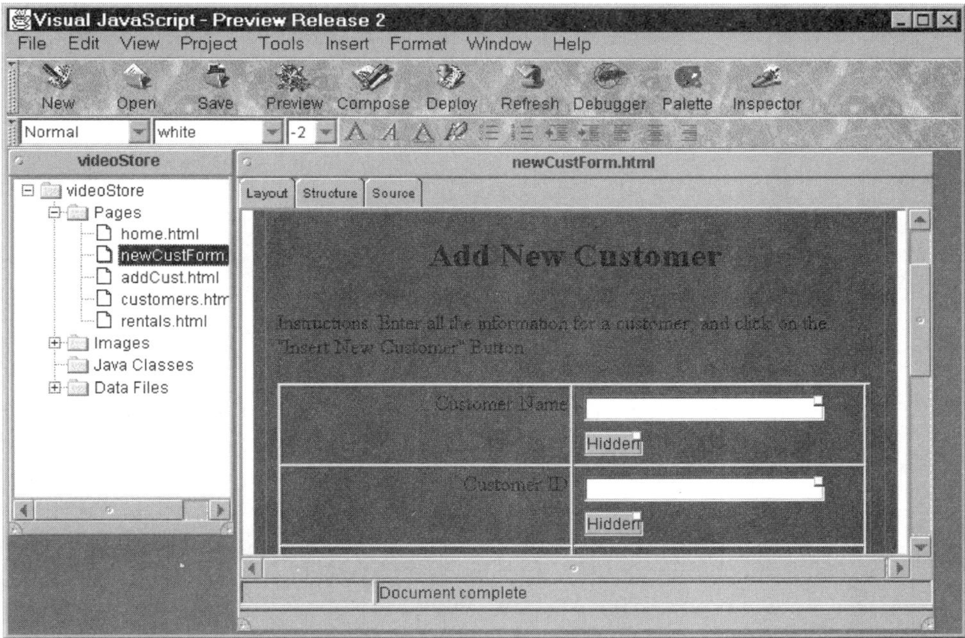

Figure 7-3: The page builder main window in layout view.

The page builder lets you view the HTML page in three different ways. Choose between the following modes from the View menu: Layout view, Structural view, and Source view.

Layout View

The Layout view is the closest to "what you see is what you get" among the display/editing views provided. In fact, it is designed to be what you'll see in Navigator 4 when deploying your final application. You can select objects on the page, and the selection is preserved in the Structural view. See Figure 7-4 for an example of the Layout view.

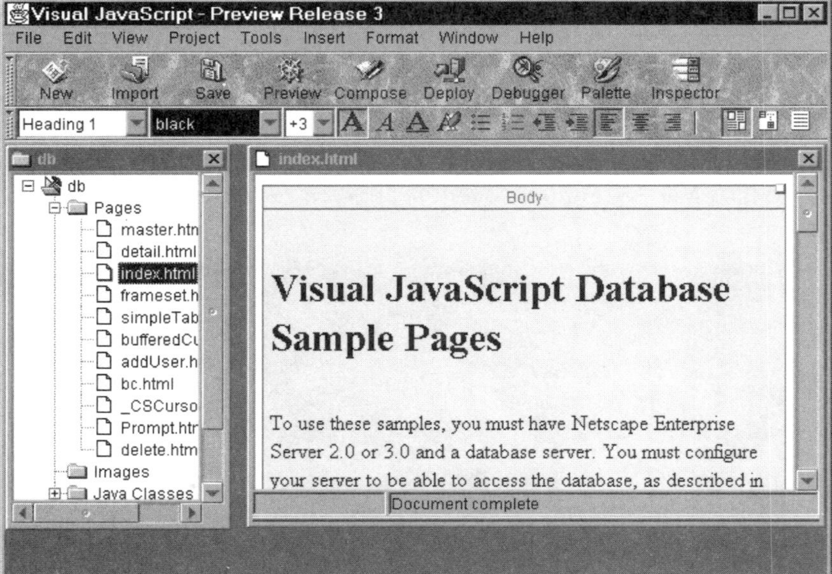

Figure 7-4: The layout view in Visual JavaScript's page builder.

Structural View

The structural view may be a little less familiar than the layout view, which is, after all, the view seen by readers of an HTML page. This view shows you a structural representation of how your page is laid out. This could also be called a hierarchical display. The page is laid out in node form, one node expanding to the next. In a sense, this view does for the HTML page what the project view does for projects.

At the top of the structural view you'll see a tag called TOP. As you add paragraphs, text, images, HTML tags, and components, you'll see the structure expand (new tags will be added). Figure 7-5 shows some of tags you'll see in Structural view, representing the overall structure of the page.

Clicking a node in the structural view shows the next level within the first level. For example, when you first see the structural view for a page, you may just see the TOP tag mentioned above, which may be expanded to show HEAD, TITLE, and BODY tags.

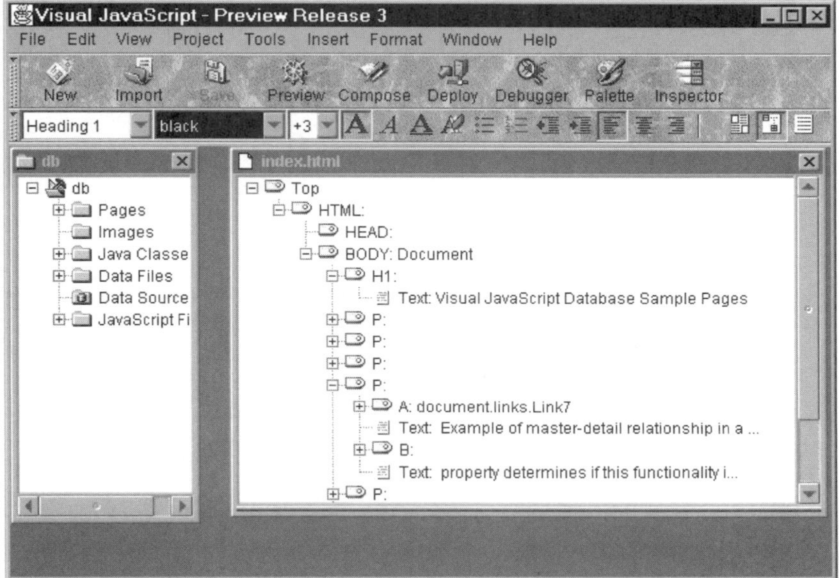

Figure 7-5: Visual JavaScript's structural view showing the indentation of various tag levels.

NOTE

In the Preview Release 3 of Visual JavaScript (PR-3) the selection is preserved between the layout and the structural view. That is, if you select an item in the structural view and go back to the layout view, that object is still selected. This selection is not preserved across the source view, however. Selection across all *views may be implemented in a future release. If you select an object in one view, the selection will be maintained over the three different views.*

Source View

This view is to what you are most used if you've written HTML with a text editor or viewed the source HTML of a page you are visiting on the Web. Source view displays the HTML text. In the Visual JavaScript Preview Release 3, the HTML cannot be edited from this view; that is, the source text you see in this view is read-only. Figure 7-6 shows a screen shot of the source view.

On the upper right-hand corner of the source view window there is a button labeled reformat source; this reformats the HTML source so it looks better to the eye.

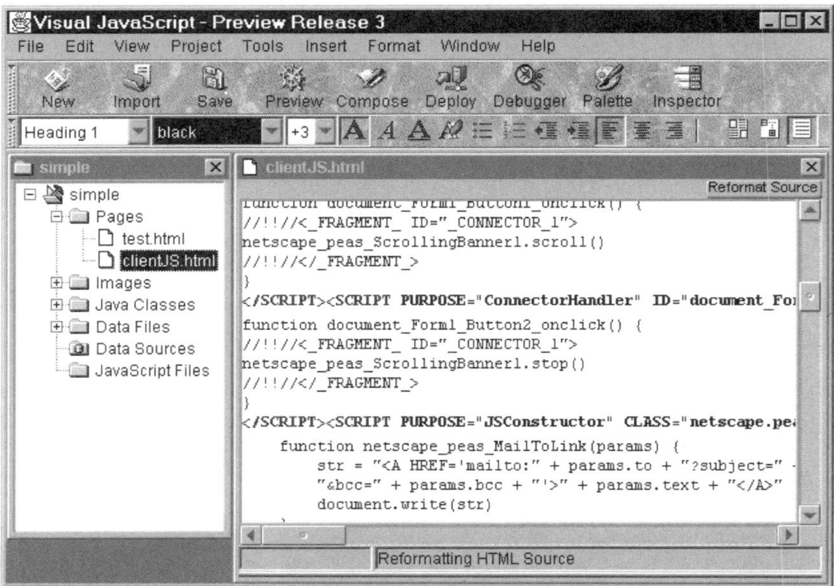

Figure 7-6: The source view of a page.

Inspector Feature

You can open an Inspector on a component by double-clicking on it in the layout view or in the palette. In fact, you can click on other features in the application environment, like a node in the project tree, and open an inspector on it. We've seen in previous chapters the importance of beanbox tools being able to discover and display the properties and events of a component. The inspector is such a display. Figure 7-7 shows an inspector window displaying the properties and events of the NervousText bean.

One very interesting feature of the inspector window is its ability to display events with the ". . ." notation. At the bottom of the inspector window, there is a section describing default events, such as Focus and Component events. Clicking on the . . . at the end of an event row displays the current handler for that particular event (if one has been defined). The code displayed is in JavaScript and can be customized by the developer.

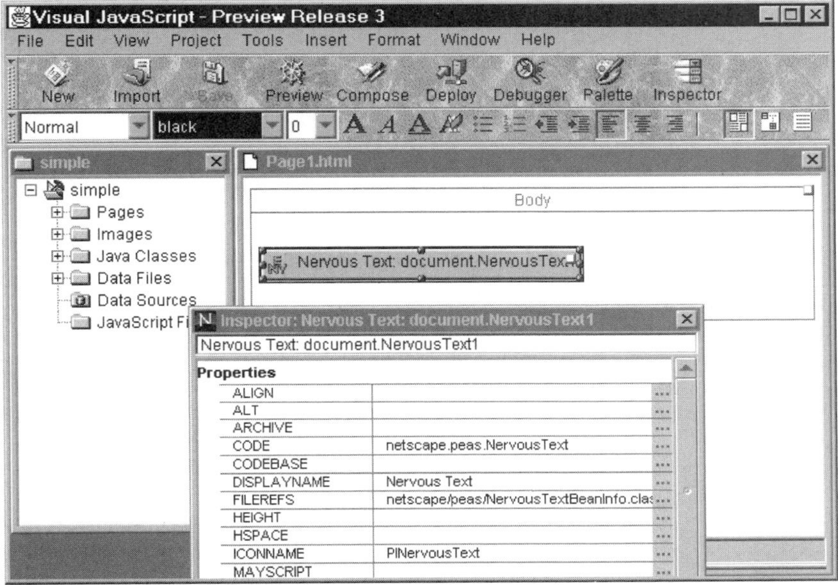

Figure 7-7: An inspector window showing the properties and events of the NervousText applet-bean.

Interacting With Components

You work with components in Visual JavaScript by dragging them from the palette to the page builder window to include them in your project. You can also copy components from the layout view of a page to the palette by dragging and dropping. The palette contains the components presently loaded in your application session (see Figure 7-8). When you first start Visual JavaScript, the palette is not yet loaded. Load it by clicking on the palette button or choosing Tools | Load. You'll see the message, "loading Palette for default user."

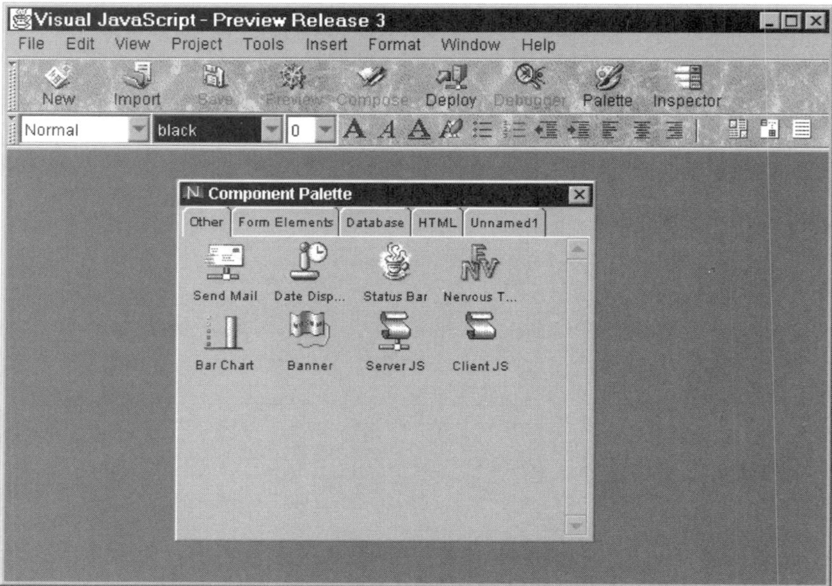

Figure 7-8: The palette.

Visual JavaScript is delivered with some pre-installed components. We'll talk about a few of them as examples in this chapter. Chapter 13, "Netscape Component Reference," will provide more reference material about Netscape's components. These components will be loaded with the palette when it starts up. Different categories of components are on different tab "pages" and can be selected by clicking different tabs. The four tab pages in Visual JavaScript PR-3 are:

- **Other:** JavaScript components not interacting with a database.
- **DataBase:** Java and JavaScript components for linking with LiveWire databases.
- **HTML:** HTML tags like mailto and IMG for image.
- **Form Elements:** HTML form elements such as text fields and buttons.

TIP

You can also insert new components using Tools | Insert to palette command from the menu bar. This is discussed in the section, "New Beans with Visual JavaScript."

Let's see an example of creating a project and then dragging and dropping a component onto a page.

Creating a Project

Open an existing project or create a new project. You can create a new project as follows:

1. Select Project | New.
2. Enter the name of the project in the project dialog box.
3. Close the dialog box.

Dragging & Dropping

Once you have an open project, go to the project window and open one of the HTML pages in the project. You do this by going to the Pages node in the project and double-clicking on the name of the page you want. Load the palette by clicking its icon—if it hasn't been already loaded. Find and then select the NervousText applet-bean from the palette (it should be on the blank tab page).

TIP

Components can be cut and pasted between tab pages, and they can be dragged from the layout view to the palette.

You should see the NervousText bean in the layout view (see Figure 7-9).

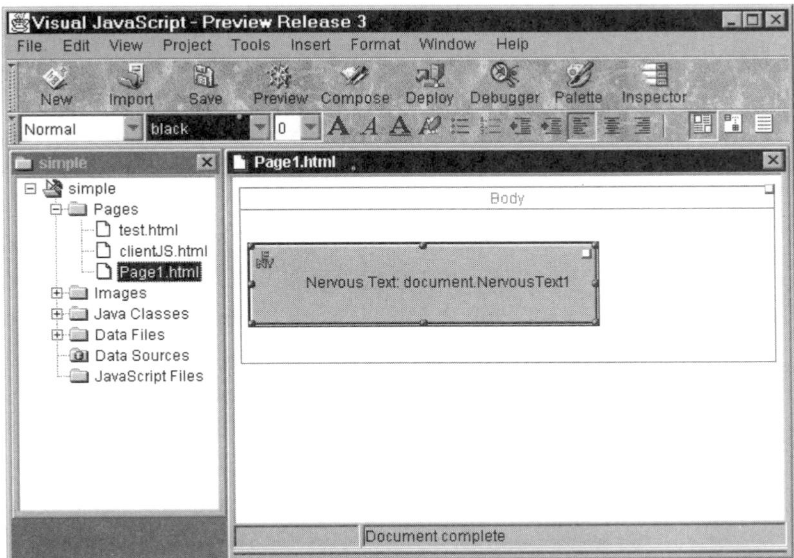

Figure 7-9: The layout view of a page with NervousText selected.

Note that the NervousText bean is surrounded by a rectangle. The rectangle contains a label for the component such as: NervousText: document.NervousText1. This selection rectangle can be used to size the component. Also, the upper right-hand corner of the rectangle is important for creating connections with other components. It invokes the Connection Builder. We'll describe connections in more detail in the section, "Connecting Components."

We can test the NervousText bean in Navigator by clicking the Preview icon in the toolbar or by choosing Preview from the menu.

Directory Structures

To preview the page, Visual JavaScript will have to find the class file NervousText.class. NervousText is in the package netscape.peas. Navigator will try to find the code for NervousText.class in the same directory in which the HTML page resides. When installing a new component to the palette, Visual JavaScript should create a new directory under its own directory, corresponding to the package name of your bean.

Connecting Components

Visual JavaScript has a component connection feature that is very similar to action events in JavaBeans. To connect components, you use the Connection Builder. Suppose you have a page with a button and an HTML form on it and you wish to connect the button to a field in the form. Here's how to do that:

1. Click the mouse on the upper right corner of a component.
2. Hold the left mouse button down over the upper right corner and drag the component. You can tell you are over the correct spot if the cursor turns into an up arrow.
3. As you drag, you will see a green and red plug connector. This tells you that you are in connection mode.
4. Drop the connector on the field in your form that you want to connect to.
5. You should see the Connection Builder dialog appear; it will have two parts. One part describes from where you are coming, the source of the event. The other to where you are going, the target of the event.

New Beans With Visual JavaScript

A user of Visual JavaScript doesn't have to be content with using the built-in components. If you've created your own bean or JavaScript component, it can be loaded into the application (by way of the palette). You can drag and drop your own components just like the built-in ones we've seen so far. Three kinds of new components can be used (there is a fourth type, HTML components, that we won't cover in this book):

- Java applets, including Java 1.02 applets.
- Java components, all of which are JavaBeans.
- JavaScript beans (also called JSB).

Netscape Web browsers since Navigator 2.0 have supported applets on a Web page, so the inclusion of Java 1.02 applets in Visual JavaScript is not surprising. Use of these pre-Java 1.1 applets requires that you use the APPLET tag—just as you would have for Java 1.0. But you would have to use a text editor to type in the APPLET tag. (You would use the Applet tag CODE parameter to reference the class file of the applet.) Listing 7-1 is an example of a short HTML file that loads an applet.

Listing 7-1: An HTML file containing an APPLET tag.

```
<HTML>
<BODY>
<APPLET code="anApplet.class" width=250 height=200>
</APPLET>
</BODY>
</HTML>
```

If you convert your applet into a bean, largely by including setter and getter methods for your properties, compile your applet with javac.exe, and archive the result into a Jar file. You can then load the applet into the component palette. A summary of these two options is as follows:

- **Java 1.0 applets**: They can be used in your Web page as before by typing in the APPLET tag with a text editor.
- **JavaBean applets**: Applets that have been converted to JavaBeans and archived into a Jar file can be loaded to the component palette in Visual JavaScript.

One important difference between using an applet as a bean and the 'old way' is that Visual JavaScript will do a lot of the work for you with applet-beans. You can see this if you open the palette and pick the tab page labeled

Other. One of the applet-beans is the NervousText applet bean, that I mentioned previously. This NervousText applet will likely be familiar to anyone who has used Java 1.0; it was one of Sun's example applets with the JDK. An interesting and helpful thing is that you can drag the NervousText bean to the page builder; the applet tag is inserted in the page for you (you must go to source view to be able to view it). Listing 7-2 shows the HTML text that was generated by Visual JavaScript by creating a new HTML page, loading the palette, and then dragging the NervousText applet into the body of the page. I then chose View | Source from the View menu to put the page builder in source view.

Listing 7-2: An HTML file generated by Visual JavaScript.

```
<HTML><HEAD>
</HEAD><BODY><P><APPLET NAME="NervousText1" CODE="netscape.peas.NervousText"
FILEREFS="netscape/peas/NervousTextBeanInfo.class,netscape/peas/
NervousText.class" DISPLAYNAME="Nervous Text" SHORTDESCRIPTION="Nervous
Text" ICONNAME="PINervousText"><PARAM NAME="message">
</APPLET></P><SCRIPT PURPOSE=ConnectorInfo>
</SCRIPT></BODY>
</HTML>
```

In Listing 7-2, you can see some familiar features. The CODE parameter of the APPLET tag references the class file of the applet we are loading. The FILEREFS parameter may be less familiar. As we've discussed in previous chapters, applets and beans may come with support files. For beans in particular, BeanInfo classes, Customizers, and PropertyEditors might be required. And if you have written an applet that does animation, you'll know that the image being animated is often in the form of a Graphics Interchange Format file (.GIF).

Visual JavaScript handles these files with the FILEREFS parameter. The FILEREFS parameter associates various data files with the applet. FILEREFS is a list of file names separated by commas. For example, the NervousText applet requires the following list of files for its FILEREFS.

```
FILEREFS="netscape/peas/NervousTextBeanInfo.class,netscape/peas/
NervousText.class"
```

NOTE

A bean in Visual JavaScript must have a BeanInfo object available. We discussed creating BeanInfo classes using the BeanInfo interface in Chapters 5 and 6. Beans also must be applets in the preview releases of Visual JavaScript (this may be changed later).

Loading a New Component

The MyAnimation class is an applet that performs an animation. It has a delay variable that controls how fast the animation will take place. It can be turned into a bean by giving it a set and a get method for its delay property, creating a BeanInfo class for it, and then archiving it in a Jar file. The code listing for the main animation class (MyAnimation.java) is in Listing 7-3:

Listing 7-3: MyAnimation.java.

```
package sunw.demo.myanim;

/** An animation java program
*
*/
import java.awt.*;
import java.applet.Applet;


public class MyAnimation extends Applet implements Runnable
{
    Thread animator;
    Image anImage[] = new Image[4];
    int currentImage;

    /* public (null) Constructor */
    public  MyAnimation()
    {
    ;
    }

    public void init()
    {
    animator = new Thread(this);
    currentImage = 0;
    int cnt = 0;

    for (cnt = 0; cnt < 3; cnt++)
        anImage[cnt] = getImage(getDocumentBase(), "dougbw" + (cnt) +
".gif");
    } // init
    public void start()
    {
        if (animator.isAlive())
        {
            animator.resume();
```

```
    }
    else
    {
        animator.start();
    }
} // start

public void stop()
{
    animator.suspend();
}
public void destroy()
{
    animator.stop();
}

public void run()   {
for(int w=0;w < 20;w++) {
    repaint();
    try {
        Thread.sleep(m_delay);
    }
    catch (Exception e) {
    return;
    }

    // advance to the next frame
    currentImage++;
 if (currentImage > 2)
        currentImage = 0;
} //for
} // run method

public void paint(Graphics g)
{
    // just draw the current image
    g.drawImage(anImage[currentImage], (int)15, (int)10, null);
} // paint

public long  getDelay()
{
    return m_delay;
}
public void setDelay(long inDelay)
{
```

```
        m_delay = inDelay;
    }
   private long m_delay =750;

} // myAnimation
```

MyAnimation.java is a fairly typical Java animation applet. It uses a thread to run the animation. Most of the action is in the run( ) method which we override when we implement the Runnable interface. Note that the MyAnimation class needs a BeanInfo if it wants to be used in Visual JavaScript applets (see Listing 7-4). The BeanInfo class for MyAnimation just provides a beanbox tool with information about the "delay" property.

Listing 7-4: MyAnimationBeanInfo.java.

```
package sunw.demo.myanim;

import java.beans.*;


/**
 * BeanInfo for MyAnimation
 *  Simply returns the "delay" property
 * @see sunw.demo.myanim.MyAnimation
*/
public class MyAnimationBeanInfo extends SimpleBeanInfo
{
    // override getPropertyDescriptors
    public PropertyDescriptor[]     getPropertyDescriptors()
    {
    try {
        PropertyDescriptor pd = new PropertyDescriptor("delay",
MyAnimationBeanInfo.class);
        PropertyDescriptor result[] = { pd };

        return result;
    }
    catch (Exception ex) {

        System.err.println("MyAnimationBeanInfo: an exception occurred: " +
ex);
        return null;
    }
}

} /// beaninfo class
```

The java files for this animation have been put in a package called sunw.demo.myanim. I used the following make file to compile MyAnimation.java and MyAnimationBeanInfo.java, and load the class files and images into a Jar file (see Listing 7-5):

Listing 7-5: Make file for MyAnimation.java.

```
CLASSFILES= \
    sunw\demo\myanim\MyAnimation.class \
    sunw\demo\myanim\MyAnimationBeanInfo.class \


DATAFILES= \
        sunw\demo\myanim\dougbw0.gif \
        sunw\demo\myanim\dougbw1.gif \
        sunw\demo\myanim\dougbw2.gif  \

JARFILE= ..\jars\myanim.jar

all: $(JARFILE)

# Create a JAR file with a suitable manifest.

$(JARFILE): $(CLASSFILES) $(DATAFILES)
        jar cfm $(JARFILE) <<manifest.tmp sunw\demo\myanim\*.class
$(DATAFILES)
Name: sunw/demo/myanim/MyAnimation.class
Java-Bean: True
<<keep

.SUFFIXES: .java .class

{sunw\demo\myanim}.java{sunw\demo\myanim}.class :
    set CLASSPATH=.
    javac $<
```

You can use this animation applet-bean (or any new Java component that you've created as a bean) in Visual JavaScript using the following steps:

1. Compile the files MyAnimation.java and MyAnimationBeanInfo.java.
2. Archive the class files to a Jar file with any data files that are needed. In this example we need the data files dougbw0.gif, dougbw1.gif, and dougbw2.gif.

3. Once the Jar file has been created, load the Jar file into Visual JavaScript palette by choosing Tools | Install to palette | Jar file.
4. Once the Jar file has been loaded to the palette, create a new HTML page and drag the MyAnimation icon to the page.
5. Make any other additions to the page that you want.
6. Preview the page with Netscape Navigation (you can use the Preview icon on the toolbar).
7. Deploy your application.

You can see the MyAnimation applet-bean loaded to the palette in Figure 7-10.

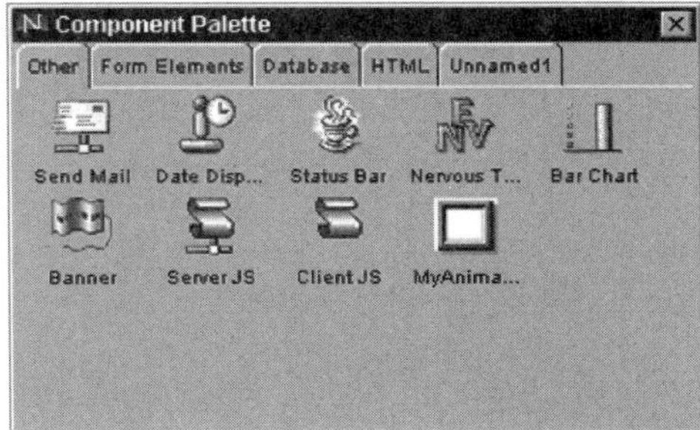

Figure 7-10: The MyAnimation applet-bean loaded on the palette.

Figure 7-11 shows a display of the Inspector window on the MyAnimation applet once it has been loaded into the palette and then dragged to a page.

Inspector: MyAnimation: document.MyAnimation1

MyAnimation: document.MyAnimation1

ALIGN	
ALT	
ARCHIVE	
CODE	sunw.demo.myanim.MyAnimation
DISPLAYNAME	MyAnimation
FILEREFS	sunw/demo/myanim/MyAnimation.class,sunw/c
HEIGHT	100
HSPACE	
ICONNAME	PIDefault
ID	MyAnimation1
MAYSCRIPT	MAYSCRIPT
SHORTDESCRIPTION	MyAnimation
VSPACE	
WIDTH	300

Figure 7-11: The inspector window showing the properties of the MyAnimation applet-bean in Visual JavaScript.

Moving On

You learned about Netscape's Visual JavaScript environment in this chapter and about its support for components: JavaBeans, Java applets, JavaScript, and HTML.

The next chapter focuses on how to create JavaScript components.

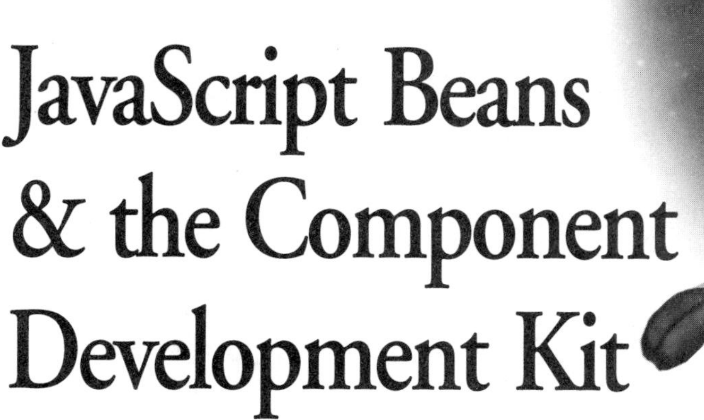

8

JavaScript Beans & the Component Development Kit

This chapter discusses Netscape's Component Development Kit (CDK), and the new JavaScript components, sometimes called JavaScript beans. CDK is made up of documentation and examples designed to be used in conjunction with Visual JavaScript. It provides documentation about how to develop JavaScript beans, examples of JavaScript beans, and other component examples that demonstrate features of CORBA and CORBA/IIOP.

This chapter begins with an introduction to the CDK and JavaScript beans, and continues with information on how to use and develop JavaScript components. JavaScript beans are written using a combination of JavaScript code and HTML-like tags. They are then stored in a JavaScript bean file (JSB file). Understanding the JSB file structure is crucial to creating your own JavaScript beans, so I also provide information about how these files are put together.

About the Component Development Kit

CDK works in conjunction with Visual JavaScript to provide the documentation and examples you need to create JavaScript beans. A summary of the features of the Component Development Kit are as follows:

- Documentation in HTML format on how to create JavaScript beans.
- The Acadia JavaScript bean development tool, called Acadia's JavaScriptBean Builder.

- Example components, including sample JavaScript JSB files, and CORBA IDL components.
- Documentation on how to use CORBA IDL-created components and BeanConnect objects with Visual JavaScript.

The Acadia JavaScriptBean Builder, included with the kit, is an automated GUI environment for developing JavaScript beans.

CORBA IDL

CORBA's Interface Definition Language (IDL) is at the heart of the CORBA concept. With CORBA you create distributed objects that can communicate and interoperate across networks, regardless of where they reside or in what language they are written. IDL is the means of describing the methods and services of a CORBA object and making it accessible to the CORBA environment (for example, an Object Request Broker (ORB)). Microsoft's competing distributed object model specification, DCOM, has its own version of IDL.

What Are JavaScript Beans?

Chapter 7 discusses the various types of components designed to be used with Visual JavaScript. You may recall that in addition to using applets or 'applets as beans' in Visual JavaScript, there was a new category of component called a JavaScript bean. JavaScript beans are written in JavaScript, but they have many of the features of JavaBeans such as properties, methods, and events.

NOTE

JavaScript beans can simply be called JavaScript components or, taking the cue from the file extension for JavaScript bean files, JSB, they can be referred to as JSBs. I'll refer to them in this chapter as JavaScript beans.

JavaScript beans support most of the features expected of component architectures. They are similar in make-up and behavior to JavaBeans. They are, however, written in JavaScript, a scripting language that some may find easier to learn than Java. Once a JavaScript bean is written, it is packaged into a JSB file and used in a builder tool environment (such as Visual JavaScript).

JavaScript beans can also be put into Jar files using the Jar packager (the same Jar compiler we've used throughout the book, for example in Chapter 4). In particular, some of the features of JavaScript beans are:

- They can have properties that can be changed at design-time by way of an inspector.
- They have methods that can be called.
- They can be linked together with events.
- They can be stored using their own file format (the JSB file).
- They can be integrated into a Web project using Visual JavaScript.

You can see the ready similarities with 'ordinary' beans, especially the support for properties, methods, and events. JavaScript beans even have their own type of listener interface. In the next section, we'll see how these features are implemented in JavaScript.

NOTE

If a JavaScript bean has no support files, it can be stored in a JSB file and used in the Visual JavaScript palette. However, JavaScript beans can be made up of more than one file, and you can package these files into a Jar using Sun's Jar packager. The support files can be JavaScript code or external Java .class files; the class files would be archived in the Jar file, too. Once the Jar file is loaded into the Visual JavaScript palette, the end user cannot tell the difference between these JavaScript components and other components (such as JavaBeans).

JSB Files

JavaScript beans are written in a special format, using a file format called the JSB file. The rules for and appearance of this file format will be familiar to people who know HTML; the format is implemented using various HTML-like tags. These tags aren't standard HTML, however. Netscape has come up with some new tags for the JSB file.

JSB files comply with the rules of a Standard Generalized Markup Language (SGML) file. SGML, a precursor to HTML, had its origins in the publishing world; 'markup' is a publishing term. SGML is more generalized than HTML; it defines general rules for tags and their syntax. It is also more complex. Some scientists at CERN in Switzerland developed HTML when they needed a simpler SGML-like language that also supported TCP/IP.

JavaScript code is included in a Web page by embedding it in the HTML text for the page. The most common place to embed JavaScript code is between the <SCRIPT> </SCRIPT> tags. These tags signal to a browser loading a page that a JavaScript script is being included. JavaScript code can be embedded in other tags in certain cases too, such as <BODY>. In picking SGML to encapsulate JavaScript beans, Netscape has hit on an approach that meshes well with existing JavaScript scripting and will be familiar to users of JavaScript and HTML.

Tip

JavaScript scripts will behave differently depending upon where they're placed in an HTML page. For example, if you put JavaScript code in the <HEAD> </HEAD> section of a page, the code is loaded when the Web page is first loaded— before a script that is in the <BODY> section.

Scripting Languages Vs. Other Languages

JavaScript is a scripting language. Perhaps the biggest difference between a scripting language and a compiled language such as Java is the process of compilation. JavaScript code is loaded as your Web page is, so the Web browser environment must understand JavaScript. The JavaScript version in Navigator 4 is version 1.2.

In the next section we'll look at an example JSB file that defines a JavaScript bean.

An Example JSB File

The 'concat' bean is distributed with Netscape's CDK. It's a fairly simple JavaScript component that concatenates two strings and returns the result. The JSB file for this bean is in Listing 8-1.

Listing 8-1: Code for the 'concat' JavaScript bean.

```
<JSB>
<JSB_DESCRIPTOR
    name="netscape.peas.Concat"
    displayName="Concat"
    shortDescription="Concatenate two string together with three static
strings"
    ENV="client">
```

```
<JSB_PROPERTY NAME="result" DISPLAYNAME="Result" PROPTYPE="JS" TYPE="string"
    ISBOUND
    SHORTDESCRIPTION="The resulting concatenated value">

<JSB_PROPERTY NAME="in1" DISPLAYNAME="Input 1" PROPTYPE="JS" TYPE="string"
    WRITEMETHOD="setIn1"
    SHORTDESCRIPTION="Input string number 1">

<JSB_PROPERTY NAME="in2" DISPLAYNAME="Input 2" PROPTYPE="JS" TYPE="string"
    WRITEMETHOD="setIn2"
    SHORTDESCRIPTION="Input string number 2">

<JSB_PROPERTY NAME="stat1" DISPLAYNAME="Static 1" PROPTYPE="JS"
TYPE="string"
    SHORTDESCRIPTION="String that will come at beginning of result">
<JSB_PROPERTY NAME="stat2" DISPLAYNAME="Static 2" PROPTYPE="JS"
TYPE="string"
    SHORTDESCRIPTION="String that will come between two input values">
<JSB_PROPERTY NAME="stat3" DISPLAYNAME="Static 3" PROPTYPE="JS"
TYPE="string"
    SHORTDESCRIPTION="String that will come at end of result">

<JSB_METHOD NAME="setIn1" TYPE="void">
    <JSB_PARAMETER name="newin" type="string">
</JSB_METHOD>
<JSB_METHOD NAME="setIn2" TYPE="void">
    <JSB_PARAMETER name="newin" type="string">
</JSB_METHOD>
<JSB_EVENT NAME="onChange" LISTENERMETHODS="onChange"
LISTENERTYPE="onChangeListener" EVENTMODEL="JS">

<JSB_CONSTRUCTOR>
function netscape_peas_concat_setin1( s ) {
    this.in1 = s
    this.recalc()
}
function netscape_peas_concat_setin2( s ) {
    this.in2 = s
    this.recalc()
}

function netscape_peas_concat_recalc() {
    this.result = "" + this.stat1 + this.in1 + this.stat2 + this.in2 +
this.stat3;
    this.onChange("result", "", this.result)
}
```

```
function netscape_peas_Concat(params) {
    this.stat1 = params.stat1
    this.stat2 = params.stat2
    this.stat3 = params.stat3
    this.in1   = params.in1
    this.in2   = params.in2
    this.setIn1 = netscape_peas_concat_setin1;
    this.setIn2 = netscape_peas_concat_setin2;
    this.recalc = netscape_peas_concat_recalc;
}
</JSB_CONSTRUCTOR>
</JSB>
```

Note the HTML-like syntax of Listing 8-1. The listing uses some tags that are not standard HTML: <JSB>, <JSB_PROPERTY>, <JSB_DESCRIPTOR>, and <JSB_CONSTRUCTOR.> The concat example demonstrates most of the features of the JSB file. In this file are specified properties, methods, and a bean constructor; a single event, onChange, is specified using the JSB_EVENT tag. We will discuss the layout and meaning of JSB file tags in the next section, "Reference to JSB Tags."

The <JSB> </JSB> pair open and close the listing and identify the file as a JSB file. The other tags in the file are embedded between these two tags. The <JSB_DESCRIPTOR> tag contains attributes that describe general information about the concat bean such as NAME and DISPLAYNAME. The NAME attribute of the concat bean uses a package name separated by periods. The concat bean is in the netscape.peas package. (JavaScript beans can be put in packages just as JavaBeans can.)

TIP

You can find the JSB file for the concat bean and the other example JavaScript beans in the subdirectory netscape\peas underneath your main Component Development Kit (CDK) directory. For example: c:\cdk\netscape\peas\concat.jsb.

The <JSB_PROPERTY> tags define properties for the bean. There is one <JSB_PROPERTY> tag for each property that the bean wants to make public. The <JSB_PROPERTY> attributes define features such as DISPLAYNAME, PROPTYPE, and TYPE. A type can be a JavaScript or a Java type (including a Java user-defined class).

The <JSB_CONSTRUCTOR> </JSB_CONSTRUCTOR> pair provides the actual code for the constructor and all other methods. In the concat bean, not only is the constructor defined; concat uses the <JSB_METHOD> tag to specify other methods; then their code is placed in the <JSB_CONSTRUCTOR> section.

In the body of the constructor the parameters passed into netscape_peas_Concat( ) are assigned to the object, with statements such as the following:

```
this.stat1 = params.stat1
this.stat2 = params.stat2
this.stat3 = params.stat3
```

The assignment statements above make use of the "this" keyword to refer to the current concat object—much as they would in Java. More about creating objects in JavaScript is in the section "About JavaScript Objects" later in this chapter.

NOTE

Since a JavaScript component is required to have a constructor, the <JSB_CONSTRUCTOR> tag pair is required in the JSB file.

Concat defines one event, onChange. The definition of the event is in the JSB_EVENT section. Attributes of the JSB_EVENT tag provide an event name, a listener method, and listener type. The following code shows this:

```
<JSB_EVENT NAME="onChange" LISTENERMETHODS="onChange"
LISTENERTYPE="onChangeListener" EVENTMODEL="JS">
```

Creating a JSB File

You begin by designing your component in the abstract. That is, decide what properties, methods, and events your component requires. Then using a text editor, specify all this information in a JSB file. The following sections provide some more details about how to specify properties, methods, and events in a JSB file.

Setting Up Properties

Once you've decided the properties of your component and their names and types, you need to define JSB_PROPERTY sections for each property. The type of the property will be specified (it can be a JavaScript or Java type such as java.lang.String). If you want to provide external Read/Write methods for a property (setters and getters), then the READMETHOD or WRITEMETHOD attributes need to be filled in.

Setting Up Methods

Define JSB_METHOD sections for each method you want. Specify return types, if needed, using one of the JSB_METHOD attributes. All parameters of the method are specified using the JSB_METHOD tag. An example JSB_METHOD section (from the concat bean again) follows. It defines a method named setIn1( ) that returns a void type (has no return value).

```
<JSB_METHOD NAME="setInl" TYPE="void">
    <JSB_PARAMETER name="newin" type="string">
</JSB_METHOD>
```

Setting Up the Constructor

The JSB_CONSTRUCTOR section contains the code for the constructor—and for all methods. The name of the constructor must be made up of the package name plus the name of the object; all periods are replaced with underscores. Here's the constructor for the 'mailto' (a JavaScript bean that writes a mailto link to the current page):

```
function netscape_peas_MailToLink(params) {
        str = "<A HREF='mailto:" + params.to + "?subject=" + params.subject
+ "&cc=" + params.cc +
        "&bcc=" + params.bcc + "'>" + params.text + "</A>"
        document.write(str)
}
```

The package name that includes the mailto component is netscape.peas; therefore the complete name of the constructor function is netscape_peas_MailToLink. Also note that the constructor references the params parameter by breaking it up into its component parts, for example:

```
params.subject
params.cc
```

The convention is to reference parameters as a single variable, rather than passing a number of individual parameters such as 'subject,' 'cc,' and 'text.' The parameters to the constructor may be initialized if appropriate, as for the concat bean:

```
this.statl = params.statl
this.stat2 = params.stat2
this.stat3 = params.stat3
this.inl   = params.inl
this.in2   = params.in2
this.setInl = netscape_peas_concat_setinl;
this.setIn2 = netscape_peas_concat_setin2;
this.recalc = netscape_peas_concat_recalc;
```

The functions setin1, setin2, and recalc are assigned to the concat objects—just like properties. This is similar to the way JavaScript objects are created; see the section "About JavaScript Objects," later in this chapter.

Setting Up Events

Define an event using the JSB_EVENT tag. If you are not using JavaScript for the EVENTMODEL attribute, you may need to define a listener using the JSB_LISTENER tag. The JSB_LISTENER tag makes reference to the external Java class. Here is an example for setting up an event for the JavaScript onChange event:

```
<JSB_EVENT NAME="onChange" LISTENERMETHODS="onChange"
LISTENERTYPE="onChangeListener" EVENTMODEL="JS">
```

The name is onChange, the listener method name is onChange, and the listener type is onChangeListener. The EVENTMODEL attribute shows that the event being used is of type JS—a JavaScript event. Java event listeners can also be specified, in that case the EVENTMODEL of AWT11 is used. If an HTML event is being used, then EVENTMODEL is given the value HTML. The JSB_LISTENER tag is used to specify a method name to be called when the appropriate event occurs. The JSB_LISTENER tag comes after the closing </JSB> for the file. Here is an example of using the JSB_LISTENER tag for the onChangeListener:

```
<JSB_LISTENER NAME="onChangeListener">
    <JSB_METHOD NAME="onChange" TYPE="void">
        <JSB_PARAMETER NAME="propertyName" TYPE="string">
        <JSB_PARAMETER NAME="oldValue" TYPE="undefined">
        <JSB_PARAMETER NAME="newValue" TYPE="undefined">
    </JSB_METHOD>
</JSB_LISTENER>
```

About JavaScript Objects

If you've used JavaScript before, you may be familiar with the concept of JavaScript *objects*. The constructor code of a JavaScript bean is really an adaptation of the syntax used for JavaScript objects. This section has details about objects in JavaScript. If you are already familiar with JavaScript and creating objects using the new statement, this will be review.

We've seen examples of individual JavaScript statements in this chapter. In addition to embedding individual JavaScript statements between <SCRIPT> </SCRIPT> tags, JavaScript also lets you define stand-alone functions and functions bound to an object (these are called methods). JavaScript objects are of two types: built-in JavaScript objects and user-defined objects.

Built-In Objects

An example of a built-in JavaScript object is the document object, which always represents the current page in which a script is executing. For example, inside a JavaScript script, you may write the following:

```
document.write("This is a terribly wonderful Web page.")
```

The preceding statement would write the message "This is a terribly wonderful Web page," to the current Web page. The document object's write method is being called; it takes a string of characters as a parameter. Calling the write method is accomplished by using the dot notation followed by the method name. In general, if you have an object called objectname, the syntax for calling a method is:

```
objectname.methodname()
```

This calls the method called methodname for the object named objectname. The parentheses are necessary to show that methodname is a method. Objects can also have properties, and they are accessed in a similar way. Properties are similar to instance variables in Java. Property names of an object can be accessed as follows:

```
objectname.property1 = 12;
document.write("The property value: " objectname.property1)
```

This statement assigns the value 12 to property1, and then uses the (built-in) document write method to write the value of property1 to the page.

User-Defined Objects

In addition to built-in JavaScript objects such as document, you can define your own objects by providing a constructor function for the object. A constructor function for a user-defined object called Person is as follows:

```
function Person(name, address)
{
this.name= "FRED"
this.address="12 Sycamore Street"
}
```

The preceding code actually defines a class of object, called Person. Now the Person class of object can be used in a JavaScript program similarly to a built-in object. The statements this.name and this.address declare that the Person class has two properties, name and address. Although this is similar to defining a Java class, there are no Java class statements or variable types given for the properties. Later in a JavaScript program, you can declare a variable of type Person by using the new keyword.

```
aPerson = new Person("Sally", "15 Manor Rd.)
```

You can then use the variable aPerson in your program. User-defined objects can have methods, too. To define a method, you simply supply a function in a JavaScript, and then assign the function name in the constructor for your object class.

```
function printFields()
{
    document.write(this.name + "<BR>" + this.address)
}

function Person(name, address)
{
this.name= "FRED"
this.address="12 Sycamore Street"
this.printFunction = printFields
}
```

In the constructor, the function printFields is assigned to a property of the Person class. The printFunction property of the Person class now contains the value printFields. printFields is now a method of class Person, so when you declare a variable of type Person in your program, you can call the printFields method by referring to the printFunction method. Perhaps an example will make this clearer:

```
aPerson = new Person("Sally", "11 Manor Rd.)
aPerson.printFunction
```

The preceding call to aPerson.printFunction writes the following to the Web page:

```
Sally
11 Manor Rd.
```

JavaScript Beans & User-Defined Objects

As I mentioned, the creation of JavaScript user-defined objects is similar to defining a JavaScript bean in a JSB file. If you've ever created your own objects in JavaScript using the keyword "new," perusing the code of a JSB file will seem familiar. Let's look at the similarities between JavaScript objects and JavaScript beans. Some features of JavaScript user-defined objects are:

- They have constructors with zero or more parameters. The parameters are assigned to the properties of the object in the body of the constructor.
- Properties are referenced in the body of the constructor by assigning them values using the "this" keyword.
- Methods are first defined with the same syntax as stand-alone functions. Then the method is associated with the object class by assigning the function name to a property in the constructor.
- User-defined objects are created using the new JavaScript keyword.

Some main features of JavaScript beans are:

- They have constructors that are defined in a JSB_CONSTRUCTOR tagged section of a JSB file. The constructor initializes properties and methods for the JavaScript bean. Function names are assigned to the bean the same as for other properties.
- The names and types of properties are declared using the JSB_PROPERTY tag in a JSB file. One JSB_PROPERTY tag is used per property. Properties are often initialized inside their constructors.
- They can have methods that are specified in the JSB_METHOD section; the code for the methods is defined in the JSB_CONSTRUCTOR section. Methods are assigned like properties in the code for the constructor.

JavaScript beans are created in an HTML page using the new keyword.

Using a JavaScript Bean

Using a JavaScript bean with Visual JavaScript is much like using a JavaBean component. If the bean is one of the existing beans provided with Visual JavaScript, drag it from the palette as you would a JavaBean or an HTML form component. Figure 8-1 shows the result of dragging the scrolling banner component into a new blank HTML page and then double-clicking on the component to open an inspector window. The inspector window shows the current values of the properties and displays events (if any are defined).

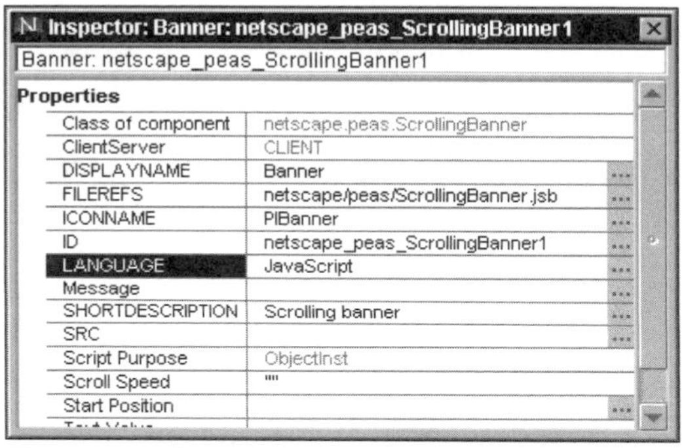

Figure 8-1: The inspector window for the Scrolling Banner component in Visual JavaScript's page builder.

You may want to create a new JavaScript bean using a JSB file. In that case, follow these steps:

1. Create the JSB file with a text editor.
2. Load the JSB file into the palette with the menu item: Tools | Load to palette | JavaScript component.
3. Drag and drop the component from the palette to a new HTML page.
4. Click on the component on the page to open an inspector window. Use the inspector window to set values for the component's properties.
5. Link the component up with other components on the page if you wish.
6. Preview your page with Navigator 4.

Once a JSB file is loaded into Visual JavaScript, it doesn't look exactly like the raw JSB file. After you've loaded the file, it can be viewed in source mode by choosing View | Source from the View menu, (see Figure 8-2).

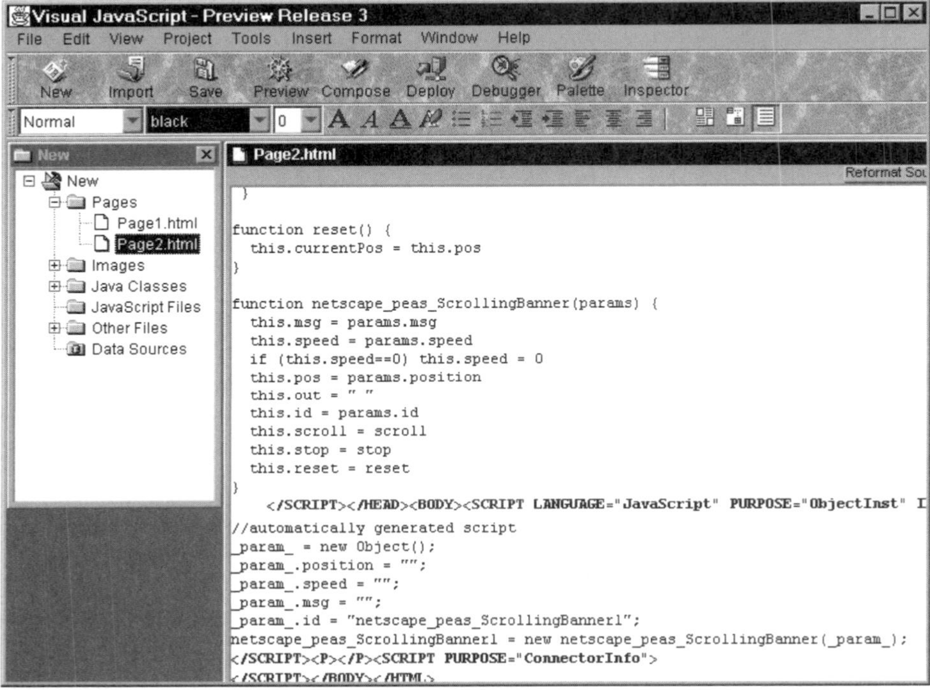

Figure 8-2: The scrolling banner JSB file loaded into Visual JavaScript.

If you look at the code you'll see that Visual JavaScript does some work for you, creating <SCRIPT> </SCRIPT> tags in the page and loading the constructor function and code for the other methods. It also initializes the parameters and uses the new keyword to create the component. Listing 8-2 is an example of how parameters are initialized and the component created. I created Listing 8-2 by dragging the scrolling banner bean to a blank page and then editing the HTML file for the page with a text editor. Note in particular the section that begins with the comment "automatically generated script." In this section Visual JavaScript creates an object to represent the parameters, initializes the parameters, then passes this object to the netscape_peas_ScrollingBanner constructor.

Listing 8-2: Parameter initializations that Visual JavaScript creates when loading a JSB file.

```
<SCRIPT LANGUAGE="JavaScript" PURPOSE="ObjectInst"
ID="netscape_peas_ScrollingBanner1" CLASS="netscape.peas.ScrollingBanner"
FILEREFS="netscape/peas/ScrollingBanner.jsb" DISPLAYNAME="Banner"
SHORTDESCRIPTION="Scrolling banner" ICONNAME="PIBanner">
//automatically generated script
_param_ = new Object();
_param_.position = "";
_param_.speed = "";
_param_.msg = "";
_param_.id = "netscape_peas_ScrollingBanner1";
netscape_peas_ScrollingBanner1 = new netscape_peas_ScrollingBanner(_param_);
</SCRIPT>
```

Reference to JSB Tags

The JSB file for creating JavaScript beans is an ASCII text file with tags resembling HTML code. This section is a reference to the tags required to create a JSB file. The tags are presented with their name, description, attributes, and other information—such as whether a particular tag is required or optional.

JSB Tag

This required tag marks the beginning and ending of a JSB file. The matching </JSB> is required to end the JSB file. The JSB tag has no attributes. Most other tags are embedded inside the <JSB> </JSB> pair; the only tag that is not inside this pair is the JSB_LISTENER tag.

JSB_DESCRIPTOR Tag

The <JSB_DESCRIPTOR> tag defines some basic features of the JavaScript bean, such as its name, display name, and where the component will be used—client-side or server-side. The attributes for the <JSB_DESCRIPTOR> tag follow.

NAME

The name of the component functions as an identifier for this component. It usually contains a package name and a period-separated name:
`NAME="packagename.componentname"`

DISPLAYNAME

This required attribute is the display name displayed by Visual JavaScript in the inspector. The DISPLAYNAME attribute has the following form:
`DISPLAYNAME="displayname"`

SHORTDESCRIPTION

This optional attribute is displayed in the tool tips feature of Visual JavaScript:
`SHORTDESCRIPTION="text description"`

CUSTOMIZER

This optional attribute specifies whether a Java customizer is used for the component. It has the following form:
`CUSTOMIZER="packagename.customizerclassname"`

ENV

A component can run on the client or the server, or both. The ENV attribute specifies this information, and can have the values: "client," "server," "both," or "either" (the default). This attribute has the following form: `ENV="value"`

ISJAVA

This is an attribute that is no longer used. According to the CDK documentation, it may appear in some older JSB files, but is no longer necessary.

JSB_PROPERTY Tag

The <JSB_PROPERTY> tag describes a single property in the bean. Information such as name and type is provided between the property tags. The attributes for the <JSB_PROPERTY> tag follow.

NAME

This required attribute is the name of the property. This is the name that is used when referring to the property (getting and setting the property for example): `NAME="propertyname"`

DISPLAYNAME

This required attribute is displayed by Visual JavaScript in the inspector:
`DISPLAYNAME="displayname"`

SHORTDESCRIPTION

This optional field is displayed in the Visual JavaScript tool tips:

```
SHORTDESCRIPTION="text"
```

TYPE

This required attribute is the type of the property. A type can be a JavaScript type, a Java primitive type, or a Java class type. The attribute has the following forms:

```
TYPE="datatype" // a Java primitive type
TYPE= "package.classname" // A Java class containing the type
TYPE="JavaScript data type" // JS types are string,
number, boolean, or void
```

PROPTYPE

This is how the property is dealt with in an HTML document. It can be one of:

- **JS:** stores the property in <SCRIPT> tags.
- **JS-expr:** <SCRIPT> tags are used, and a JavaScript expression assigns a value for the property.
- **TagAttribute:** an option for .HI files, used to store HTML form element type components.
- **AWT11:** The AWT11 type describes a property that is accessed through getter and setter methods.

READMETHOD

A property may be supplied with a JavaBean-style read method to read the property. The method name supplied using this attribute needs to be supplied elsewhere in the JSB using the <JSB_METHOD> tag. This attribute is optional:

```
READMETHOD="methodname"
```

WRITEMETHOD

A property may be supplied with a JavaBean-style write method (setter method). The method name supplied using this attribute needs to be supplied elsewhere in the JSB using the <JSB_METHOD> tag. This optional attribute has the form: `WRITEMETHOD="methodname"`

ISDEFAULT

If used, the property being described is the default property for the component. This attribute is optional. If you don't use this attribute, the first property listed will be the default.

VALUESET

This optional attribute specifies a range of permitted values. It has the form:

```
VALUESET="range"
```

The value in "range" can be a range of string values or a numeric range. String values are specified as a comma-delimited list of strings. Numeric ranges can be specified in the form "1,2,4" (the specific values: 1,2, and 4) or "0:10" (min:max, values from 0 to 10).

PROPERTYEDITOR

A JavaBeans-style propertyeditor class can be specified using this optional attribute. This attribute has the form:

```
PROPERTYEDITOR="packagename.properteditorclassname"
```

ISRUNTIME

This optional attribute, if used, specifies that a property can only be accessed at runtime.

ISBOUND

This optional attribute defines whether or not the property is bound. Bound properties require that you define the onChange listener interface.

ENV

A property can be accessed on the client or the server, or both. The ENV attribute for a property is ignored if the <JSB_DESCRIPTOR> tag for the component is not set to "both." This optional attribute can have the values: "client," "server," or "both." This attribute has the following form: `ENV="value"`

JSB_METHOD Tag

The <JSB_METHOD> tag is used to define a method associated with a component. The closing </JSB_METHOD> tag is required. A list of the attributes of this tag follow:

NAME

This required attribute is the name of the method. This attribute has the form:

```
NAME="methodname"
```

DISPLAYNAME

This required attribute is displayed by Visual JavaScript in the inspector. This attribute has the form: `DISPLAYNAME="displayname"`

SHORTDESCRIPTION

This optional field is displayed in the Visual JavaScript tool tips and provides a short description of the method. This attribute has the form:

```
SHORTDESCRIPTION="text"
```

TYPE

This required attribute is a return type for the method. This attribute has one of the following forms:

```
TYPE="datatype" // a Java primitive type
TYPE="package.classname" // A Java class containing the type
TYPE="JavaScript data type" // JS types are string,
number, boolean, or void
```

ENV

The ENV attribute specifies whether a method can be called on the client or the server, or both. This optional attribute can have the values: "client," "server," "both" (the default). The ENV attribute is ignored if the <JSB_DESCRIPTOR> tag for the component is not set to "both." This attribute has the following form: `ENV="value"`

JSB_EVENT Tag

This tag is used to provide event information about the component being defined.

NAME

This required attribute is the name of the event. This attribute is used to refer to the event inside JavaScript code. This attribute has the form:

```
NAME="methodname"
```

DISPLAYNAME

This required attribute is displayed by Visual JavaScript in the inspector. This attribute has the form: `DISPLAYNAME="displayname"`

SHORTDESCRIPTION

This optional field is displayed in the Visual JavaScript tool tips and provides a short description of the method. This attribute has the form:

```
SHORTDESCRIPTION="text"
```

EVENTMODEL

The event model can take on the value of: JS (JavaScript), AWT11(Java), or HTML (uses existing JavaScript events such as those generated from HTML form elements). This attribute tells Visual JavaScript how to manage events for this component. This attribute has the form: `EVENTMODEL="model"`

ADDLISTENERMETHOD

Method used to add listeners from this component. This corresponds to JavaBean-style add/remove listener methods. This attribute is used with the AWT11 event model: `ADDLISTENERMETHOD="methodname"`

REMOVELISTENERMETHOD

Method used to remove listeners from this component. This corresponds to JavaBean-style add/remove listener methods.
`REMOVELISTENERMETHOD="methodname"`

LISTENERMETHODS

This required field is a list of listener methods. The list of method names is separated by commas: `LISTENERMETHODS="eventHandler1" [, "eventHandler2" . . .]`

LISTENERTYPE

A listener type attribute is required when using the AWT11 event model. The name of the listener interface is specified using this tag. The name given will match the listener defined in a <JSB_LISTENER> section at the end of the JSB file. The <JSB_LISTENER> section specifies the listener methods between <JSB_METHOD> tags embedded inside the <JSB_LISTENER> and </JSB_LISTENER> tags: `LISTENERTYPE="packagename.listenername"`

ISDEFAULT

This optional field specifies whether the event is the default for the component.

JSB_PARAMETER Tag

This is a parameter of a method. If a method has parameters, the <JSB_PARAMETER> section defining the parameter is inside the <JSB_METHOD> </JSB_METHOD> pair for that method.

NAME

This optional attribute is the name of the parameter. This attribute is used to display the parameter inside Visual JavaScript. This attribute has the form: `NAME="parametername"`

DISPLAYNAME

This optional attribute is displayed by Visual JavaScript in the inspector. This attribute has the form: `DISPLAYNAME="displayname"`

SHORTDESCRIPTION

This optional field is displayed in the Visual JavaScript tool tips and provides a short description of the parameter. This attribute has the form: `SHORTDESCRIPTION="parameter description"`

TYPE

This required field is the type of a parameter's return type. It can be a Java class (package.class) or a JavaScript data type.

```
TYPE= "package.classname" // A Java class containing the type
TYPE="JavaScript data type" // JS types are string,
number, boolean, or void
```

JSB_CONSTRUCTOR Tag

The constructor tag defines the code for the component's constructor. The constructor's name is the name of the component and includes the package name. This constructor name is the same as the name given in the <JSB_DESCRIPTOR> section, where underscores are substituted for periods in the package name. Code for other functions can be defined in the <JSB_CONSTRUCTOR> section. These functions are assigned to the object being created in the constructor and become methods of the object. The section must end with the matching </JSB_CONSTRUCTOR> tag. This tag is required and has no attributes.

JSB_INTERFACE Tag

A Java listener interface can be used to manage events for a JavaScript bean. This tag specifies a Java listener interface for a component. This tag is optional and has one attribute. The NAME attribute is described below.

NAME

This is the packagename of the interface class. If the <JSB_INTERFACE> tag is used, the NAME attribute is required. The NAME attribute takes the following form: `NAME="packagename.listenerclassname"`

JSB_LISTENER Tag

This attribute defines the name of a listener interface that is also referenced in the <JSB_EVENT> tag. The <JSB_EVENT> event tag can have three different event models. The event model being used dictates which parameters are supplied with the <JSB_LISTENER> tag.

The JS (JavaScript) event model requires three parameters: a property name, the property's current value, and the property's new value. The AWT11 event model requires the event object as the only parameter. If the event model is HTML, no parameters are required. <JSB_LISTENER> tag requires one attribute.

NOTE

The <JSB_LISTENER> tag is used and is included at the end of the JSB file after the closing </JSB> tag.

NAME

Name to identify the listener interface. This required attribute describes the package name and interface name of the listener interface. It has the following form: `NAME="packagename.interfacename"`

Moving On

JavaScript beans are a new type of component from Netscape. Many of their features are based upon JavaBeans. They are written using a new file format called the JSB file. In this chapter you learned about JavaScript beans and how they are created using the JSB file. You also saw many similarities between JavaScript beans and JavaBeans, including properties, methods, events, and the ability to use event listeners.

In the next chapter we'll look at what CORBA support Netscape has provided with the CDK.

CORBA & Visual JavaScript

9

With its announcement in 1996 that it would provide an *Object Request Broker* (ORB) in future products, Netscape committed itself to supplying Common Object Request Broker Architecture / Internet Inter-ORB Protocol (CORBA/IIOP) support in its server software, browsers, and tools for developers. Currently, CORBA support is available in Communicator 4 and Enterprise Server 3.0.

This chapter begins with an introduction to CORBA and CORBA ORBs. I also provide some information on Interface Definition Language (IDL) and Netscape's ORB product, the Internet Service Broker (ISB). CORBA components can be integrated into HTML pages in Visual JavaScript, and the Component Development Kit gives examples of how to load IDL files to use CORBA in your crossware applications. In the last section, I describe one of these examples, HelloCORBA.

What Is CORBA?

CORBA is a product of the *Object Management Group* (OMG). OMG is a consortium of over 700 companies that creates specifications for software. It operates by soliciting proposals and recommendations from its members and then deliberates on the results. The goal of the project was to create an open architectural standard for distributing business objects across networks whose result was CORBA.

Business Objects

In the world of client-server computing, a *business object* can be thought of as an object that provides services integral to some ubiquitous business task. These business objects can be plugged together in many different applications, thus making client-server development quicker and easier.

CORBA is a category of software called *middleware*. Client/server environments (including the World Wide Web) are often made up of different computers running different operating systems. The goal of middleware is to provide a standard cross-platform specification for creating, locating, and using objects across such systems. The dream is that objects can be developed in a cross-platform way, their interactions specified clearly, and then be assembled as components to create truly platform-blind client-server applications. Objects can be retrieved across networks and perform their services without regard to operating systems or where they reside on the network.

CORBA makes these features possible. It specifies the means to create objects, locate them over networks, and send them requests and return results, all in a platform-independent way without regard to the language in which the objects are written. In addition to specifying how to design objects so they'll interoperate over networks, the specification also defines other support services important for managing objects, for example, a naming service and a security service. (See the section entitled "CORBA Services" in this chapter for more information.) To make seamless distribution of objects happen, CORBA needed to define a central piece of software called the ORB, which is discussed next.

The CORBA ORB

ORB is at the center of the CORBA concept. The ORB is that piece of middleware that is responsible for processing a request, finding the object to process the request, asking the object to process the request (possibly delivering some parameters), and returning any values that result.

Anyone familiar with the heterogeneous operating environments and platforms common today can appreciate the complexity of this piece of software. The ORB can be regarded as a library of services that implements everything in the CORBA specification. Perhaps more important to a developer of crossware over the Internet or intranet: it's code that you don't have to write yourself. ORBs are written by various vendors and installed on your system.

There are various ORBs on the market. Sun has an ORB called NEO/JOE, and Netscape's ORB for Communicator 4 and Enterprise Server 3.0 is called the Internet Service Broker (ISB). See the section "Netscape's Internet Service Broker," later in this chapter for more information.

Interface Definition Language (IDL)

Key to the idea of CORBA is that objects used across networks can be implemented in any language. The object's interfaces are first specified in a language-neutral form which OMG calls IDL. The syntax of IDL looks something like C++. But it's not a general-purpose programming language like C++; it's referred to as a declarative language. It describes the interface to objects without providing all the low-level details. For example, in IDL there are no control structures such as if, for, and while.

What IDL does have is a way to specify modules, interfaces, operations (methods), and type definitions. You provide an interface to an object in IDL by providing the method names along with their parameters and return types. Those familiar with C++ won't be too far afield in viewing IDL as similar to a C++ class definition.

Modula-2 & ADA

The programming language Modula-2 lets you separate interfaces from implementation by using a definition module (describing the procedure names and their return types and parameters) and an implementation module (where you fill out the code). The ADA language has a construct called "the package" that has a similar purpose.

To specify an object to be used with a CORBA-compliant system you follow steps such as these:

1. Specify the objects by creating an IDL file.
2. Use an IDL compiler to compile the specification file. This step creates client stub code and server skeleton code in Java or C++.
3. Fill out the code for stubs and the server skeleton in your chosen language, (Netscape's tools support Java or C++).
4. Compile the code created in step 3 using an appropriate compiler.

CORBA Services

As I mentioned earlier, in addition to specifying the basic method of how objects will be created on and interact with an ORB, CORBA defines some services that support specific issues that come up when dealing with distributed objects. Some of these services are:

- **Naming Service:** This service allows CORBA client programs to actually look up objects on the object bus by name.
- **Life Cycle Service:** This service defines interfaces for how CORBA components will be created, copied, moved, and deleted.
- **Persistence Service:** This service provides a standard interface to storing objects, regardless of what form the object is being stored in (to a specific database format, for example).
- **Event Service:** This service allows objects to register or unregister their interest in receiving certain events. An object called the "event channel" acts as the conduit for events among different components.
- **Transaction Service:** Database transactions can often be rolled back until the database system makes them permanent (called a commit). This service provides a two-phase commit supporting flat or nested transactions.
- **Security Service:** This service provides security features such as authentication of objects for more secure transactions.

The Internet Inter-ORB Protocol (IIOP)

With the CORBA 2.0 specification, the OMG made it a requirement that all ORBs implement IIOP, which is a communications protocol for using CORBA services over the Internet. As you know, the Internet backbone is based upon the communications protocol called TCP/IP. IIOP was designed on top of TCP/IP. CORBA was originally created with existing client-server systems in mind, before the Internet and the Web reached their current prominence. IIOP extends CORBA to the Internet; it provides a backbone of communication for applications using CORBA on the Internet.

Netscape's Internet Service Broker (ISB)

Netscape's Internet Service Broker (ISB) is both an ORB and a set of tools for creating CORBA-compliant objects. In 1996, Netscape announced that future products would contain an ORB. The ORB they chose uses technology from Visigenic Software, Inc. (http://www.visigenic.com). There is an ISB for Java and an ISB for Java and C++. You can think of ISB as Netscape's ORB, but it contains an ORB and other tools for developing CORBA-compliant solutions. Some important points about ISB are:

- ISB for Java is supported in Communicator 4.
- ISB for Java and C++ is supported in Enterprise Server 3.0.
- Netscape's IDL to Java compiler (idl2java) lets you compile IDL to Java stub code. You can then complete your implementation in Java.
- Netscape's java2iiop compiler (also called Caffeine) is included with Enterprise Server 3.0. It lets you generate CORBA IDL files from existing Java class files.

The java2iiop compiler included with Enterprise Server 3.0 actually compiles Java source code to an IDL interface file. For developers with an existing Java code base this can be an advantage; it also means that developers don't necessarily have to learn IDL to program crossware applications with CORBA.

There are two parts to ISB. ISB for Java is available on the client side with Netscape Communicator 4. ISB for Java and C++ is available for developing server-side code with Enterprise Server 3.0. The ORB in Netscape systems was originally developed at Visigenic Software (and was once called VisiBroker for Java). This ORB was developed entirely in Java. Please consult Netscape's DevEdge site at: http://developer.netscape.com, for more information about developing crossware with Netscape's ISB environment.

ISB for Java, Netscape's ORB, offers the following additional features:

- **Caffeine:** As mentioned previously, this lets you create interfaces from Java code without learning IDL.
- **Dynamic Invocation Interface:** A client can get an object's interface and dynamically create requests.
- **Dynamic Skeleton Interface:** DSI lets you create objects that do not inherit from a skeleton interface (it is usual for classes to derive from a skeleton class generated by idl2java).

- **Enhanced thread management:** 'Thread-per-session' and 'thread pooling' maximize efficiency of connection management.
- **Fault tolerance:** ISB identifies server crashes and tries to restart the server or create a different server connection.
- **Interface repository:** The IR contains information about objects, their interfaces and operations. The client inquires about interfaces stored in the IR, or the ORB can check the type of values in a client's request.
- **Optimized binding:** ISB uses the most efficient means to connect to an object.
- **Web naming service:** This allows an object reference to be obtained by a URL.

CORBA With Visual JavaScript

CORBA components are loaded into the Visual JavaScript tool (VJS) much as Java or JavaScript beans are. Once an IDL file is loaded into VJS, each IDL specified interface is converted into a JSB file. The CORBA component becomes available in the VJS palette. You use the component as you would other components in Visual JavaScript, as described in Chapter 8. Once you have set up your client Web page using CORBA components, JavaScript components, and possibly HTML form elements and JavaBeans, you deploy the application. At run time, the CORBA component sends a request to the ORB in Communicator, which finds an object to service the request.

You load CORBA components using the Visual JavaScript environment as follows (see Figure 9-1 for a screen shot of the Tools | Install to palette menu item):

1. Choose Tools | Install to palette | CORBA Object from the Visual JavaScript menu.
2. The component appears in the palette with a CORBA icon.
3. Drag and drop the component as you would other Visual JavaScript components.
4. Use the inspector to inspect and modify the properties of the CORBA object.

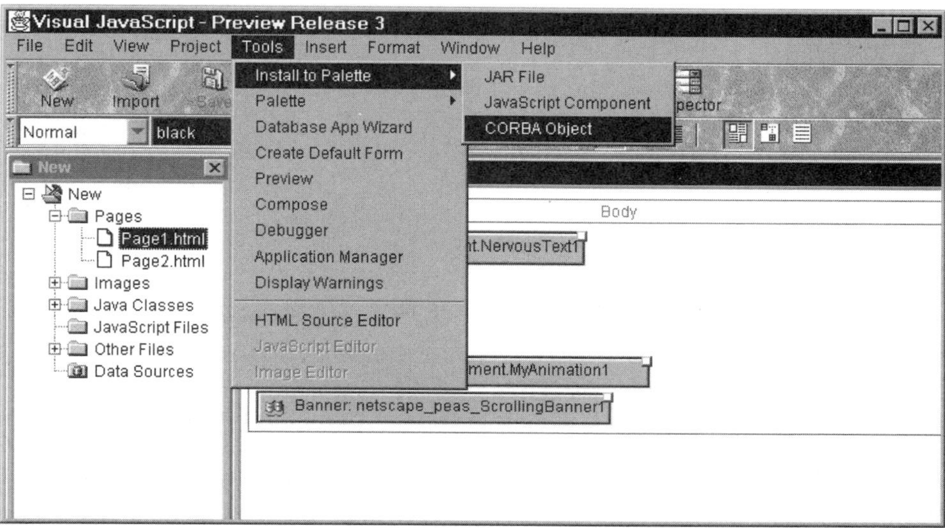

Figure 9-1: Loading a CORBA IDL file by choosing Tools | Install to palette.

JavaScript Properties & Methods

When Visual JavaScript loads an IDL file it creates a JSB file. IDL files can contain multiple interface definitions, so VJS creates a JSB file for each interface definition in the IDL file. There is some mapping or translation between interfaces in IDL and the JSB file format. From the IDL file, Visual JavaScript gets information which it translates to JavaScript properties and methods. This section discusses how the contents of the IDL file are interpreted in Visual JavaScript.

Properties

After loading a CORBA component into Visual JavaScript, the component is translated to a JavaScript component with properties that can be edited in the inspector. Some properties are derived from attributes in the IDL file and some from other sources. Properties come from the following:

- Attributes that are in the IDL file.
- Attributes of SCRIPT or APPLET tags. Some example attributes that will be translated are PURPOSE, CLASS, SRC, WIDTH and HEIGHT.
- Properties created by Visual JavaScript.

Visual JavaScript creates an 'ObjectURL' property for every object imported as a CORBA component. This property lets the user specify a URL which in turn specifies the actual location of the CORBA object. The JavaScript component acts as a wrapper for the CORBA object. At run time the actual CORBA component will be found using the value of ObjectURL. I provide further information on how this connection works in the section "Connecting To CORBA Components," later in the chapter.

Methods

In IDL terminology, a method is called an operation. Interfaces have operations as Java classes have methods. When loading into Visual JavaScript, operations are converted to JavaScript method declarations. The data types for parameters and return types will be converted to Java data types. (More information about this type conversion is in the section "JavaScript & CORBA Data Types," later in this chapter.) The methods in the JSB file are wrappers for the methods of the CORBA object. At run time, the component will be connected to an actual CORBA object on the server. How does the JavaScript program reference this object? JavaScript defines a variable (called "corbaObject") which is the ORB's Java representation of the object. When referring to the CORBA object the JavaScript code needs to reference it via corbaObject. The JavaScript wrappers use the corbaObject variable to call the actual CORBA object.

NOTE

CORBA components in Visual JavaScript do not support events.

JavaScript & CORBA Data Types

CORBA IDL defines various data types that can be used in an IDL file. JavaScript's data types are not as numerous as CORBA's. It's natural that some IDL data types need to be mapped to Java and JavaScript types. Some types may not map directly to Java or JavaScript types. For example, the CORBA struct and union types are mapped to java.lang.Object. Table 9-1 shows the mapping between IDL data types and Java data types. Also, Java does not have unsigned types, so types such as ushort and ulong are converted to Java types Short and Long. In this section, two tables show the usual mappings of data types, first from IDL to Java, then from Java to JavaScript.

Data type (IDL)	Data type (Java)
null	java.lang.Object
void	java.lang.Void
short	java.lang.Short
long	java.lang.Long
ushort	java.lang.Short
ulong	java.lang.Integer
float	java.lang.Float
double	java.lang.Double
Boolean	java.lang.Boolean
char	java.lang.Char
octet	java.lang.Byte
any	java.lang.Object
TypeCode	java.lang.Object
Principal	java.lang.Object
objref	java.lang.Object
struct	java.lang.Object
union	java.lang.Object
enum	java.lang.Object
string	java.lang.String
sequence	java.lang.Object
array	java.lang.Object
alias	java.lang.Object
except	java.lang.Object
longlong	java.lang.Long
ulonglong	java.lang.Long
longdouble	java.lang.Double
wchar	java.lang.Char
wstring	java.lang.String
fixed	java.lang.Object
estruct	java.lang.Object

Table 9-1: Data type mapping from CORBA IDL to Java.

NOTE

Netscape's documentation warns that some aspects of these mappings may change. They encourage you to check the "Netscape ISB for Java Programmer's Guide" for current information at http://developer.netscape.com/library/documentation/enterprise/javapg/title.html.

You may notice the prevalence of the type java.lang.Object in Table 9-1. This is because IDL data types that have no equivalent type in Java are all mapped to java.lang.Object. Also, the mapping between the unsigned types in IDL and signed types in Java could cause some unexpected results if you are unaware of it. That is, very large positive IDL values will be represented as signed in Java, and therefore as negative numbers. There is also some mapping that occurs between Java and JavaScript data types. A list of these mappings is in Table 9-2.

Java data type	JavaScript data type
java.lang.Object	object
java.lang.Short	number
java.lang.Long	number
java.lang.Integer	number
java.lang.Float	number
java.lang.Double	number
java.lang.Boolean	boolean
java.lang.Char	number
java.lang.Byte	number
java.lang.String	string

Table 9-2: Mapping of data types from Java to JavaScript.

JavaScript does not have its own character data type, and this could cause some problems when converting characters from Java. You can note from Table 9-2 that the java.lang.Char type is translated to the JavaScript number type. In general, if you are writing an application that requires converting character types between Java and JavaScript (or vice versa), you need to do the conversion yourself.

Connecting to CORBA Components

Suppose you have loaded a CORBA component from an IDL file into Visual JavaScript. This component has been converted to a JSB file and is now represented as a JavaScript wrapper. How does the JavaScript bean actually connect to a CORBA object? There are two connection methods:

- Use the ObjectURL property of the JavaScript component to specify the URL of the CORBA object. The Netscape Enterprise Server 3.0 must be installed and running to use this option.
- Use the corbaObject property. corbaObject must be set using a custom Java method; it's called setCorbaObject( ).You must have a custom Java library for handling CORBA objects.

The first approach to connecting, using the ObjectURL property, is the recommended one. The ObjectURL property is created for every CORBA component when it is loaded into VJS. As a property of the component, it can be edited in design mode through the inspector. It can also be set from a JavaScript script using a method called setObjectURL( ).

In a previous section, "CORBA Services," we discussed the naming service that lets CORBA find an object by name. Whenever the value of ObjectURL is changed, whether in the inspector or at run time by using the setObjectURL( ) method, the local component is bound to the CORBA object "on the fly." It is the CORBA naming service that accomplishes this binding. The local environment looks up the CORBA object in the naming service's list of objects.

The HelloCorba Example

The Component Development Kit (CDK) comes with documentation and examples to help in creating JavaScript beans and CORBA components. The Preview Release 3 of the CDK contains the HelloCorba example component along with instructions on how to build it. This example is designed to demonstrate how a client application would establish a connection to the ORB and use its services. The files contained with HelloCorba are an IDL file (HelloCorba.idl) and a Java source file (HelloCorbaDaemon.java) that acts as a support file. In this section we'll look at the IDL file and then at the Java files created from it.

NOTE

If you have the CDK installed to directory c:\cdk, the samples folder is c:\cdk\samples. The HelloCorba example is in c:\cdk\samples\HelloCorba.

The IDL File

The IDL file for this example is fairly short and defines the method names for HelloCorba. A listing of this IDL file is in Listing 9-1. If you have not seen IDL before, this listing gives you an idea of its appearance.

Listing 9-1: The IDL file for the HelloCorba example.

```
module idl {

    interface HelloCorba {

        void setOneString(in string value1);
        void setTwoStrings(in string value1, in string
value2);
        void setThreeStrings(in string value1, in string value2, in string
value3);
        string getOneString();
        string getTwoStrings(out string value2);
        string getThreeStrings(out string value2, out string value3);
        void  setLong(in long value);
        long  getLong();
        void  outLong(out long value);
        void  setShort(in short value);
        short getShort();
        void  outShort(out short value);
        void  setULong(in  unsigned long value);
        unsigned long  getULong();
        void  outULong(out unsigned long value);
        void  setUShort(in unsigned short value);
        unsigned short getUShort();
        void  outUShort(out unsigned short value);
        void  setChar(in char value);
        char  getChar();
        void  outChar(out char value);
        void  setBoolean(in boolean value);
        boolean  getBoolean();
        void  outBoolean(out boolean value);
        void  setOctet(in octet value);
        octet  getOctet();
        void  outOctet(out octet value);
    };

};
```

Listing 9-1 begins with a module statement with the form:

```
module idl { ... }
```

When the Java files are created from this IDL file using the idl2java utility, they will be in package idl. The interface statement encloses the various methods. Inside the interface definition, the statements look similar to Java method definitions without the Java code filled in. In IDL, parameters can be specified with some information about whether they are input parameters, output parameters, or both. Parameters are prefaced by either IN, OUT or both IN and OUT. All of the parameters in Listing 9-1 are either IN or OUT.

Building the Java Support Files

The Java support file (HelloCorbaDaemon.java) is provided with the CDK. You must build the HelloCorba example from the IDL file using the idl2java utility. The steps are:

1. Run the idl2java utility on HelloCorba.idl. This will create the Java source files in Table 9-3.
2. Compile the resulting Java source files using javac.exe.

The CDK provides a batch file (BuildHelloCorba.bat) to accomplish the steps above. The idl2java utility takes as input an IDL file and outputs Java source files. A number of support Java files are created by this step. Table 9-3 lists the Java source files; these files are created by the idl2java utility.

Filename	Description
HelloCorba.java	Interface HelloCorba.
HelloCorbaHelper.java	Reads/writes and returns an identifier for HelloCorba objects.
HelloCorbaHolder.java	Implements persistence using HelloCorbaHelper.
HelloCorbaOperations.java	Interface declaring all HelloCorba operations.
_example_HelloCorba.java	Stub code to be implemented by developer.
_sk_HelloCorba.java	Code skeleton file extended by HelloCorbaDaemon.
_st_HelloCorba.java	Implements the methods defined in HelloCorbaOperations.
_tie_HelloCorba.java	Implements HelloCorba operations using delegation code.

Table 9-3: The Java source files used by the HelloCorba example.

As an example of the output of the idl2java utility, Listing 9-2 is HelloCorbaHolder.java, one of the generated Java source files. It uses a Streamable class from the CORBA library and class HelloCorbaHelper to implement some persistence (read and write) methods.

Listing 9-2: HelloCorbaHolder.java.

```
final public class HelloCorbaHolder implements
org.omg.CORBA.portable.Streamable {
  public idl.HelloCorba value;
  public HelloCorbaHolder() {
  }
  public HelloCorbaHolder(idl.HelloCorba value) {
    this.value = value;
  }
  public void _read(org.omg.CORBA.portable.InputStream input) {
    value = HelloCorbaHelper.read(input);
  }
  public void _write(org.omg.CORBA.portable.OutputStream output) {
    HelloCorbaHelper.write(output, value);
  }
  public org.omg.CORBA.TypeCode _type() {
    return HelloCorbaHelper.type();
  }
}
```

Running HelloCorba as Crossware

To run this example you need the Enterprise Server installed and running. I won't go through all the steps you'd need to connect this component to the server, but this section will provide an overview to give you an idea of what you need to get going with CORBA. These steps are taken from the CDK. The recommended steps are:

1. Set up Enterprise Server with a directory (iiop_objects, for example) for CORBA objects with read/write permissions granted to 'all.'
2. Run the HelloCorbaDaemon. You can run RunHelloCorbaDaemon.bat. First you may need to edit it to point to appropriate directories on your machine.

After running the daemon program you'll see output like this:

```
HelloCorba: initializing...
HelloCorba: starting CORBA...
HelloCorba being registered to: http://dougie/iiop_objects/HelloCorba
HelloCorba Daemon ready for service
```

3. Start Visual JavaScript, and load the HelloCorba.idl file to the palette using Tools | Load to palette | CORBA Object.
4. Drag the HelloCorba component to a new HTML page.
5. Double-click on the HelloCorba object on the page to open the inspector, and set the "Object URL Address." For example: http://mymachine.mydomain.com/iiop_objects/HelloCorba.

To continue with the example you need to set up a form on the HTML page. Drag two buttons and two text fields to the page. Change the first button's label to "Set String" and the second button's label to "Get String."

You may recall the connection builder from the section "Interacting with Components" in Chapter 7. Connect the first button to the HelloCorba object by dragging the connection point of the button. You'll see the connection builder dialog open. Choose the "new event connection" option. For the target of the connection, press "view parameters," and select an action of setOneString. For value1 enter:

```
document.Form1.Text1.value
```

Press "Apply" and "Close" to create the connection. Connect the second button to the HelloCorba object as you did the first. This time select an action of getOneString in the connection builder, and enter edit mode by pressing the "View JavaScript" button. Modify the text in the "JavaScript event handler" box from: idl_HelloCorba1.getOneString( ) to read:

```
document.Form1.Text2.value = idl_HelloCorba1.getOneString()
```

The preceding statement uses the CORBA object's getOneString method. If you still have the connection builder dialog open, press "Apply" and then "Close." You can now deploy the project with the deploy button and test it by loading the page you created in Navigator. Type **Hello Corba** in the first text field, and click the "Set String" button. If everything went as planned, it will retrieve the string from the CORBA object.

Moving On

In this chapter I've presented information about the CORBA. Netscape supports CORBA in their current product line through ORBs available in Communicator 4 and Enterprise Server 3. CORBA components can also be used in Visual JavaScript, giving developers another important building block for creating crossware applications.

The next chapter will talk about some other important features of Netscape's component support, such as using Customizers and Plug-ins with Visual JavaScript.

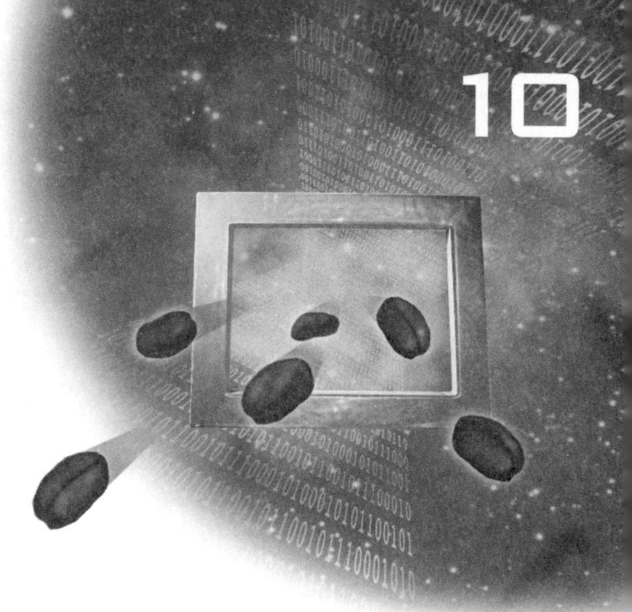

Using Plug-ins, Customizers & PropertyEditors

Those familiar with Netscape Communicator or previous Navigator versions will be familiar with the idea of Netscape *plug-ins*. Plug-ins extend the file types Communicator can read by providing code modules that are loaded when a different file type is read. An example of a plug-in already available would be one that reads Adobe Acrobat files which are in the Portable Document Format (PDF). Plug-ins can be written for use with Visual JavaScript and with Netscape ONE technologies. These plug-ins are written to comply with the Netscape Composer plug-in specification. Composer plug-ins for Visual JavaScript and Netscape ONE are written in Java; previous Netscape plug-ins may have been written in languages such as C or C++.

JavaBeans Customizers and PropertyEditors can be considered Visual JavaScript plug-ins, too. We've talked about Customizers and PropertyEditors in Chapter 5, but not their use with Visual JavaScript.

Plug-ins With Communicator

Plug-ins are available for use with Netscape Communicator 4 (and have been available for use with Navigator for some time). If you are a user of the Navigator browser, you know that plug-ins let a browser read file and MIME types that it ordinarily cannot process. (MIME stands for Multipurpose Internet Mail Extensions.) A plug-in is always associated with a file type. When Navigator downloads a file with a special format it cannot read, a plug-in is needed. Plug-ins reside in a particular plug-in directory or folder on your system. For example, when a PDF file (these are usually read by Adobe Acrobat) is downloaded, the PDF plug-in is enabled in Navigator if it is installed in your plug-in directory. If it's not installed in your plug-in directory, a dialog box queries you to download the plug-in.

Plug-ins come in two varieties: *embedded* and *page-oriented*. Embedded plug-ins are embedded in an HTML page. The process of using them is analogous to embedding images with the IMG tag. They can be embedded in a page using the EMBED and OBJECT tags:

- **EMBED** is used only to embed plug-ins. Plug-ins are handled similarly to the way images are displayed with the IMG tag.
- **OBJECT** can be used to embed plug-ins; it also is used to embed Java applets or ActiveX controls.

Embedded plug-ins function like images in that they are part of the page. They display as a rectangle on the page.

The other category, page-oriented plug-ins (also called *full page* plug-ins), require an entire page to do their work. That is, when you download a document requiring a page-oriented plug-in, you see a full document displayed in a window by itself. Documents requiring Adobe Acrobat or Microsoft Word would be handled by page-oriented plug-ins.

There are many plug-ins already available. Netscape has a plug-in page accessible from http://home.netscape.com. For more complete information about developing plug-ins in C and C++, consult *Official Netscape Technologies Developer's Guide* by Luke Duncan and Sean Michaels (Ventana 1997).

Visual JavaScript Plug-ins

There are three types of objects that Netscape considers Visual JavaScript plug-ins. The first type is a page-oriented plug-in similar to what we described in the preceding section. These page-oriented plug-ins must be written to the Composer plug-in specification. The two other object types considered to be plug-ins are Customizers and PropertyEditors. These two are considered plug-ins because they can be 'plugged-in' to Visual JavaScript to add customization features for Visual JavaScript components. Here is a summary of the three types of Visual JavaScript plug-ins:

- **Composer-style plug-ins:** These are page-oriented plug-ins written in Java and using the Composer interface API.
- **Property editors:** These are Java property editors, written to conform with Visual JavaScript.
- **Customizer classes:** These are Java classes implementing java.beans.Customizer and conforming with Visual JavaScript.

Composer is the Web page editor component of Netscape Communicator. Composer plug-ins are written in Java using interfaces provided with the Composer Plug-in Kit. Other plug-ins in the past were often written in other languages, for example C or C++.

NOTE

The Composer Plug-in Kit and more information about the Composer Plug-in API can be obtained from Netscape's DevEdge Web site at http://developer.netscape.com. Also, some of the information about Visual JavaScript plug-ins is subject to change. That is, complete information was not available at the time of writing about integrating Composer plug-ins with VJS. Netscape recommends that developers become familiar with the Composer Plug-in API to be ready to develop plug-ins to work with Visual JavaScript and Netscape ONE.

Composer Plug-in API

The support provided by Netscape to develop Composer plug-ins is in three Java packages. You write the plug-in using Java, using the classes and interfaces in these three packages. The packages are as follows:

- **The netscape.plugin.composer package:** The classes of this package implement the basic functionality for Composer plug-ins. They implement basic operations needed by all plug-ins.
- **The netscape.plugin.composer.io package:** The classes in this IO package support input and output in an HTML page.
- **The netscape.test.plugin.composer package:** This package contains the Testbed classes for you to test Composer plug-ins.

The following sections describe the classes and interfaces that make up these Java packages.

Composer Package

The netscape.plugin.composer package contains classes that handle basic features required for every plug-in. Table 10-1 shows the classes and interfaces in the netscape.plugin.composer package.

Class Name	Description of Class
Plugin	This class is a base-class for Composer plug-ins.You derive your plug-in from this class.
Document	This class represents an entire HTML document for page-oriented Composer plug-ins to operate on.
Factory	This supports plug-ins that act as wrappers and supports foreign plug-in types.
ImageEncoder	This class provides support for different image file formats.
ImageEncoderFactory	This class is a factory class for creating ImageEncoder objects.

Table 10-1: Classes in the netscape.plugin.composer package.

IO Package

The IO package defines functions that have to do with reading and writing the HTML page in your plug-in. Table 10-2 lists the classes in the netscape.plugin.composer.io package:

Class Name	Description of Class
Comment	This class represents comments that might appear in an HTML document.
Entity	This class is used to represent the escape characters that are used in HTML to represent special characters.The character "&" is used in HTML, for example, as an escape character.
JavaScriptEntity	This class represents parameters in JavaScript tags.
LexicalStream	This class parses Strings or Unicode streams and converts them to tokens.
SelectedHTMLReader	This class supports the filtering of text from an HTML document.
Tag	This class is a token representing HTML tags.
Text	This class is a token representing HTML text.
Token	This class is the base class for other token classes in the system.

Table 10-2: Classes in the netscape.plugin.composer.io package.

Test Package

The Composer plug-in API has facilities for testing your plug-in. The classes to support the Testbed are in netscape.test.plugin.composer. You can run a plug-in in the Testbed as you would another application. The following classes make up the netscape.test.plugin.composer package:

- **Test:** This class provides support for testing the plug-in as an application.
- **ImageEncoderTest:** This class provides support for testing image encoders.

How to Write Composer Plug-ins

Once you've decided what you want your plug-in to do, you implement the plug-in in Java using the packages in the preceding sections. You are implementing a page-oriented plug-in; the entire HTML document will be passed to the perform( ) method (discussed later in this chapter in the section "Adding Informational Methods & Perform( )"). Your primary task is to implement this perform( ) method, implementing any code that's required to modify the document. The following sections describe some necessary tasks associated with implementing a Composer plug-in.

Importing Packages

To use the packages in the Composer plug-in API, you need to import them into your Java code as you would for other Java packages. In fact, you may use other packages of the Java API as you need them. An example that includes the composer and IO packages follows:

```
import netscape.plugin.composer.*;
import netscape.plugin.composer.io.*;
import java.util.*;
```

Extending the Plug-in Class

All plug-ins using the Composer interface need to derive their plug-in from the netscape.plugin.composer.Plugin class. This class provides support common to all plug-ins. You do this in the normal Java way, by extending the plug-in class using the "extends" keyword.

```
import netscape.plugin.composer.*;

public class ComposerPlugin extends Plugin {
}
```

Adding Informational Methods & Perform( )

There are two categories of methods that are overridden when writing a plug-in class. The first category includes more than one method. This group of methods is called the informational methods. The second category contains one method, the perform( ) method. The perform( ) method is where the functional code for the plug-in is placed; the actual work is done in perform( ).

Informational Methods

The signature for the informational methods is given in this section. The information methods all describe information about the plug-in. By default all these methods return the name of the plug-in; you override them in your plug-in class to return the information you want. The names of the methods are getName( ), getCategory( ), and getHint( ). The signature for getName( ) is as follows:

```
public String getName();
```

getName( ) returns a string that is the name end users see in the menu when using the plug-in from Composer. Composer creates a menu of plug-in names and uses this method to get that name. You override this method with your own name for the plug-in.

```
public String getCategory();
```

Plug-ins can be organized into groups called *categories*. This method returns a string that becomes an option on the Tools menu when running in Composer.

```
public String getHint();
```

You implement the getHint( ) method in your plug-in by returning a one-line description in the body of the code of this method. This description describing the purpose of the plug-in is displayed by the status line of the Communicator window when the plug-in is selected in the menu.

Perform Method

This method performs the work of the plug-in. In this method, which you override from the netscape.plugin.composer.Plugin class, you are passed the entire HTML document. The signature of the perform( ) method is:

```
public boolean perform(Document d) throws IOException;
```

When your plug-in is called, perform( ) is called with the current document. Then your code can read and modify the document in any way needed. The perform( ) method can call other methods you can define in your plug-in class. In fact, when you define other methods in your plug-in class, they can only be called from this method.

Listing 10-1 is an example of a perform method from the Composer Plug-in Kit's EditRaw example. This example requests user input by way of a dialog box and the input is placed back in the document.

Listing 10-1: The EditRaw example's perform( ) method.

```
public boolean perform(Document doc) throws IOException {
    // create a dialog
    MyDialog dialog = new MyDialog("Edit Raw HTML", doc);

    dialog.reshape(50, 50, 300, 300);
    dialog.show();
    dialog.requestFocus();

    // wait for user to exit
    boolean result = dialog.waitForExit();

    // Dispose of the dialog
    dialog.dispose();

    // write changed data back to the document
    if (result)
    {
        doc.setText(dialog.getText());
    }
}
```

Testing Plug-ins

The Composer environment provides an option to test plug-ins outside of Composer. They are tested as stand-alone applications. If you want to take this option, define a main method just as you would for a Java stand-alone application:

```
public static void main (String args[])
{
    netscape.test.plugin.composer.Test.perform(args, new plugInName());
}
```

The implementation of the preceding main( ) method uses the Test class in the netscape.plugin.composer package. Any arguments that you pass on the command line will be passed to the plug-in. Once you have written this method, you've effectively prepared the plug-in for testing in the Testbed. In order to actually test the plug-in, you would execute it using the Java command line, as you would execute a Java stand-alone program.

Packaging Plug-ins

Netscape will allow you to package a plug-in as a Zip or Jar archive (creating Jar file archives is discussed in Chapter 14). This archive file will contain all the classes associated with the plug-in. Name the file cpXXX.jar (for a Jar file) or cpXXX.zip (for a Zip file) where XXX is unique. That is, the string XXX cannot conflict with other plug-ins on your system or other plug-ins downloaded to your system. For these reasons, you may want to include your company name for the archive name. The length of the file name cannot exceed eight characters. That is, "cp" plus "XXX" must be less than or equal to eight characters in length. The Jar or Zip archive should be uncompressed.

For a Jar file, at the top level of the archive, place the configuration file called netscape_plugin_composer.ini. This configuration file, in Java Properties file format, contains names and user interface strings of the plug-in classes. The following properties are required for this property file:

- **netscape.plugin.composer.factory:** The classname of a Factory class.
- **netscape.plugin.composer.classes:** A list of classnames of the plug-ins in the archive. Multiple classnames are separated in the list by colons.

Once you have zipped or archived your plug-in, put it in the plug-in directory of your system to install it.

Plug-in Security

Composer plug-ins use the Communicator 4 security model for security features. In this regard, Composer plug-ins are restricted to the same security privileges as are Java applets. The applet or plug-in is required to ask the Netscape Security Manager (NSM) for permission when it wants to do some risky action such as writing a file. The NSM then asks the user for permission. If it receives permission from the user, it can continue reading or writing files.

Since the NSM is new with Communicator 4, you may have to upgrade your code to take advantage of this security model. To provide a link to the security manager for developers who have not upgraded, the Composer Plug-in Kit contains the class netscape.security.SecurityManager. This class is implemented in stub form, so a developer can use an existing Java environment to call the NSM.

The Java Runtime Interface

The Java Runtime Interface (JRI) is a C/C++ interface to the functionality of the Java Virtual Machine. It lets Java run native C/C++ code methods and C/C++ code call into the Java runtime. This is important for Composer plug-in developers because you can write your plug-in in Java and then call native methods in C/C++ to do other work.

PropertyEditor Classes

I described some aspects of creating a property editor class in Chapter 5—about JavaBean's property support. You also learned in Chapter 7 that beans conforming to the JavaBeans specification can be used in Visual JavaScript. Netscape will provide support for property editors in Visual JavaScript, although it is not fully implemented in the Component Development Kit PR-3 that I tested. These property editors will interact with the inspector window displaying properties of a selected bean. The property editor support follows all the guidelines for JavaBeans property editors.

You recall that in order to implement a JavaBeans property editor class, you implemented the java.beans.PropertyEditor interface. This interface has a number of methods that you must implement. The java.beans.PropertyEditorSupport class can also be extended. The PropertyEditor interface methods are identical when using property editors with Visual JavaScript. The methods in Netscape's support for properties are almost the same as those of the java.beans.PropertyEditor interface. They are listed here along with their behavior when using a Visual JavaScript inspector:

- **addPropertyChangeListener:** This method behaves the same as the JavaBeans specification.
- **removePropertyChange Listener:** This method behaves the same as the JavaBeans specification.
- **getAsText:** Visual JavaScript uses the getAsText value to retrieve Unicode strings from the inspector. The string will be converted into HTML after having been retrieved from the inspector.
- **setAsText:** The inspector gives the text to the property editor with this method.
- **getValue:** Preliminary documentation states that this method will probably not be used.

- **setValue:** Not used.
- **supportsCustomEditor:** This method returns a Boolean stating whether a custom editor is supported. See the following method.
- **getCustomEditor:** This returns a custom editor. In Visual JavaScripts's inspector, this will be invoked by clicking on the button to the right of the inspected value.
- **getIFCEditor:** This returns an IFC View class representing a pop-up dialog. This dialog will allow custom editing of a property.
- **isPaintable:** This value states whether the property is drawable in a GUI.
- **paintValue:** If the value of the property is paintable, this method is called to render it to the screen.
- **getJavaInitializationString:** This method may not be used.
- **getTags:** Will probably not be used.

Most of these methods are similar to the java.beans.PropertyEditor support. They just have slightly different meanings in the context of Visual JavaScript inspectors. Perusing these methods with the java.beans.PropertyEditor interface in mind, you can see one method Netscape has added is:

```
Get IFCEditor();
```

The method Get IFCEditor returns an IFC View class that supports a pop-up dialog for custom editing of the property value. This is so that IFC-oriented customizers can be added.

Customizer Classes

We also looked at JavaBean Customizer classes. You recall that a Customizer was a Java class that implemented the java.beans.Customizer interface. There is one difference between JavaBeans Customizer classes and those designed to work with Visual JavaScript: Composer plug-in developers may be using the Internet Foundation Classes for their Graphical User Interface (GUI) support. One of the notes about the Customizer classes in the JavaBeans specification is that Customizers need to inherit from java.awt.Component so that they can be added to a window or dialog box. This constraint is dropped if you are developing a Customizer for use with Visual JavaScript. This will not be the case for Customizers developed for Netscape.

BeanConnect

BeanConnect programs will be used with Visual JavaScript and Netscape ONE tools. BeanConnect lets Java applications function among different HTML pages and frames. Although Netscape envisions support for BeanConnect, its full implementation was not available in the Preview Release-3 version of the Component Development Kit (CDK) that I tested.

Normally BeanConnect objects use the <OBJECT> tag. You embed them in an HTML page as you would Java applets with the <APPLET> tag. Applets are subject to an arbitrary limit on a page; there can only be about ten applets on a page at a time. BeanConnect programs are made up of linked Java objects; there is no limit to the number of BeanConnect programs on a page.

Because a BeanConnect program consists of one or more linked Java objects, it is possible to import a BeanConnect program to a VJS palette. They will be imported to the VJS palette similarly to JavaBeans or Java applets.

Moving On

This chapter provided information on Visual JavaScript plug-ins. Plug-ins can be developed according to the Composer plug-in specification (using classes from Netscape's Composer plug-in libraries). These plug-ins are developed in Java and are page-oriented—they operate on an entire HTML page. PropertyEditors and Customizers were discussed previously in Chapter 5, and in this chapter we considered how these classes can function as Visual JavaScript plug-ins.

The next chapter describes the persistence and synchronization support that is available in JDK 1.1.

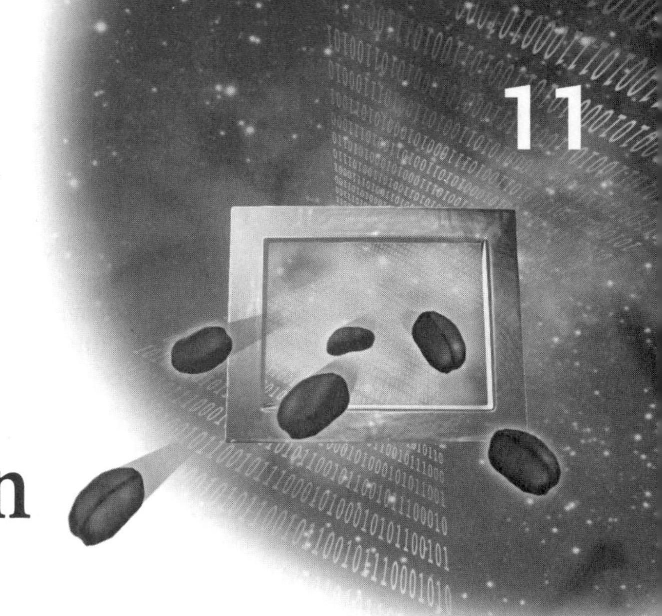

Persistence & Synchronization

A truly flexible component architecture supports the persistence of components. Using persistence, a developer can use a component in a builder tool, connect it with other components, customize it, and store it for later use. This makes the architecture more flexible and enables components to be used on a wider range of platforms. JavaBeans includes such a persistence mechanism. In fact, the storage of beans is done using the same built-in serialization support used for other Java objects.

This chapter discusses the Java API for storing beans. Code synchronization is another important Java topic that will be discussed. Beans will often be run in a multi-threaded environment. Using the synchronized keyword, you can make sure your beans operate safely in an environment using threads.

Persistence Support in Java 1.1

The input/output support in Java 1.0 (in package java.io) bases its storage style upon byte streams. Classes such as BufferedInputStream and BufferedOuputStream let you write primitive data objects to and from a *stream*. Java 1.1 has extended this concept to include support for objects. The classes and interfaces that support this are new in the java.io package and can be thought of as the serialization API.

You use the same Java serialization support for JavaBeans as for other objects. You can also customize this support to gain more control over what fields are stored. Support centers around the classes ObjectOutputStream and ObjectInputStream, and interfaces Serializable and Externalizable. We'll first look at the stream classes used to serialize objects: ObjectOutputStream and ObjectInputStream; then we'll look at the interfaces.

Class ObjectOutputStream

Java 1.0 has a class named DataOutputStream that lets you store a stream of bytes or data of various types—integers or floats, for example. Class ObjectOutputStream extends this idea to let you store objects as you would other data types in Java. Objects may contain references to other objects, and any storage mechanism must take that into account. Classes ObjectOutputStream and ObjectInputStream address this problem by following a 'graph' of objects—if an object contains other objects, these objects will be stored (as well as any objects that these objects may contain).

Class ObjectOutputStream is a subclass of OutputStream in the package java.io. Two important methods in class ObjectOutputStream are writeObject and defaultWriteObject. Both these methods are declared as final and cannot be overridden. The writeObject method is used to write out the state of an object. defaultWriteObject is used when you are customizing the default serialization and adding some serialization code of your own (discussed further in the section "The Serializable Interface" later in this chapter).

The following example demonstrates using the writeObject method. The example code opens a file stream of type FileOutputStream, then creates an ObjectOutputStream object and outputs two strings and some integers to the stream using writeObject. The strings and integers are written out as a stream of bytes. Note that the flush method is called to flush the stream before closing it. The writeObject method is used to write out object types (like class String); ObjectOutputStream also supports writing of primitive types such as short integers (writeShort), long integers (writeLong), and characters (writeChar, writeChars). Here's the example:

```
FileOutputStream fileStream = new FileOutputStream("FileOut");
ObjectOutputStream objStream = new ObjectOutputStream(fileStream);
objStream.writeObject("Fred Smith");
objStream.writeObject(new String("Hi"));
objStream.writeShort(3);
objStream.writeLong(32000);
objStream.flush();
objStream.close();
```

Class ObjectInputStream

Class ObjectInputStream is also a subclass of OutputStream in the package java.io. Two methods you need to use in class ObjectInputStream are readObject and defaultReadObject. These methods are declared as final, as are writeObject and defaultWriteObject. The readObject method performs the inverse of writeObject, reading in an object that's been serialized and taking care to reconstruct the complete object 'graph.' You can use defaultReadObject to customize default serialization to read the custom fields you write with your customized version of writeObject.

The following example demonstrates the use of the readObject method. The example code opens a file stream of type FileInputStream, then creates an ObjectInputStream object. It reads a string and some integers from the stream using readObject.

```
FileInputStream fileStream = new FileInputStream("FileIn");
ObjectInputStream inStream = new ObjectInputStream(fileStream);
String hiStr = (String)inStream.readObject();
int anInt = inStream.readInt();
long aLong = inStream.readLong();
inStream.close();
```

The Serializable Interface

In order to make an object readable and writable by readObject and writeObject, you must implement the Serializable interface or the Externalizable interface. The Serializable interface, which is in Java package java.io, is interesting because it contains no methods; its only function is to identify a class as serializable. This provides more compatibility than Externalizable if you expect your bean classes may change. Serializable will always correctly serialize objects if what Sun calls a "compatible version" of the class is present. That is, when reading a serialized class, the class definition in the reading environment need not be the same as when the class was originally stored, but it must be compatible.

Since this interface has no methods, to mark a class as serializable all you really need to do is the following:

```
public class MyBeanClass extends Canvas implements Serializable
{
// class code
}
```

Once you've implemented this interface as in the preceding, the fields of the bean will be written and read correctly when writeObject/readObject is called. Of course, you may not want to write all fields to storage; some fields may not be meaningful when serialized. The section "Custom Bean Storage," later in this chapter, discusses these issues.

The Externalizable Interface

You implement the Externalizable interface (in java.io) to truly customize the storage of an object. This approach is the most flexible (in that you can create your own file format, for example) but also more work than using the Serializable interface. Externalizable has two methods: readExternal and writeExternal. You must provide code for these two methods to read and write your object. For example, if you create your own file format when writing out an object using writeExternal, you must implement a compatible readExternal method that reads the same format. The prototypes for these methods are as follows:

```
public interface Externalizable extends Serializable
{
    public void writeExternal(ObjectOutput o) throws IOException;
    public void readExternal(ObjectInput I) throws IOException,
java.lang.ClassNotFoundException;
}
```

Special Considerations for Storing Beans

Since beans use the standard Java 1.1 serialization techniques, the simplest approach to making a bean persistent is to implement the Serializable interface. This is the approach that is taken for any object in Java (not just beans). JavaBeans may have some unique requirements with regard to serialization, however. Sun suggests in their JavaBeans specification that the following are important issues to consider:

- Beans may not want to store pointers to other beans.
- Beans may not want to store references to a list of event listeners.
- Beans might occasionally need their storage to be completely customized. The Externalizable interface can be used to implement this custom storage.

The running of a bean in a beanbox tool is a dynamic process. An end user may select any number of beans and cause them to interact in various ways. A beanbox tool is expected to keep track of connections that the developer may have set up among beans before serializing them. So the storing of pointers to other beans or lists of event listeners is something you may want to prevent. For details on how to prevent bean fields from being stored, see the next section, "Custom Bean Storage."

Custom Bean Storage

There are several ways to customize the storage of a bean. Instead of merely making the bean class serializable, you may want to implement the Serializable interface as before, but then implement your own writeObject and readObject methods. You can also prevent fields from being stored for reasons of security (to hide certain fields) or because they won't be meaningful when read in a new environment. And, as I mentioned, the advanced features provided by the Externalizable interface give you the control to create your own file format. In this section I'll describe creating your own writeObject/ readObject and preventing fields from being stored.

Providing Your Own writeObject & readObject

Implementing the Serializable interface and using writeObject and readObject works well for normal serialization. But if you have fields that need to be preprocessed before being saved or processed after being read in, you can add this processing to your own versions of the writeObject and readObject methods.

For example, suppose your bean has an integer field that is always changing. Rather than relying upon the default writeObject method, you may want to update this field before writeObject is called. In this case you write your own writeObject method, compute the field's current value, write it out using a primitive method (such as writeInt), then call ObjectOutputStream.defaultWriteObject to store the rest of the fields. A short example that implements a writeObject method using this approach is in Listing 11-1. The example class declares a field that contains the current width of the class (the object is derived from Canvas). Before calling defaultWriteObject, the example calls a method to update the width to the current width.

Listing 11-1: Example1.java.

```
import java.io.*;
import java.awt.*;
import java.util.*;

public class Example1 extends Canvas
{
        long timeOfDay;
        Date aDate;
        public int aChangeableWidth=0;

        public Example1()
        {
        // field that contains width
        aChangeableWidth = this.getSize().width;
        // other fields
        long timeOfDay = 0;
        aDate = new Date();
        }

        private void writeObject(ObjectOutputStream s)
     throws IOException
        {
        // calculate current value of a field
        updateField();
        // then store it
        s.writeInt(aChangeableWidth);
        // then store the rest of object
        s.defaultWriteObject();
        }
        protected void updateField()
        {
         aChangeableWidth = this.getSize().width;
        }
}
```

For reading (still continuing with a similar example), you could read in whatever special fields are required, then call ObjectInputStream.defaultReadObject to read the rest. Whatever post-processing you need could also be done in readObject:

```
private void readObject(ObjectInputStream s)
     throws IOException, ClassNotFoundException
{
s.readInt(aChangeableField);
```

```
s.defaultReadObject();
// maybe do some processing on other fields
// to make sure they're up to date
}
```

The prototypes of the methods readObject and writeObject that you write need to match the following:

```
import java.io.*;
private void readObject(ObjectInputStream s)
     throws IOException, ClassNotFoundException;
 private void writeObject(ObjectOutputStream s)
     throws IOException;
```

The next section describes how you would prevent fields from being stored.

Transient & Static Fields

JavaBeans specifies that fields that are declared with the keyword transient are not written out by writeObject. Therefore, fields that you don't want to store may be declared as follows:

```
private transient int i;
private transient String filename;
```

This declaration will prevent the fields "i" and "filename" from being saved. Static fields will also not be stored, for example:

```
static String filename;
```

Making Beans Thread-Safe

Java is a multi-threaded environment. This means two (or more) different threads might be calling the methods in your code at the same time. The JavaBeans specification recommends a few guidelines to be aware of when writing code for beans. Two situations important to bean development come up when processing events: synchronization when sending events and synchronization when adding or removing listeners.

Synchronization When Sending Events

The first synchronization guideline comes up when coding an event source. You recall that an event source sends an event by calling a method on an event listener. The event source must maintain a list of the event listeners. The actual delivery of the event is usually implemented as a for loop that cycles through a list of listeners, calling the target method upon each. (This is sometimes called *broadcasting* events.) The recommendation for thread-safe code is this: you must "clone" (make a copy of) the list of listeners and call the target methods using the copy of the list. Perhaps an example will make this more clear:

```
Vector w;
synchronized (this) {
    w = (Vector) listOfListeners.clone();
} // end of  synchronized block

for (int i = 0; i < w.size(); i++) {
    ListenerType x = (ListenerType) w.elementAt(i);
    x.callTargetMethod(); //call method on listener
}
```

The first statement in this code uses a synchronized block statement. When it sees a synchronized block statement, Java locks the expression in the parentheses, and then runs the code in the block. In the example code the expression in parentheses is the keyword 'this,' so the current object would be locked (the current object is the one containing the example code) while executing the clone statement.

Critical Sections

The clone statement between { and } is executed as a "critical section." A critical section is a term for code that should not be interrupted by another process until it is done executing. Critical sections often turn up in operating system code where important code may be interrupted, by a system interrupt, for example.

Why clone the list? Cloning the list 'etches it in stone' while you are using it. You use a copy of the list rather than the list itself. What might happen if you don't clone the list? Suppose that another bean added or removed a listener while you were in the for loop sending events. Then the list of listeners would not reflect the current state. Also, adding or removing listeners would certainly change the length of the list. But the code of the for loop uses w.size( ) in order to tell when to terminate the loop. This inconsistency could cause a problem. It is also possible that you could get into a *deadlock* situation.

What Is Deadlock?

A deadlock occurs when a program cannot continue because two sections of code are waiting for a resource and that resource is unavailable (and will continue to be unavailable). For example, suppose that the listener, as a result of your target method call, had called a method back on the source of the event. If this source method could not return because it was waiting for a resource, this is a deadlock.

It is possible to declare your entire event broadcasting method to be synchronized. Then, another thread could not call this method until you are finished broadcasting events. Rather than do this however, Sun recommends that you clone the list and make the actual section that calls the listener's target method unsynchronized. The preceding example code is in agreement with the recommended approach.

Synchronization When Adding/Removing Listeners

Earlier I mentioned the difficulties that could occur if a listener is added while you are broadcasting events. It's also important that the add/remove listener methods themselves be declared as synchronized, too. These, too, must be 'thread-safe.' As an example, suppose we have a source of events containing an addXYZListener( ) method, and the following sequence occurs:

1. Thread A starts adding listener 1 by calling addXYZListener( ).
2. Thread B starts adding listener 2 by calling addXYZListener( ).
3. Thread A finishes adding listener 1.

The problem is that when thread B begins adding listener 2, thread A is not finished adding listener 1. So what list does thread B use? For those familiar with database updates, this is similar to difficulties that can happen when two people are trying to update the same record in a database concurrently. To get around these possible problems, the add/remove methods are declared synchronized. Look at the following definitions of add/remove listener methods:

```
public synchronized void addWWWListener (WWWListener);
public synchronized void removeWWWListener(WWWListener);
```

The synchronized keyword is used to declare these methods. This assures us that no other thread will make calls to these methods while they are executing.

Moving On

Being able to save components is an important feature of any component architecture. JavaBeans supplies persistence support accessible from a fairly easy API. You may use the default storage by declaring your beans using the Serializable interface, or customize bean storage by providing your own read/write methods. In this chapter you also learned about a few cases in which it is important to make your code 'thread-safe' using synchronization.

The next chapter provides a reference to the package containing most of the JavaBeans API, java.beans.

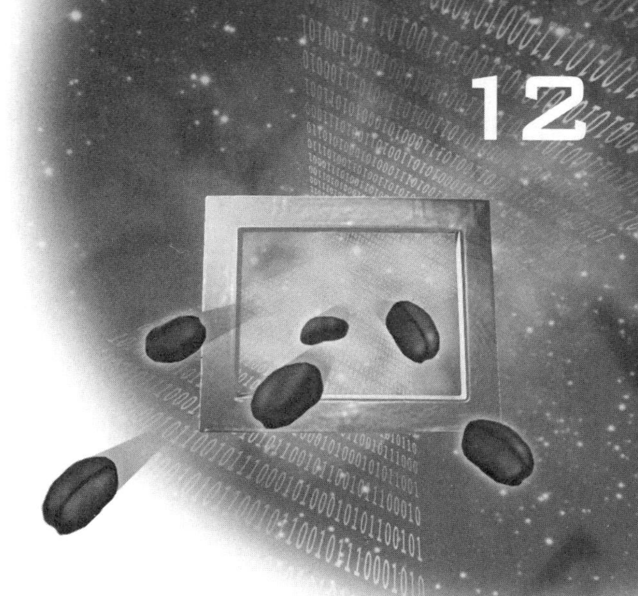

Reference to JavaBeans API

This chapter is a reference chapter to the JavaBeans API. JavaBeans support is primarily in the Java package java.beans.

Each section in this chapter takes a parallel form: I present the class or interface name followed by a description of the class and its uses. Then a listing of the constructors, methods, and private or public variables follows.

In the descriptions, I try to highlight what you might find most useful about a class. The features highlighted will often be the ones you'll want to learn first, either for your own development of beans or to be able to read the code of beans developed by others.

Of course, as the rest of this book has made clear, not all the support for JavaBeans is contained in the single java.beans package. In particular, the JDK 1.1 event model is important for developing beans. However, this chapter is a good place to look for Java 1.1 support that is unique to JavaBeans.

Package java.beans

The new classes, interfaces, and exceptions providing support for JavaBeans are in the package java.beans. This package, new with Java version 1.1, is divided into classes, interfaces, and exceptions; following is a section for each of these categories.

The Classes

Class java.beans.BeanDescriptor

Class BeanDescriptor is a subclass of FeatureDescriptor. During introspection, a beanbox tool will call the getBeanDescriptor method in a BeanInfo object to return a BeanDescriptor object if it is available. One major use of the BeanDescriptor constructor is to associate a customizer class (a class that implements the Customizer interface) with your bean. The methods getBeanClass and getCustomizerClass provide access for a beanbox tool to the bean class and its customizer.

```
// Listing for BeanDescriptor
public class BeanDescriptor
extends FeatureDescriptor {
// Constructors
public BeanDescriptor(Class beanClass);
public BeanDescriptor(Class beanClass, Class customizerClass);
// Methods
public Class getBeanClass();
public Class getCustomizerClass();
}
```

Class java.beans.Beans

This is an abstract class with methods mostly applicable to beanbox tools. It provides some general methods for inquiring about beans. Beans.instantiate in particular is used by a beanbox tool to create and initialize a bean. Beans.instantiate looks for a no argument constructor for the bean it's trying to load. Beans.instantiate could also be used in code in which you are hand-coding the inclusion of a bean. The isDesignTime and setDesignTime methods access whether the bean is being used in 'design mode' in a beanbox.

```
// Listing for Beans
public class Beans extends Object {
// no argument constructor
public Beans();
// Methods
public static Object getInstanceOf(Object bean,Class targetType);
public static Object instantiate(ClassLoader cls,String beanName) throws
IOException, ClassNotFoundException;
public static boolean isDesignTime();
public static boolean isGuiAvailable();
public static boolean isInstanceOf(Object bean, Class targetType);
public static void setDesignTime(boolean isDesignTime) throws
SecurityException;
```

```
public static void setGuiAvailable(boolean isGuiAvailable) throws
SecurityException;
}
```

Class java.beans.EventSetDescriptor

This class is a subclass of FeatureDescriptor, as are many other BeanInfo helper classes—such as PropertyDescriptor, MethodDescriptor, and ParameterDescriptor. An event set is the methods of one listener interface. For an event listener interface with one or more methods, the event set is the methods that are specified in that interface. The various EventSetDescriptor constructors require the name of the class that produces the event, the name of the event type, the name of the event listener, and the name of the listener method (or methods).

```
// Listing for EventSetDescriptor
public class EventSetDescriptor
extends FeatureDescriptor {
// Constructors
public EventSetDescriptor(Class sourceClass, String eventSetName,Class
listenerType, String listenerMethodName) throws IntrospectionException;
public EventSetDescriptor(Class sourceClass,
String eventSetName, Class listenerType,
String listenerMethodNames[],
String addListenerMethodName,
String removeListenerMethodName) throws IntrospectionException;
public EventSetDescriptor(String eventSetName, Class listenerType, Method
listenerMethods[], Method addListenerMethod, Method removeListenerMethod)
throws IntrospectionException
public EventSetDescriptor(String eventSetName,
Class listenerType,MethodDescriptor listenerMethodDescriptors[],Method
addListenerMethod, Method removeListenerMethod) throws
IntrospectionException
// Methods
public Method getAddListenerMethod();
public MethodDescriptor[] getListenerMethodDescriptors();
public Method[] getListenerMethods();
public Class getListenerType();
public Method getRemoveListenerMethod();
public boolean isInDefaultEventSet();
public Method getAddListenerMethod();
public Method getRemoveListenerMethod();
public boolean isUnicast();
public void setInDefaultEventSet(boolean inDefaultEventSet);
public void setUnicast(boolean unicast);
}
```

Class java.beans.FeatureDescriptor

This class is important to introspection, because it is the superclass of classes like PropertyDescriptor and MethodDescriptor that are used with BeanInfo classes. Some of the methods in this class may also be used by a beanbox tool to perform its introspection upon a bean.

```
// Listing for FeatureDescriptor
public class FeatureDescriptor
extends Object
{
// no argument constructor
public FeatureDescriptor();
// Methods
public Enumeration attributeNames();
public String getDisplayName();
public String getName();
public String getShortDescription();
public Object getValue(String attributeName);
public boolean isExpert();
public boolean isHidden();
public void setDisplayName(String displayName);
public void setExpert(boolean expert);
public void setHidden(boolean hidden);
public void setName(String name);
public void setShortDescription(String text);
public void setValue(String attributeName, Object value);
}
```

Class java.beans.IndexedPropertyDescriptor

This is a subclass of PropertyDescriptor that represents an indexed property. An indexed property is a property of a bean that behaves like an array (can be read and written using integer indexes). The constructors for IndexedPropertyDescriptor require at a minimum the property name and a Class object representing the class the property belongs to. Other constructors let you specify the names of the get/set methods for the property.

```
// Listing for IndexedPropertyDescriptorpublic class
IndexedPropertyDescriptor
extends PropertyDescriptor
{
// constructors
public IndexedPropertyDescriptor(String propertyName, Class beanClass)
throws IntrospectionException;
public IndexedPropertyDescriptor(String propertyName, Class beanClass,
String getterName, String setterName, String indexedGetterName, String
```

```
indexedSetterName) throws IntrospectionException;
public IndexedPropertyDescriptor(String propertyName, Method getter, Method
setter, Method indexedGetter, Method indexedSetter) throws
IntrospectionException;
// methods
public Class getIndexedPropertyType();
public Method getIndexedReadMethod();
public Method getIndexedWriteMethod();
}
```

Class java.beans.Introspector

Class Introspector contains the facilities to enable a beanbox tool to analyze or introspect upon a bean. The getBeanInfo method is used to return a BeanInfo object, if one is available, for the bean being introspected. The decapitalize method is a utility method that follows appropriate Java capitalization rules for names. That is, Java method names often begin with a small letter, with capitals used for subsequent 'words'.

```
// Listing for Introspector
public class Introspector
extends Object
{
// methods
public static String decapitalize(String name);
public static BeanInfo getBeanInfo(Class beanClass) throws
IntrospectionException;
public static BeanInfo getBeanInfo(Class beanClass, Class stopClass) throws
IntrospectionException;
public static String[] getBeanInfoSearchPath();
public static void setBeanInfoSearchPath(String path[]);
}
```

Class java.beans.MethodDescriptor

MethodDescriptor is a subclass of FeatureDescriptor that represents a method in a bean. Its two constructors use either a single instance of class Method or the method information plus an array of ParameterDescriptor objects. This array represents the parameters of the method being described.

```
// Listing for MethodDescriptor
public class MethodDescriptor
extends FeatureDescriptor
{
// constructors
public MethodDescriptor(Method method);
public MethodDescriptor(Method method, ParameterDescriptor
parameterDescriptors[]);
```

```
// methods
public Method getMethod();
public ParameterDescriptor[] getParameterDescriptors();
}
```

Class java.beans.ParameterDescriptor

ParameterDescriptor is a subclass of FeatureDescriptor that provides information about parameters. Most of the functionality of this class derives from the superclass FeatureDescriptor.

```
// Listing for ParameterDescriptor
public class ParameterDescriptor
extends FeatureDescriptor
{
// constructor
public ParameterDescriptor();
}
```

Class java.beans.PropertyChangeEvent

A PropertyChangeEvent is derived from java.util.EventObject. This class represents the event fired when a bound property changes its value. The getOldValue and getNewValue methods can be used to retrieve the before and after values of a bound property.

```
// Listing for PropertyChangeEvent
public class PropertyChangeEvent
extends EventObject
{
// constructors
public PropertyChangeEvent(Object source,
String propertyName, Object oldValue, Object newValue);
// methods
public Object getNewValue();
public Object getOldValue();
public Object getPropagationId();
public String getPropertyName();
public void setPropagationId(Object propagationId);
}
```

Class java.beans.PropertyChangeSupport

When implementing bound property code for a bean, class PropertyChangeSupport can be useful. Like other support classes in java.beans, it's easier to use PropertyChangeSupport than it would be to implement bound properties from scratch. When trying to support bound properties in a bean, you can have your class extend PropertyChangeSupport or declare a local variable (an instance variable) in your class of type PropertyChangeSupport.

```
// Listing for PropertyChangeSupport
public class PropertyChangeSupport
extends Object
implements Serializable
{
// constructors
public PropertyChangeSupport(Object sourceBean);
// methods
public synchronized void addPropertyChangeListener(PropertyChangeListener
listener);
public void firePropertyChange(String propertyName, Object oldValue, Object
newValue);
public synchronized void removePropertyChangeListener(PropertyChangeListener
listener);
}
```

java.beans.PropertyDescriptor

This subclass of class FeatureDescriptor provides support for representing bean properties. It is used by the introspection process; BeanInfo objects can contain an array of PropertyDescriptor objects. Each PropertyDescriptor object represents a property belonging to some bean. This is how information about a property in a BeanInfo class is specified.

```
// Listing for PropertyDescriptor
public class PropertyDescriptor
extends FeatureDescriptor
{
// constructors
public PropertyDescriptor(String propertyName, Class beanClass) throws
IntrospectionException;
public PropertyDescriptor(String propertyName,
Class beanClass, String getterName,
String setterName) throws IntrospectionException;
public PropertyDescriptor(String propertyName,
Method getter, Method setter) throws IntrospectionException;
// methods
public Class getPropertyEditorClass();
public Class getPropertyType();
public Method getReadMethod();
public Method getWriteMethod();
```

```
public boolean isBound();
public boolean isConstrained();
public void setBound(boolean bound);
public void setConstrained(boolean constrained);
public void setPropertyEditorClass(Class propertyEditorClass);
}
```

Class java.beans.PropertyEditorManager

This class is used to find the property editor that's associated with a given bean. The registerEditor method can be used to register a property editor class for a bean.

```
// Listing for PropertyEditorManager
public class PropertyEditorManager
extends Object
{
// constructor
public PropertyEditorManager();
// methods
public static PropertyEditor findEditor(Class targetType);
public static String[] getEditorSearchPath();
public static void registerEditor(Class targetType, Class editorClass);
public static void setEditorSearchPath(String path[]);
}
```

Class java.beans.PropertyEditorSupport

One of the support classes, PropertyEditorSupport implements the PropertyEditor interface and provides some default implementations of its methods. If you are creating a property editor class for a bean, it may be easier to use this class than to implement the PropertyEditor interface directly. The getTags and setAsText methods can be used when providing property editors for non-simple types, such as enumerated types represented as strings. The addPropertyChangeListener and removePropertyChangeListener methods manage a list of listeners for bound properties. This is how a property editor notifies interested listeners when properties in the editor are modified.

```
// Listing for PropertyEditorSupport
public class PropertyEditorSupport
extends Object
implements PropertyEditor
{
// constructors
protected PropertyEditorSupport();
protected PropertyEditorSupport(Object source);
```

```
// methods
public synchronized void addPropertyChangeListener(PropertyChangeListener
listener);
public void firePropertyChange();
public String getAsText();
public Component getCustomEditor();
public String getJavaInitializationString();
public String[] getTags();
public Object getValue();
public boolean isPaintable();
public void paintValue(Graphics gfx, Rectangle box);
public synchronized void removePropertyChangeListener(PropertyChangeListener
listener);
public void setAsText(String text) throws IllegalArgumentException;
public void setValue(Object value);
public boolean supportsCustomEditor();
}
```

Class java.beans.SimpleBeanInfo

This support class is very useful when creating a BeanInfo class for a bean. SimpleBeanInfo implements the methods in the BeanInfo interface and provides default implementations for them. It will be easier to derive your BeanInfo class from SimpleBeanInfo than to implement the BeanInfo interface directly. Using SimpleBeanInfo, the developer can just override those methods that are needed. SimpleBeanInfo returns null for many of the methods it implements. When a beanbox receives null from a BeanInfo method, it means no information is available on that feature (for example property, event, or method). Low-level reflection using design patterns then reveals more information about the property, method, or event.

```
// Listing for SimpleBeanInfo
public class SimpleBeanInfo
extends Object
{
// constructor
public SimpleBeanInfo();
// methods
public BeanInfo[] getAdditionalBeanInfo();
public BeanDescriptor getBeanDescriptor();
public int getDefaultEventIndex();
public int getDefaultPropertyIndex();
public EventSetDescriptor[] getEventSetDescriptors();
public Image getIcon(int iconKind);
public MethodDescriptor[] getMethodDescriptors();
```

```
public PropertyDescriptor[] getPropertyDescriptors();
public Image loadImage(String resourceName);
}
```

Class java.beans.VetoableChangeSupport

This class provides support for constrained properties. The support it provides is similar to that provided to bound properties by class PropertyChangeSupport. It includes methods to add and remove VetoableChangeListener objects, and a method to fire a vetoable change event: fireVetoableChange. The fireVetoableChange method will throw a PropertyVetoException if the property change is vetoed.

```
// Listing for VetoableChangeSupport
public class VetoableChangeSupport
extends Object
implements Serializable
{
// constructor
public VetoableChangeSupport(Object sourceBean);
// methods
public synchronized void addVetoableChangeListener(VetoableChangeListener
listener);
public void fireVetoableChange(String propertyName, Object oldValue,
Object newValue) throws PropertyVetoException;
public synchronized void removeVetoableChangeListener(VetoableChangeListener
listener);

}
```

The Interfaces

Interface java.beans.BeanInfo

A BeanInfo class can be written to accompany a bean and give special information to a beanbox about properties, methods, and events. A BeanInfo class is a class that implements the java.beans.BeanInfo interface. The getBeanDescriptor method returns a BeanDescriptor object with information about a bean, including a possible bean Customizer. A beanbox tool can call the BeanInfo class's getPropertyDescriptors, getMethodDescriptors, and getEventSetDescriptors to get the properties, methods, and events of a bean. BeanInfo classes can implement the getIcon method to return an image for use in beanbox toolbars or menu bars.

The static final int constants are provided to represent icons; the getIcon method returns the icon appropriate to the system. Different icon constants represent 16 x 16 or 32 x 32 pixels; color and monochrome icons.

```
// Listing for BeanInfo
public interface BeanInfo {
// constants
public static final int ICON_COLOR_16x16;
public static final int ICON_COLOR_32x32;
public static final int ICON_MONO_16x16;
public static final int ICON_MONO_32x32;
// Methods
public abstract BeanInfo[] getAdditionalBeanInfo();
public abstract BeanDescriptor getBeanDescriptor();
public abstract int getDefaultEventIndex();
public abstract int getDefaultPropertyIndex();
public abstract EventSetDescriptor[] getEventSetDescriptors();
public abstract Image getIcon(int iconKind);
public abstract MethodDescriptor[] getMethodDescriptors();
public abstract PropertyDescriptor[] getPropertyDescriptors();
}
```

Interface java.beans.Customizer

The Customizer interface provides methods that Customizer classes should implement. A Customizer class lets a developer provide a GUI representation for interacting with a bean. The Customizer class is associated with a bean by way of a BeanDescriptor. The setObject method associates the Customizer with the bean it is designed to customize. Customizer classes need to be supplied with a null constructor.

```
// Listing for Customizer
public interface Customizer
{
// public methods
public abstract void addPropertyChangeListener(PropertyChangeListener
listener);
public abstract void removePropertyChangeListener(PropertyChangeListener
listener);
public abstract void setObject(Object bean);
}
```

Interface java.beans.PropertyChangeListener

PropertyChangeListener is a listener interface for use with bound properties. A PropertyChangeEvent is sent when a bound property changes its value.

```
// Listing for PropertyChangeListener
public interface PropertyChangeListener
extends EventListener
{
// public method
public abstract void propertyChange(PropertyChangeEvent evt);
}
```

Interface java.beans.PropertyEditor

This interface provides the necessary methods for creating a PropertyEditor class. A PropertyEditor class is a class that implements this interface and supports the custom editing of properties. The isPaintable and paintValue methods provide support for properties whose values admit of a graphical representation. The getTags and setAsText methods can be used to edit a property that takes on one of a finite set of (possibly non-primitive) values, such as an enumerated type. A PropertyEditor class should be provided with a null constructor.

```
// Listing for PropertyEditor
public interface PropertyEditor
{
// methods
public abstract void addPropertyChangeListener(PropertyChangeListener
listener);
public abstract String getAsText();
public abstract Component getCustomEditor();
public abstract String getJavaInitializationString();
public abstract String[] getTags();
public abstract Object getValue();
public abstract boolean isPaintable();
public abstract void paintValue(Graphics gfx, Rectangle box);
public abstract void removePropertyChangeListener(PropertyChangeListener
listener);
public abstract void setAsText(String text) throws IllegalArgumentException;
public abstract void setAsText(String text) throws IllegalArgumentException;
public abstract void setValue(Object value); public abstract boolean
supportsCustomEditor();
}
```

Interface java.beans.VetoableChangeListener

This is a listener interface implemented by beans listening for vetoable changes. A vetoable change event is sent when a bean changes a constrained property.

```
// Listing for VetoableChangeListener
public interface VetoableChangeListener
extends EventListener
{
// public methods
public abstract void vetoableChange(PropertyChangeEvent evt) throws
PropertyVetoException;
}
```

Interface java.beans.Visibility

In cases where beans run on non-graphical environments, this interface provides some methods to check the availability of a GUI. These methods will probably be of most use to the container running the bean. The methods dontUseGui and okToUseGui tell a bean to use a GUI or not, respectively. avoidingGui returns true if the bean is currently not using the GUI.

```
// Listing for Visibility
public interface Visibility
{
// public methods
public abstract boolean avoidingGui();
public abstract void dontUseGui();
public abstract boolean needsGui();
public abstract void okToUseGui();
}
```

The Exceptions

Class java.beans.IntrospectionException

Thrown by the introspection process when an exception occurs, such as when a method name in a class does not match an expected signature.

```
// Listing for IntrospectionException
public class IntrospectionException
extends Exception
{
    public IntrospectionException(String msg);
}
```

Class java.beans.PropertyVetoException

This exception is used for constrained property support. Constrained properties are those that can only take on certain values. When a constrained property takes on a value outside its set of values, this exception is thrown by the class owning the property.

```
// Listing for PropertyVetoException
public class PropertyVetoException
extends Exception
{
public PropertyVetoException(String message, PropertyChangeEvent evt);
public PropertyChangeEvent getPropertyChangeEvent();
}
```

Moving On

This chapter has been a reference to the java.beans package. The next chapter will provide reference information on the components that are part of Netscape's Component Development Kit.

Netscape Component Examples

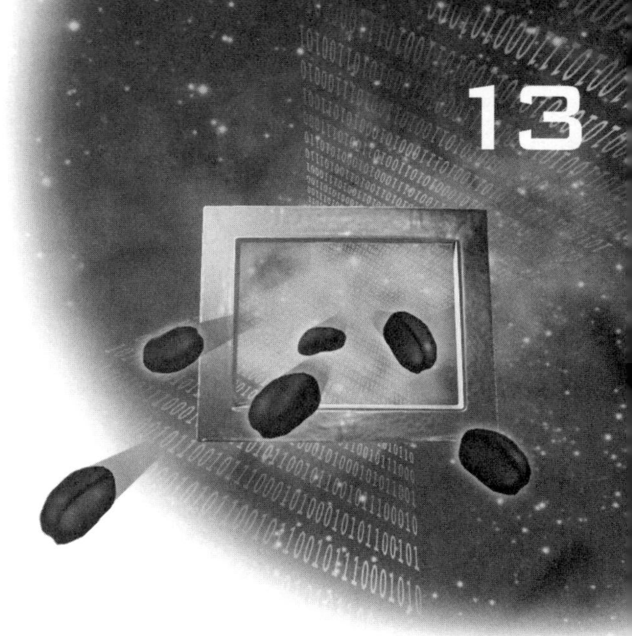

Visual JavaScript and the Component Development Kit (CDK) both come with example components for you to study and include in your projects. There are Java, JavaScript, CORBA, and HTML components. This chapter provides you with reference information on some of these example components. The purpose is to present the examples to demonstrate different features possible in Visual JavaScript with different types of components.

Examples From the CDK

This section discusses examples available with the CDK. Both Java and JavaScript example components are included in this section.

ShowText Applet

The ShowText applet is a Java applet example that displays a string to the screen. The string is a property of the applet and can be modified. The public property "message" is accessed with the SetMessage( ) , GetMessage( ) methods. The example code initializes the message to "Netscape." This example also demonstrates a BeanInfo class called ShowTestBeanInfo.java. The purpose of the example is to demonstrate an applet with a setter and getter method for a simple property. Listing 13-1 shows the code for ShowText.java and Figure 13-1 shows the ShowText applet running in the BeanBox.

Listing 13-1: ShowText.java.

```
import java.awt.*;

public class ShowText extends java.applet.Applet {
    public String  message = null;

    public void init() {
        String textVal = getParameter("message");
    setMessage(textVal);
    setFont(new Font("TimesRoman",Font.ITALIC | Font.BOLD,36));
    }

    public void paint(Graphics g) {
        g.setColor(Color.gray);
        g.drawString(message,20, 45);
        g.setColor(Color.black);
        g.drawString(message,17, 40);
    }

    /**
     * getter method for the message property
     */
    public String getMessage() {
        return message;
    }

    /**
     * setter method for the message property
     */
    public void setMessage(String newVal) {
        message = newVal;
    if (message == null) {
        message = "Netscape";
    }
    repaint();
    }
}
```

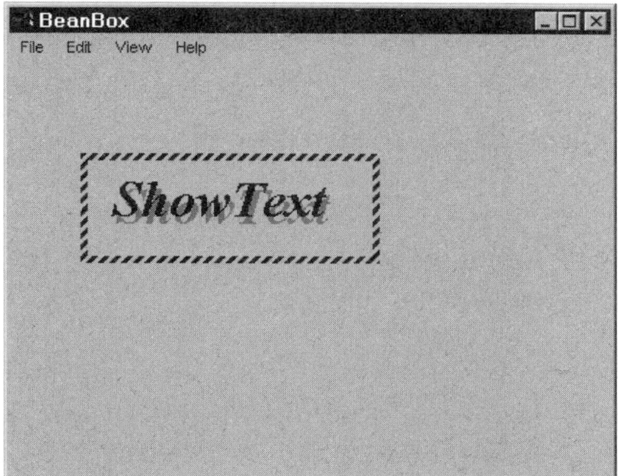

Figure 13-1: The ShowText applet running in the BeanBox.

Adding a Customizer to ShowText

The ShowTextCustom example augments the preceding ShowText example with a Customizer. This Customizer class provides a custom property editor for the message property—otherwise, the Visual JavaScript inspector is the default. The files associated with this example are ShowTextCustom.java, ShowTextCustomBeanInfo.java, and ShowTextCustomizer.java. ShowTextCustom.java is identical to ShowText.java, except for the class declaration:

```
import java.awt.*;

public class ShowTextCustom extends java.applet.Applet
```

Listing 13-2 is *ShowTextCustomBeanInfo.java*, which provides a BeanInfo object for the ShowTextCustom object:

Listing 13-2: ShowTextCustomBeanInfo.java.

```
import java.beans.*;

public class ShowTextCustomBeanInfo extends SimpleBeanInfo {
private final static Class customizerClass = ShowTextCustomizer.class;
private final static Class beanClass = ShowTextCustom.class;

public ShowTextCustomBeanInfo() throws Exception
```

```
{
    // methods
    _methodDescriptor = new MethodDescriptor[0];
    // properties
    _propertyDescriptor = new PropertyDescriptor[1];
    _propertyDescriptor[0] = new    PropertyDescriptor("message",
Class.forName("ShowTextCustom"));
    // events
    _eventSetDescriptor = new EventSetDescriptor[0];
}

public BeanDescriptor getBeanDescriptor )
{
    try {
    // associate customizer class with bean
    return new BeanDescriptor(beanClass, customizerClass);
    }
    catch (Exception e) {
        return null;
    }
}

public EventSetDescriptor[] getEventSetDescriptors ()
{
    return _eventSetDescriptor;
}

public MethodDescriptor[] getMethodDescriptors ()
{
    return _methodDescriptor;
}

public PropertyDescriptor[] getPropertyDescriptors()  {
    return _propertyDescriptor;
}

public BeanInfo[] getAdditionalBeanInfo()  {
    return null;
}

public int getDefaultEventIndex() {
    return -1;
}

public int getDefaultPropertyIndex() {
    return -1;
}
```

```
private EventSetDescriptor[] _eventSetDescriptor;
private MethodDescriptor[]   _methodDescriptor;
private PropertyDescriptor[] _propertyDescriptor;

} // class ShowTextCustomBeanInfo
```

The file *ShowTextCustomizer.java* defines the Customizer class for the ShowTextCustom *bean. ShowTextCustomizer.java* is shown in Listing 13-3:

Listing 13-3: ShowTextCustomizer.java.

```
import java.beans.*;
import java.awt.*;
import java.awt.event.*;

public class ShowTextCustomizer extends Panel implements Customizer,
KeyListener {

private ShowTextCustom target;
private TextField textField;
public Font textFont = new Font("TimesRoman",Font.ITALIC | Font.BOLD,26);
public Color textColor = new Color(80,80,180);
public Color backgroundColor = new Color(200,200,255);

public ShowTextCustomizer() {
    setBackground(backgroundColor);
    setLayout(null);
}

public void setObject(Object obj) {
    target = (ShowTextCustom) obj;
Label textLabel = new Label("Caption:", Label.RIGHT);
add(textLabel);
textLabel.setBounds(10, 45, 60, 30);

Label previewLabel = new Label("Preview:", Label.LEFT);
add(previewLabel);
previewLabel.setBounds(10, 85, 60, 30);

textField = new TextField(target.getMessage(), 20);
add(textField);
textField.setBounds(80, 45, 100, 30);

textField.addKeyListener(this);
}
```

```
public void paint(Graphics g) {
    g.setFont(textFont);
    g.setColor(textColor);
    g.drawString("ShowText Customizer",20,30);

    g.setColor(Color.gray);
    g.drawString(textField.getText(),23, 145);
    g.setColor(Color.black);
    g.drawString(textField.getText(),20, 140);
}

public Dimension getPreferredSize() {
    return new Dimension(300, 175);
}

public void keyTyped(KeyEvent e) {
    repaint();
}

public void keyPressed(KeyEvent e) {
    repaint();
}

public void keyReleased(KeyEvent e) {
    String txt = textField.getText();
    target.setMessage(txt);
    support.firePropertyChange("", null, null);
}

/**
* 1.0 method used only for older layout managers
*/
public Dimension preferredSize() {
    return getPreferredSize();
}

// add / remove listener methods
public void addPropertyChangeListener(PropertyChangeListener listener)
{
    support.addPropertyChangeListener(listener);
}
```

```
public void removePropertyChangeListener(PropertyChangeListener listener)
{
support.removePropertyChangeListener(listener);
}
// use a local PropertyChangeSupport object
private PropertyChangeSupport support = new PropertyChangeSupport(this);
}
```

Listing 13-3 sets up a Customizer class for the ShowTextCustom bean. You can see that the Customizer class extends Panel. In the setObject method, label fields and a text field are set up to manage the editing of ShowTextCustom's message property. Figure 13-2 shows the property editor created by this Customizer class.

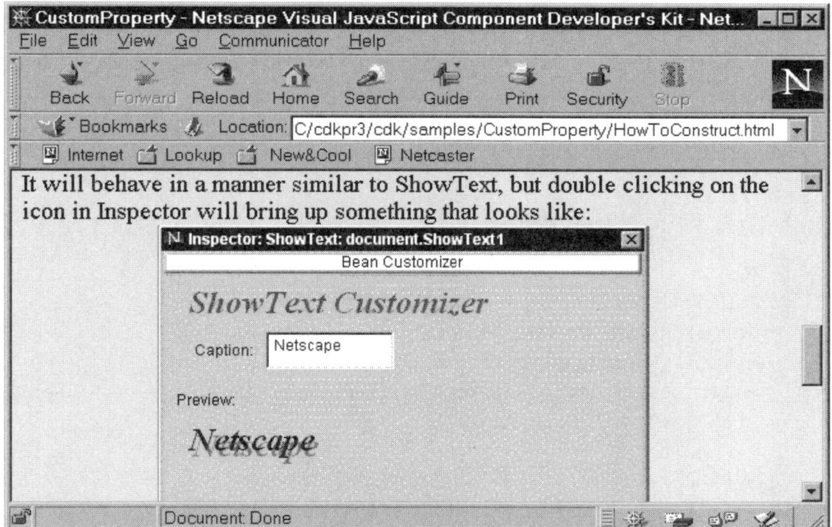

Figure 13-2: Editing the message property with the property editor created by ShowTextCustomizer.

The Calc Components

The Calc components are three JavaScript components. These three examples demonstrate how to construct JavaScript components and how to use properties, methods, and events. For example, *BiCalc.jsb* component uses a JavaScript onChange event to decide when to recalculate a formula in one of its fields. The example also shows how to integrate three example JSB files into a Jar file. The three JavaScript beans are in the following files:

- **BiCalc.jsb:** An example that implements a bi-directional calculation between two fields. The two fields are dependent on each other; when an onChange event occurs in one field, the other is recalculated.
- **Calc4.jsb:** Calculates a formula from four input values.
- **Concat.jsb:** Concatenates two strings using three static strings.

These three components can be loaded into Visual JavaScript one at a time using Tools | Load to palette, or they can be packaged into a Jar file. When the Jar file is loaded into the palette, the JSB files will appear as individual components. The source for the BiCalc component, *BiCalc.jsb*, is in Listing 13-4.

Listing 13-4: BiCalc.jsb.

```
<JSB>
<JSB_DESCRIPTOR
    name="netscape.peas.BiCalc"
    displayName="Bidirectional Calculation"
    shortDescription="Bidirectional Calculation"
    ENV="client">

<JSB_PROPERTY NAME="prop1" DISPLAYNAME="Property 1" PROPTYPE="JS"
TYPE="string"
    WRITEMETHOD="set1" ISBOUND
    SHORTDESCRIPTION="This is property 1">

<JSB_PROPERTY NAME="prop2" DISPLAYNAME="Property 2" PROPTYPE="JS"
TYPE="string"
    WRITEMETHOD="set2" ISBOUND
    SHORTDESCRIPTION="This is property 2">
```

```
<JSB_PROPERTY NAME="formula1" DISPLAYNAME="Formula 1" PROPTYPE="JS"
TYPE="string"
SHORTDESCRIPTION="Formula that calculates property 1 from property 2">
<JSB_PROPERTY NAME="formula2" DISPLAYNAME="Formula 2" PROPTYPE="JS"
TYPE="string"
SHORTDESCRIPTION="Formula that calculates property 2 from property 1">

<JSB_METHOD NAME="set1" TYPE="void">
<JSB_PARAMETER name="newVal" type="string">
</JSB_METHOD>
<JSB_METHOD NAME="set2" TYPE="void">
<JSB_PARAMETER name="newVal" type="string">
</JSB_METHOD>
<JSB_EVENT NAME="onChange"
LISTENERMETHODS="onChange" LISTENERTYPE="onChangeListener" EVENTMODEL="JS">

<JSB_CONSTRUCTOR>
function netscape_peas_BiCalc_set1(s) {
    this.prop1 = s
    this.prop2 = eval(this.formula2)
    this.onChange("prop1", "", this.prop1)
    this.onChange("prop2", "", this.prop2)
}

function netscape_peas_BiCalc_set2(s) {
    this.prop2 = s
    this.prop1 = eval(this.formula1)
    this.onChange("prop1", "", this.prop1)
    this.onChange("prop2", "", this.prop2)
}

function netscape_peas_BiCalc(params) {
    this.prop1 = params.prop1
    this.formula1 = params.formula1
    this.formula2 = params.formula2
    this.prop2 = eval(this.formula2)
    this.set1 = netscape_peas_BiCalc_set1;
    this.set2 = netscape_peas_BiCalc_set2;
}
</JSB_CONSTRUCTOR>
</JSB>
```

ValidatedText & ValidatedForm

ValidatedText is a JavaScript component that needs to be used inside an HTML form. It provides a way to validate client-side input on a form. ValidatedText is implemented in a JSB file in the package netscape.peas. (It is located in \samples\netscape\peas under the current installation directory.) Using the ValidatedText component with an HTML form, the validity of a text field can be checked as a result of these JavaScript events:

- **onblur:** End user removes focus from text field.
- **onchange:** Field value has been changed, and the end user has left the field.
- **onsubmit:** End user has clicked a submit of the ValidatedForm containing the ValidatedText field.

This JavaScript component gives you two types of validation to apply to the text field: "Required," or "Expression." "Required" means that the end user must enter data into the text field. Using the "Expression," option, you select an expression that the field should match. Figure 13-3 is a design mode picture of setting up a form with ValidatedText.

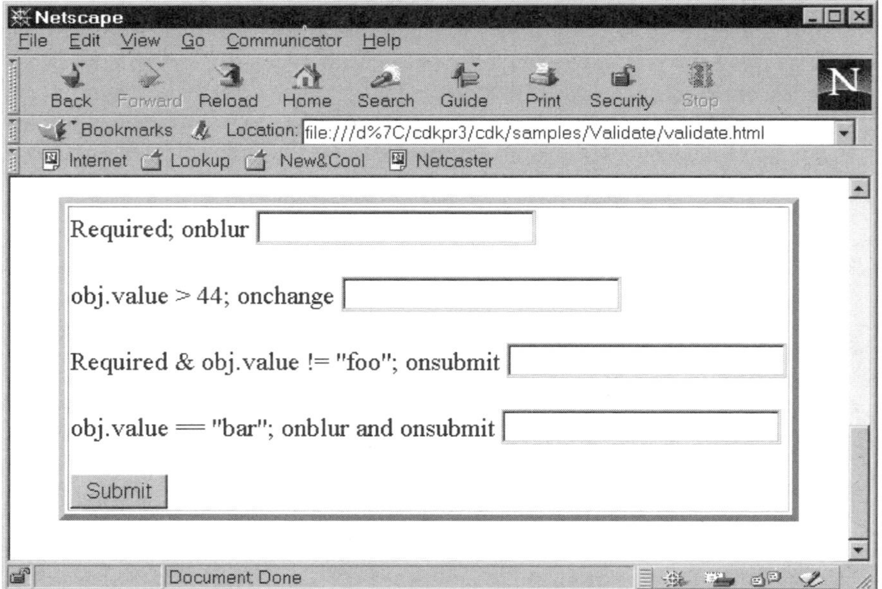

Figure 13-3: An HTML form in design mode using ValidatedText components.

The ValidatedForm component is an HTML form containing an onSubmit button. ValidatedForm can cooperate with ValidatedText components via the onsubmit event. ValidatedText responds to an onsubmit event by validating its text.

CustomDisplay JavaScript Component

CustomDisplay is a JavaScript component that demonstrates the packaging of supporting files (an image in this case) with a JavaScript component. When loaded, the CustomDisplay component used the Circle.gif file to display an image of a circle. The component does this by creating an HTML IMG tag by writing it to the page with JavaScript's document.write( ) method. This IMG tag references the Circle.gif file. This example also makes use of a Java helper file called CircleVisual.java. See Listing 13-5 for the JSB file for CustomDisplay.

Listing 13-5: CustomDisplay.jsb.

```
<JSB>

<JSB_DESCRIPTOR NAME="CustomDisplay" DISPLAYNAME="Circle"
    ENV="client" VISUAL="CircleVisual">

<JSB_CONSTRUCTOR>
/*
 * The constructor simply writes out an image reference within
 * the HTML
 */
function CustomDisplay(params) {
    document.write("<img src=images/Circle.gif border=0>");
}

</JSB_CONSTRUCTOR>
</JSB>
```

SourceLoader Component

The SourceLoader component is written in JavaScript and makes use of Java code to retrieve a URL. It also demonstrates some server connections. This component is in the file *SourceLoader.jsb*. This example also comes with a Visual JavaScript project file that can be used to build it. The project is in the directory: c:\cdk\samples\SourceLoader*SourceLoader.prj*. (That is, if your install directory for the CDK is c:\cdk.)

In a crossware project, SourceLoader can be set up to transmit a URL from a server. The CDK documentation demonstrates crossware development with SourceLoader by setting up a text area and a button. The button invokes the SourceLoader to request transmittal of the URL, and the contents of the URL are displayed in the text area.

FloatingWindow Component

The FloatingWindow component is a client-side JavaScript component that creates a movable and resizeable window in the client page. This window can be used to display the contents of a URL. The URL is specified in the "src" property. Table 13-1 shows the properties of the FloatingWindow component, and Listing 13-6 shows how these properties are defined in the JSB file.

Property	Description
title	Title displayed in title bar of window.
src	Lets the end user specify a URL to display in the FloatingWindow.
PosX	Initial x position of the window.
PosY	Initial y position of the window.
contentWidth	Width of the scrollable area in the window.
width	Width of the onscreen window.
height	Height of the onscreen window.

Table 13-1: Properties of the FloatingWindow component.

Listing 13-6: Definitions in the JSB file for properties of the FloatingWindow.

```
<JSB_DESCRIPTOR NAME="FloatingWindow" ENV="client" DISPLAYNAME="Floating
Window"

SHORTDESCRIPTION="Scrollable, movable, resizeable window widget">

<JSB_PROPERTY NAME="title" PROPTYPE="JS" TYPE="java.lang.String"
DISPLAYNAME="Window Title" SHORTDESCRIPTION="Title to display at the top of
the window">

<JSB_PROPERTY NAME="src" PROPTYPE="JS" TYPE="java.lang.String"
DISPLAYNAME="Source URL" SHORTDESCRIPTION="URL containing the window's
content">
```

```
<JSB_PROPERTY NAME="posX" PROPTYPE="JS" TYPE="java.lang.String"
DISPLAYNAME="X Position" SHORTDESCRIPTION="X position to start window at">

<JSB_PROPERTY NAME="posY" PROPTYPE="JS" TYPE="java.lang.String"
DISPLAYNAME="Y Position" SHORTDESCRIPTION="Y position to start window at">

<JSB_PROPERTY NAME="contentWidth" PROPTYPE="JS" TYPE="java.lang.String"
DISPLAYNAME="Content Width" SHORTDESCRIPTION="Width to wrap the content at">

<JSB_PROPERTY NAME="width" PROPTYPE="JS" TYPE="java.lang.String"
DISPLAYNAME="Window Width" SHORTDESCRIPTION="Initial width of the window">

<JSB_PROPERTY NAME="height" PROPTYPE="JS" TYPE="java.lang.String"
```

Figure 13-4 shows the FloatingWindow component running in Navigator 4. This is how it looks without a URL displayed. I created this display by loading the JSB file *FloatingWindow.jsb* into Visual JavaScript, dragging the FloatingWindow icon to a blank HTML page, and then previewing the page in Navigator 4.

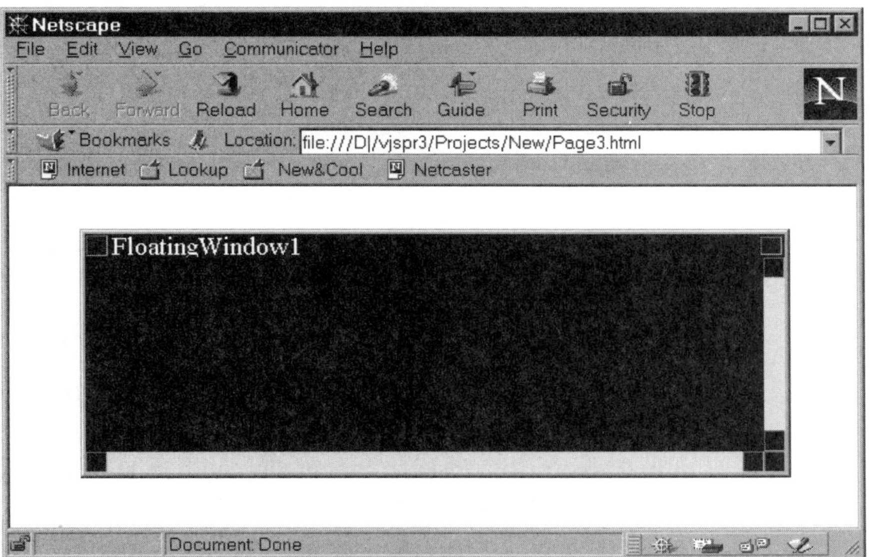

Figure 13-4: The FloatingWindow running in Navigator 4.

Examples From Visual JavaScript

Visual JavaScript ships with a number of components ready to use on its palette, including both Java and JavaScript components. This section describes some of these components.

TIP

These examples can be found in the \netscape\peas subdirectory under the Visual JavaScript installation directory.

JavaScript Database Components

Various database components are shipped with the preview release of Visual JavaScript. Some are server-side components, and some are client-side. Some make use of Java classes or other JavaScript files as helpers. A list of these sample components follows:

- **ClientCursor.jsb:** A LiveConnect component. This is a client-side database cursor that uses netscape.peas.ClientSideCursor and netscape.peas.CSCException as helper Java classes.
- **Cursor.jsb:** A server-side component. This creates a LiveWire database cursor.
- **CustomTable.jsb:** Server-side custom database HTML table display. Requires a client-side helper function, setSearch(URL or sortColumn), defined in file *cCustomTable.js*.
- **DBPool.jsb:** Manages various connections to a LiveWire database.
- **DBSelect.jsb:** Displays the results of a database query and interacts with an HTML Select element. *cSelectBox.js* is required as a helper JavaScript file.
- **DBSource.jsb:** Holds identifying information about a database being used with Visual JavaScript.
- **DummyCursor.jsb:** Works in conjunction with JSBufferedCursor by providing an example cursor that works on the client side.
- **FormAccept.jsb:** Processes data from a form and passes it to a database.
- **JavaDummyCursor.jsb:** Works in a similar way as ClientCursor.
- **JSBufferedCursor.jsb:** Creates a cursor on the server and then creates a client-side image of it in JavaScript.

- **SimpleTable.jsb:** Puts the results of a SQL query into a table.
- **SQLExec.jsb:** Works in conjunction with the server to execute a SQL statement.

Other JavaScript Components

The components in this section are JavaScript components provided with Visual JavaScript that aren't database-oriented. These components are not as "large" as the components in the previous section—they do only one thing, and they do it well.

- **DateDisplay Component:** DateDisplay is in the JSB file *DateDisplay.jsb*. This component displays a current or last modification date to a page.
- **MailToLink Component:** The *MailToLink.jsb* file creates a JavaScript component that displays a mailto link on the current page. Dragging this to a page includes a ready-made link that saves typing in the HTML code for a mailto.
- **ScrollingBanner Component:** This component, in the *ScrollingBanner.jsb* file, displays a message in the status bar of Navigator 4. The message is public property of the component and can be modified.
- **Label Component:** The file *Label.jsb* contains a component that evaluates an expression from a server, then prepares it for display in HTML. This can be used in conjunction with a server-side database to format data as it arrives.
- **SendMail Component:** This is a JavaScript component that can be integrated into your application to send mail from the server side.

Other Java Components

There are quite a few other Java components provided in the package netscape.peas. This package is found in the \netscape\peas directory under the Visual JavaScript installation directory. There are two groups of classes important for creating crossware for databases: the Table and Row classes. These Java classes work together to provide functionality such as adding or deleting data from a database table, inserting or deleting rows, and fetching rows as the result of a query. Table 13-2 shows the classes in the Table support category. (More information is accessible from http://developer.netscape.com/one/components/cdk.html.)

Class name
netscape.peas.Table
netscape.peas.TableApplet
netscape.peas.TableAppletBeanInfo
netscape.peas.TableApplication
netscape.peas.TableChangeEvent
netscape.peas.TableChangeListener
netscape.peas.TableChangeSupport
netscape.peas.TableInfo
netscape.peas.TableProvider
netscape.peas.TableReceiver
netscape.peas.TableSupport

Table 13-2: Table support classes from netscape.peas package.

Table 13-3 shows the classes in the Row support category.

Class name
netscape.peas.Row
netscape.peas.RowChangeEvent
netscape.peas.RowChangeListener
netscape.peas.RowChangeSupport
netscape.peas.RowProvider
netscape.peas.RowReceiver
netscape.peas.RowSupport

Table 13-3: Row support classes from netscape.peas package.

Moving On

This has been a whirlwind tour of some of the examples provided with Netscape's Visual JavaScript and Component Development Kit. Some examples are for instruction; others are intended as ready-to-use components. The CDK contains other components, plus examples of integrating them into crossware, that I haven't described here. Many intranet or Internet applications need to access a back-end database, so it's not surprising that the CDK is particularly rich in the area of database examples. You can continue to use and study the various JavaScript and Java components by obtaining the Netscape tools.

Packaging components for distribution and downloading on the Internet is important to both JavaBeans and Netscape components. The next chapter discusses the habitat and breeding grounds of the ubiquitous Jar file.

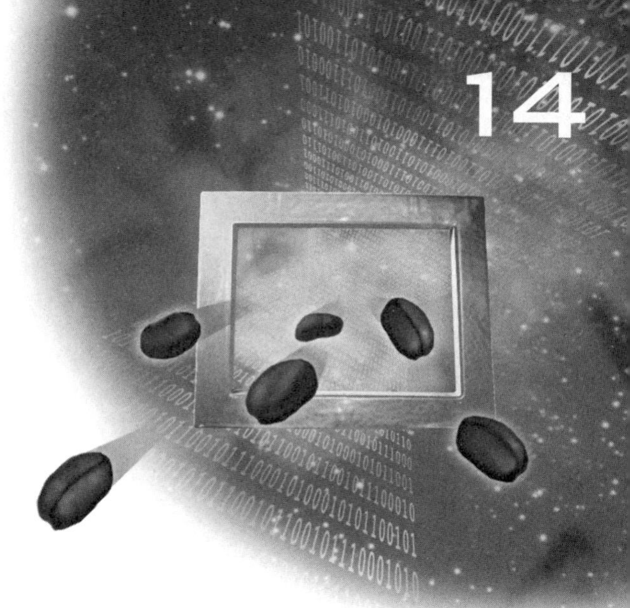

Working With Jar Files

The new Java Archive file format (Jar) has some important uses in JDK 1.1. It can be used to archive a number of related files such as the files that make up an applet. A variation on the ZIP file format that many computer users are familiar with, the Jar file also supports the inclusion of a support file called the *manifest* file. When using JavaBeans, the manifest is often used to tell whether a class is a bean or not. Manifest files also have uses in the support of signed applets.

In this chapter I discuss Jar files: how to use them and how to create them with the *jar* command. Developed by Sun with applets and JavaBeans in mind, Jars have other uses, too. Netscape's JavaScript beans can be archived with Jar files, and this chapter contains some guidelines for when to use Jars with Netscape components. This chapter also contains some information on the use of manifest files for JavaBeans and signed applets.

What Is a Jar File?

You may be familiar with the ZIP format (defined by PKWARE) often used for archiving PC files. In addition to being used to distribute commercial software on diskettes or to pass files around the office, ZIP is a popular format for downloading software over the Internet. The Java Archive file format (Jar) was introduced with JDK 1.1 and is based upon the ZIP format. The Jar file has three important features:

- It acts as an archive, combining more than one file into one.

- It acts as a compression utility. It archives, but also compresses files so they take up less space.
- It acts as an informational file. The optional manifest file provides information about the contents of the Jar and supports the signing of the Jar's contents.

Archiving and compression decrease download time for components. This was an important reason for developing the Jar format in the first place, to make downloading applets and beans quicker. It is typical for an applet to be made up of more than one file. An animation applet, for example, may require separate image or sound files while running. When a browser sees an APPLET tag in an HTML file, it downloads a Java class file containing the code for the applet. If the applet needs resources such as images or sounds, another HTTP connection for every resource is made. With Jars, all the associated files are in a single archive, thus making downloading quicker.

The same reasoning applies to compression. Internet users are aware of how long it can take to view a page when multiple images are downloading, especially if the images are large. In this regard, anything that decreases file size is a boon. The next section describes how you use Jars to load applets and beans.

Using Jar Files

Jar is a generalized format supporting the archiving of different types of objects. This section discusses some special considerations and syntax for using Jars with Java applets and JavaBeans. A separate section further on, "Using Jars With Netscape Components," describes some special considerations when using Jar files with Netscape components.

Using Jars With the APPLET Tag

The standard way of loading an applet in a Web page is by using the Applet tag in the HTML text. The Applet tag uses begin and end tags <APPLET> and </APPLET>. You specify the name of the class implementing the applet by way of the code attribute, as in the following example:

```
<APPLET code="Animation.class" HEIGHT=200
WIDTH=200> </APPLET>
```

The code is specified using the CODE attribute. The code for this applet is in the file Animation.class, a Java class file. When the browser sees this attribute, it downloads the Animation.class file from the server. The WIDTH and

HEIGHT attributes specify the rectangle the applet displays in. In addition, other parameters can also be used with the Applet tag by using the PARAM attribute. To use Jar files with applets, add the ARCHIVE attribute, which is used in addition to the CODE attribute. The following is an example using the ARCHIVE attribute:

```
<applet code="Animation.class" archive="jars/animation.jar" width=200
height=100>
</applet>
```

I've provided both CODE and ARCHIVE attributes in the preceding example. Why must you provide the CODE attribute in addition to the ARCHIVE attribute? Even though the file Animation.class may be part of the animation.jar archive, the browser still needs to know where to begin the execution of the applet. The Animation.class file contains the start( ) and init( ) methods for the applet, and the browser needs to know where to find them.

How does the browser use the Jar file? Once it reads the ARCHIVE attribute, it downloads the Jar file. The browser stores the archive, then starts the applet. When the applet loads images or sounds, it looks for them in the archive instead of establishing a new HTTP connection. If it can't find an image, it may have to download a new archive from the server. The archive attribute can support more than one Jar file; the multiple Jar files are separated in the archive tag with commas as follows (the browser ignores white space between entries):

```
<applet code="Animation.class" archive="class1.jar , image.jar,  sound.jar"
width=250 height=150>
</applet>
```

NOTE

As for all HTML tags, the ARCHIVE tag is not case sensitive, so it can be capitalized any way you like.

Using Jars With JavaBeans

When using Jars from a beanbox tool, the beanbox loads the Jar for you. Sun's BeanBox takes care of loading and separating the component of a bean. For example, the BDK's Juggler bean in Chapter 3 needs to access from Juggler.jar the Juggler.class, JugglerBeanInfo.class, and also a number of GIF file images for the coffee beans.

You assist the beanbox (Sun's or a future beanbox tool) by specifying which items in the Jar represent beans. The manifest file is used to tell whether a class is a bean or not. In the examples in Chapter 3, we used an inline manifest file embedded in the make file (between << and <<). Here is an example section of a make file showing how we used an inline manifest file, manifest.tmp:

```
CLASSFILES= \
    sunw\demo\data\DataSource.class \
    sunw\demo\data\DataSourceBeanInfo.class

datasrc.jar: $(CLASSFILES)
        jar cfm datasrc.jar <<manifest.tmp sunw\demo\data\*.class
Name: sunw/demo/data/DataSource.class
Java-Bean: True

Name: sunw/demo/data/DataSourceBeanInfo.class
Java-Bean: False
<<
```

NOTE

It is common to use the forward slash ("/") as a directory separator for the manifest portion of the preceding file, even if you're using the make file in a Windows environment. Note that the references to the class files all contain the backward slash ("\"), which is usual for Windows.

The lines in the manifest file take the form of an Attribute followed by a Value. There are two attributes here: Name and Java-Bean. The Name attribute is followed by the name of a file. The line that begins with the Java-Bean attribute tells whether the particular file in the Name statement is a bean. Note that each pair of lines is followed by an empty line.

Manifest files do not need to be inline. They can be created with a text editor and simply used with the jar command from the command line. To create a manifest file with a text editor, begin the file with the Manifest-Version attribute as follows:

```
Manifest-Version 1.0
```

The current version is 1.0; of course this version may change in the future. Once you have specified the Manifest-Version attribute, follow it with the attributes Name and Java-Bean for the various files in your archive:

```
Manifest-Version 1.0

Name: sunw/demo/data/DataSource.class
Java-Bean: True

Name: sunw/demo/data/DataSourceBeanInfo.class
Java-Bean: False
```

In this manifest file, I've used the forward slash ("/") to separate directory names as before. (Pathnames in Windows generally use the back slash "\", and pathnames in UNIX use the forward slash "/".)

NOTE

Strictly speaking, you do not have to insert a Name, Java-Bean statement in the manifest for a class or JSB that is not a bean (a support file for example). I've used the Java-Bean: False statement for files in the example for demonstration purposes.

Using Jars With Netscape Components

Jar files can be used to archive Netscape components such as JavaScript beans just as they can for JavaBeans (and applets). You'll recall from Chapter 8 that JavaScript beans are written using the JSB file—which is a text file. In addition, JavaScript beans also may use other supporting files (Java class files for example). You may use Jars with Visual JavaScript (VJS), but you don't always have to. This section discusses some issues about when to use archives for Netscape components and how to create them correctly by managing the directory structure.

To Jar or Not to Jar?

JavaBeans and JavaScript beans can both be used in VJS. Either of these component types may use Jar archives. But you may not always want to deliver your components in an archive. Netscape recommends that you may want to use an archive if:

- You are packaging a JavaScript bean that's made up of multiple files. The bean may use JavaScript functions defined in separate JavaScript files or Java classes located in separate Java class files.
- You are packaging a Java object, such as a bean or applet that requires multiple files to support it correctly.

Packaging Components for Visual JavaScript

Packaging Jar files for use with Visual JavaScript (VJS) is similar to packaging them for other environments. Above all, you must make sure that the package names of your class files match the directory structure. The steps for packaging up a component are as follows:

1. Create a working directory.
2. Copy the .class files to subdirectories matching their package names. A bean in package companyname.demo.tools would be placed into a directory: companyname\demo\tools under the working directory.
3. Create the manifest file in the working directory. Name the file MANIFEST.MF (observe capitalization). Make sure the first line of the file reads: Manifest-Version 1.0.
4. Specify the lines (Name/Java-Bean) for each file to be put in the archive as described in the preceding section "Using Jars With JavaBeans."
5. Run the Jar compiler using the jar command, specifying the Jar file name, MANIFEST.MF (observe capitalization), and the names of the various files to archive on the command line.

NOTE

The main reason for the Name/Java-Bean lines in the manifest is to distinguish which members of the archive are beans. Netscape documentation suggests you don't need the manifest file if all JSB files and .class files you have in the archive are beans.

More about the syntax of and options for the Jar compiler is in the section "The Jar Compiler" further on in this chapter.

Packaging Plug-ins

Plug-ins can be used from VJS. There are three sorts of plug-in blank and page-oriented plug-ins. VJS supports page-oriented plug-ins that are developed along the guidelines recommended by Netscape's Composer Plug-in Kit. Netscape's guidelines for developing Composer plug-ins include recommendations about how to package them in Jar files.

Once you have developed your plug-in from Java files, you compile the Java source files with javac. The resulting class files are put into a jar using the jar command. For Composer plug-ins, you need to name your Jar file cpXXX.zip, where the XXX is a string that is unique. Netscape suggests you could use your company name for the XXX string. The file name is required to begin with "cp."

TIP

There is more information about writing Composer plug-ins for VJS in Chapter 10.

Manifest File Structure

You've seen the manifest file and its use for telling what's in the Jar. The manifest file has a specification (like many things computer) that specifies it can be more general than its use in JavaBeans. Manifests have a role in signing applets, for example. This section explains a little about the manifest structure and a little about signature files.

The manifest file is made up of sections. A section is defined as a group of name/value pairs. Sections are separated by empty lines. The manifest file begins with:

```
Manifest-Version 1.0
```

followed by an empty line. Name is one of the defined attributes that we've already used. Technically, since unknown attributes are ignored, you can also create your own attributes—it's just that there may not be any program to read them. If you list a META-INF\MANIFEST.MF from a Jar you've created, you'll see the "Digest-Algorithms" attribute in the file. Digest-Algorithms: is followed by a comma-separated list of digest algorithm names. Here's an example of a section specifying digest information about a class:

```
Name: JavaClass.class
Digest-Algorithms: SHA MD5
SHA-Digest: OaZQnK6nnO/hMb757rBG8s07NcY=
MD5-Digest: tOSPuel6gD4yogvgpKnbxg==
```

The Digest-Algorithms: line in the file is followed on the next line by a name/value pair of the form "Digest algorithm name-Digest:" as in:

```
MD5-Digest: tOSPuel6gD4yogvgpKnbxg==
```

The value following "MD5-Digest:" is a binary signature (in base64) representing a digest value. Digest algorithms are used when signing downloaded objects, such as applets. The digest value is compared to another digest value in the archive, thereby providing a check. Thus, manifest files are used in support of signature files (the files that do object signing). A complete discussion of signature files is beyond the scope of this chapter. There is more information about the complete Manifest file specification accessible from the Java site at: http://java.sun.com.

The Jar Compiler

What I am calling the Jar compiler is also called the Java Archive Tool by Sun in their documentation. The Jar compiler (invoked with the jar command) has been used before in this book. The previous examples of archiving beans and loading them into the BeanBox made use of make files that may have hidden the inner workings of the command from you. So, in this section I give some more details about the Jar compiler along with the command set (or options) for this tool.

Jar Compiler Basics

There are three types of input to the Jar compiler, which is used from the command-line. The format in schematic form is:

```
jar [options] [manifestFile] jarFile inputFile [inputFiles]
```

The three types are the manifest, which is optional, the name of the Jar file, and the files that will be put in the archive.

NOTE

A default manifest file is always created by the Jar compiler and is the first entry in the file. It is created in the subdirectory META-INF and is called MANIFEST.INF. If you extract from a jar file using the command jar -xf jarfilename, *the Jar compiler will create a subdirectory META-INF in the working directory. This subdirectory will contain a file named MANIFEST.INF.*

We discussed creating your own manifest file in the preceding section "Using Jars With JavaBeans." An example of running the Jar compiler with a manifest file that you've created yourself is:

```
jar cfm jarfile.jar manifest.mf *.class
```

This command would archive all of the class files in the current directory, read from a manifest file named manifest.tmp (which you've created in the current directory), and put the results in an archive called jarfile.jar. You can see the options on the command line after the Jar command. The options "cfm" have the following meaning: create a new archive (option "c"), the command line will contain a Jar file name (option "f"), and a manifest file name is found on the command line (option "m"). There are more details on the set of available options in the next section.

TIP

As far as the Jar file specification is concerned, you can use any file extension to name your Jar files. The BeanBox tool from Sun expects the .jar extension.

The Jar Compiler Command Set

The Jar file compiler comes with a set of available options that control the behavior of the jar command. Table 14-1 shows the options available on the command line when using the Jar compiler.

c	Create a new or empty archive file on the standard output.
t	List the table of contents of an archive.
x Filename	Extract all files (or Filename) from the archive.
v	Verbose mode.
f	Specify the name of the Jar file to create, table of contents, or extract from on the command line.
m	Specify the name of a manifest file on the command line.
0	Do not compress files when archiving them.
M	Do not create a default manifest file when archiving.

Table 14-1: Jar compiler command line options.

Note from Table 14-1 that the "x" option extracts files from an archive. If the file name "Filename" is supplied with the option on the command line, then Filename is extracted. If the Filename argument is left out, then all files are extracted. Many command line programs give a list of options—usage summary—by typing the command without arguments. Typing **jar** at the C:\ prompt displays the following usage summary to the standard output:

```
C:\>jar
Usage: jar {ctx}[vfmOM] [jar-file] [manifest-file] files ...
Options:
```

```
-c  create new archive
-t  list table of contents for archive
-x  extract named (or all) files from archive
-v  generate verbose output on standard error
-f  specify archive file name
-m  include manifest information from specified manifest file
-0  store only; use no ZIP compression
-M  Do not create a manifest file for the entries
```

If any file is a directory, then it is processed recursively.
Example: to archive two class files into an archive called classes.jar:

```
jar cvf classes.jar Foo.class Bar.class
```

Note: use the '0' option to create a Jar file that can be put in your CLASSPATH.

Look at the line that begins "Usage:" in the preceding listing. The first three options {ctx} are enclosed in braces. This indicates that at least one option from this set is required at all times. Also, the three options {ctx} are mutually exclusive (you use only one of them at a time). The options in brackets [vfm0M] are optional. For example, you don't need the verbose mode (option "v") every time you use the Jar tool. The verbose mode is handy for seeing the actions of the command, so I'll use it in the examples in the next section "Examples of Using the Jar Compiler." The -0 option turns off compression. Normally the CLASSPATH environment contains a list of pathnames that are searched for class files during compilation. Uncompressed Jar files can also be used in a CLASSPATH environment variable; the uncompressed Jar file will be searched for class files as are directories.

Examples of Using the Jar Compiler

This section provides a few examples of actually using the Jar compiler to create, get the table of contents of, and extract from Jar files. I want to show the process of entering the various options and what the screen output looks like for each of these commands. The examples were run all on Windows 95.

To create a new Jar archive, use the -c option. Creating a Jar in verbose mode, and adding all the class files in the current directory gives the following output:

```
C:\book-2\src\ch2>jar -cfv captnemo.jar *.class
adding: AButtonListener.class (in=557) (out=363) (deflated 34%)
adding: BeanLoaderApplet.class (in=1361) (out=732) (deflated 46%)
adding: ButtonApplet.class (in=575) (out=370) (deflated 35%)
adding: MyFirstBean.class (in=735) (out=453) (deflated 38%)
adding: MySecondBean.class (in=849) (out=513) (deflated 39%)
```

We used the options "cfv." These options mean: create a new Jar, specify the Jar file name on the command line, and use verbose mode. You can see that in verbose mode jar displays the names and statistics about the files it is archiving. Now let's look at the -t, table of contents, option. To display a table of contents for the Jar we created in the preceding step, use the -t option. Displaying the table of contents of captnemo.jar in verbose mode gives the following output:

```
C:\book-2\src\ch2>jar -tfv captnemo.jar
   716 Wed Oct 08 18:05:28 PDT 1997 META-INF/MANIFEST.MF
   557 Sun Oct 05 18:35:46 PDT 1997 AButtonListener.class
  1361 Sun Oct 05 17:58:40 PDT 1997 BeanLoaderApplet.class
   575 Sun Oct 05 18:35:44 PDT 1997 ButtonApplet.class
   735 Sun Oct 05 17:58:40 PDT 1997 MyFirstBean.class
   849 Sun Oct 05 17:58:40 PDT 1997 MySecondBean.class
```

You can see that the file names for the items in the archive are displayed along with their dates. We can extract all the files from captnemo.jar into the current directory by using the "x" option. Here we are using verbose mode:

```
C:\book-2\src\ch2>jar -xfv captnemo.jar
 extracted: META-INF\MANIFEST.MF
 extracted: AButtonListener.class
 extracted: BeanLoaderApplet.class
 extracted: ButtonApplet.class
 extracted: MyFirstBean.class
 extracted: MySecondBean.class
```

This command displays the names of files it has extracted and writes them to the current directory (in this case). Note that the display shows that a manifest file META-INF\MANIFEST.MF has been extracted, too. A subdirectory was created under the current working directory. When we created this Jar with the -c options, we didn't explicitly create this manifest file. Let's look at the contents of META-INF\MANIFEST.MF file:

```
Manifest-Version: 1.0

Name: AButtonListener.class
Digest-Algorithms: SHA MD5
SHA-Digest: y/3Vnbv8uVEtTZwjv79hoKxH6HQ=
MD5-Digest: V6c/zrvlZKTOFE2k6jyoRA==

Name: BeanLoaderApplet.class
Digest-Algorithms: SHA MD5
SHA-Digest: LQBopPOTty95TFfOKlLr+tQrmVO=
MD5-Digest: JzcblNMKmJOufzIPrmkRgg==
```

```
Name: ButtonApplet.class
Digest-Algorithms: SHA MD5
SHA-Digest: 0aZQnK6nn0/hMb757rBG8s07NcY=
MD5-Digest: t0SPue16gD4yogvgpKnbxg==
```

I've only shown the first three sections of the file for this example (there are two other files in this archive). Recall that sections in a manifest file are separated by an empty line. In addition to the class file names of the contents of the Jar, you can see two Digest-Algorithms: SHA and MD5, and the binary digest base64 information for each.

Summary

Jar files make distributing multi-file components over the Internet more efficient. Archiving components using the Jar compiler results in files that are compressed and quicker to download since they don't use multi-file HTTP transactions. The Jar file format can be used to archive and compress both Java and JavaScript beans. The Jar file format is flexible, so it can also be used to package Netscape Composer plug-ins.

Conclusion

JavaBeans from Sun Microsystems and the new component types from Netscape give an intranet/Internet developer new opportunities to create crossware applications by piecing together component parts. Sun's Beans are based upon the cross-platform language Java and can be used in many different computing environments. They can also interact with JavaScript beans, CORBA components, HTML, Visual JavaScript, plug-ins, and other component types to make the Internet a more interesting place in which to develop crossware.

In this book I've described component architectures, JavaBeans, and demonstrated the various support available from Sun's JDK 1.1 to help you develop these new crossware components. The 'component idea' is becoming prevalent, so now a developer also has the chance to integrate Netscape components, JavaBeans, and other component types with Netscape ONE tools such as Visual JavaScript. We discussed these options too.

I certainly hope that you've learned some details about the specific component architectures in this book, but I especially hope I've helped you to come to a better appreciation of what software components are and what they can do now—and in the future . . ..

APPENDIX A

About the Companion CD-ROM

The CD-ROM included with your copy of the *Official Netscape JavaBeans Developer's Guide* includes valuable software and source code (found in the Resources directory) that relates to the examples in the book.

Navigating the CD-ROM

To find out more about the CD-ROM and its contents, please open the "README.HTM" file in your favorite browser. You will see a small menu offering several links.

Software

- **BDK 1.0**—The JavaBeans Development Kit from Sun Microsystems includes the Bean Box and a container application for Beans, which includes the example Beans. The BDK also contains Bean Box tutorial information, and source code for the Java.beans package. You must read the terms of the Binary license, found in this Appendix, before using the BDK.
- **JDK Version 1.1.4**—Sun Microsystem's JDK lets you write applets and applications that conform to the Java Core API. See the vreadme for more information. You must read the terms of the Binary license, found in this Appendix, before using the JDK software.

Binary Code License for JDK Version 1.1.4 & BDK Version 1.0:

This binary code license ("License") contains rights and restrictions associated with use of the accompanying software and documentation ("Software"). Read the License carefully before installing the Software. By installing the Software you agree to the terms and conditions of this License.

1. **Limited License Grant**. Sun grants to you ("Licensee") a non-exclusive, non-transferable limited license to use the Software without fee for evaluation of the Software and for development of Java(TM) compatible applets and applications. Licensee may make one archival copy of the Software. Except for the foregoing, Licensee may not re-distribute the Software in whole or in part, either separately or included with a product. Refer to the Java Runtime Environment Version 1.1 binary code license (http://www.javasoft.com/products/JDK/1/1/index.html) for the availability of runtime code which may be distributed with Java compatible applets and applications.
2. **Java Platform Interface**. Licensee may not modify the Java Platform Interface ("JPI", identified as classes contained within the "java" package or any subpackages of the "java" package), by creating additional classes within the JPI or otherwise causing the addition to or modification of the classes in the JPI. In the event that Licensee creates any Java-related API and distributes such API to others for applet or application development, Licensee must promptly publish an accurate specification for such API for free use by all developers of Java-based software.
3. **Restrictions**. Software is confidential copyrighted information of Sun and title to all copies is retained by Sun and/or its licensors. Licensee shall not modify, decompile, disassemble, decrypt, extract, or otherwise reverse engineer Software. Software may not be leased, assigned, or sublicensed, in whole or in part. Software is not designed or intended for use in on-line control of aircraft, air traffic, aircraft navigation or aircraft communications; or in the design, construction, operation or maintenance of any nuclear facility. Licensee warrants that it will not use or redistribute the Software for such purposes.
4. **Trademarks and Logos**. This license does not authorize Licensee to use any Sun name, trademark, or logo. Licensee acknowledges that Sun owns the Java trademark and all Java-related trademarks, logos, and icons including the Coffee Cup and Duke ("Java Marks") and agrees to: (i) comply with the Java Trademark Guidelines at http://java.com/trademarks.html; (ii) not do anything harmful to or inconsistent with Sun's rights in the Java Marks; and (iii) assist Sun in protecting those rights, including assigning to Sun any rights acquired by Licensee in any Java Mark.

5. **Disclaimer of Warranty.** Software is provided "AS IS", without a warranty of any kind. ALL EXPRESS OR IMPLIED REPRESENTATIONS AND WARRANTIES, INCLUDING ANY IMPLIED WARRANTY OF MERCHANTABILITY, FITNESS FOR A PARTICULAR PURPOSE OR NON-INFRINGEMENT, ARE HEREBY EXCLUDED.
6. **Limitation of Liability**. SUN AND ITS LICENSORS SHALL NOT BE LIABLE FOR ANY DAMAGES SUFFERED BY LICENSEE OR ANY THIRD PARTY AS A RESULT OF USING OR DISTRIBUTING SOFTWARE. IN NO EVENT WILL SUN OR ITS LICENSORS BE LIBABLE FOR ANY LOST REVENUE, PROFIT OR DATA, OR FOR DIRECT, INDIRECT, SPECIAL, CONSEQUENTIAL, INCIDENTAL, OR PUNITIVE DAMAGES HOWEVER CAUSED AND REGARDLESS OF THE THEORY OF LIABILITY, ARISING OUT OF THE USE OF OR INABILITY TO USE SOFTWARE, EVEN IF SUN HAS BEEN ADVISED OF THE POSSIBILITY OF SUCH DAMAGES.
7. **Termination**. Licensee may terminate this License at any time by destroying all copies of Software. This license will terminate immediately without notice from Sun if Licensee fails to comply with any provision of this License. Upon such termination, Licensee must destroy all copies of Software.
8. **Export Regulations**. Software, including technical data, is subject to U.S. export control laws, including the U.S. Export Administration Act and its associated regulations, and may be subject to export or import regulations in other countries. Licensee agrees to comply strictly with all such regulations and acknowledges that it has the responsibility to obtain licenses to export, re-export, or import Software. Software may not be downloaded, or otherwise exported or re-exported (i) into, or to a national or resident of, Cuba Iraq, Iran, North Korea, Libya, Sudan, Syria, or any country to which the US has embargoed goods; or (ii) to anyone on the US Treasure Department's list of Specially Designated Nations or the US Commerce Department's Table of Denial Orders.
9. **Restricted Rights**. Use, duplication, or disclosure by the United States government is subject to the restsrictions as set foth in the Rights in Technical Data and Computer Software Clauses in DFARS 252.227-7013(c)(1)(ii) and FAR 52.227-19(c)(2) as applicable.
10. **Governing Law**. Any action related to this License will be governed by California law and controlling US federal law. No choice of law rules of any jurisdiction will apply.

11. **Severability**. If any of the above provisions are held to be in violation of applicable law, void, or unenforceable in any jurisdiction, then such provisions are herewith waived to the extent necessary for the License to be otherwise enforceable in such jurisdiction. However, if in Sun's opinion deletion of any provisions of the License by operation of this paragraph unreasonably compromises the rights or increases the liabilities of Sun or its licensors, Sun reserves the right to terminate the License and refund the fee paid by Licensee, if any, as Licensee's sole and exclusive remedy.

Technical Support

Technical support is available for installation-related problems only. The technical support office is open from 8:00 A.M. to 6:00 P.M. Monday through Friday and can be reached via the following methods:

- Phone: (919) 544-9404 extension 81
- Faxback Answer System: (919) 544-9404 extension 85
- E-mail: help@vmedia.com
- FAX: (919) 544-9472
- World Wide Web: **http://www.vmedia.com/support**
- America Online: keyword *Ventana*

Limits of Liability & Disclaimer of Warranty

The authors and publisher of this book have used their best efforts in preparing the CD-ROM and the programs contained in it. These efforts include the development, research, and testing of the theories and programs to determine their effectiveness. The authors and publisher make no warranty of any kind expressed or implied, with regard to these programs or the documentation contained in this book.

The authors and publisher shall not be liable in the event of incidental or consequential damages in connection with, or arising out of, the furnishing, performance, or use of the programs, associated instructions, and/or claims of productivity gains.

If there is software on this CD-ROM, then it may be shareware. There may be additional charges (owed to the software authors/makers) incurred for their registration and continued use. See individual program's README files for more information.

APPENDIX B

JavaScript Bean Builder

Acadia Software (www.acadians.com) has developed the JavaScriptBean Builder application to assist with the creation of JavaScript beans. An early version of this bean builder (Version 1.0, Preview Release 2) is provided with the Component Development Kit (CDK). This appendix describes some preliminary information on how to use the bean builder.

Component & Source Views

Similar to Visual JavaScript, Acadia Software's Bean Builder lets you structure your JavaScript bean with a project construct and view it in different views. The two views I want to describe are the Component and Source views.

Component View

This view is where you create your component and add properties, methods, events, and method parameters. There is also an attribute pane that lets you define properties associated with a component descriptor. See Figure B-1 for the component view.

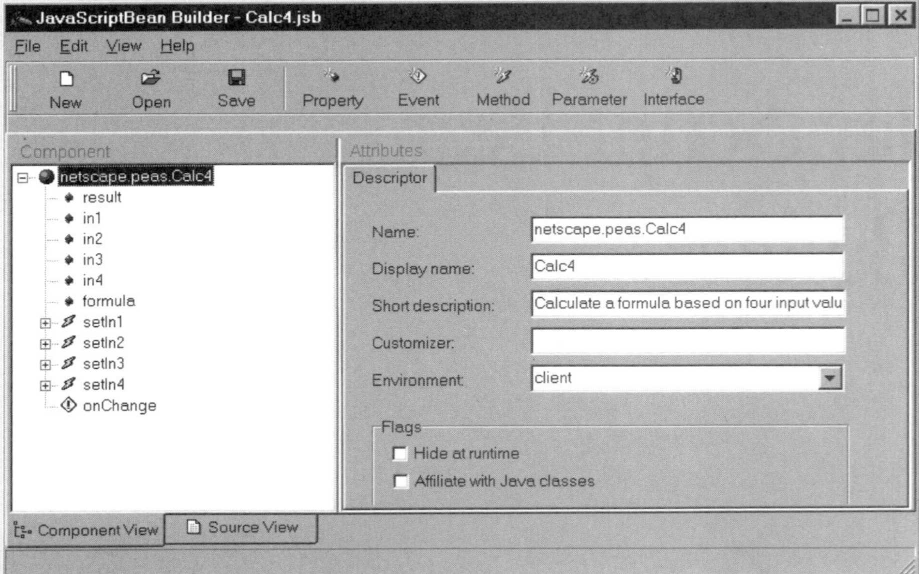

Figure B-1: The Component View mode of Acadia's JavaScriptBean Builder.

Source View

This view displays the HTML source of the JavaScript bean. The source for the JSB file can then be edited. This is where you provide the code (in JavaScript) for your constructor function and other methods. The Bean Builder places the code between JSB_CONSTRUCTOR tags for you. The source view lets you save your source to a JSB file. See Figure B-2 for the appearance of the source view.

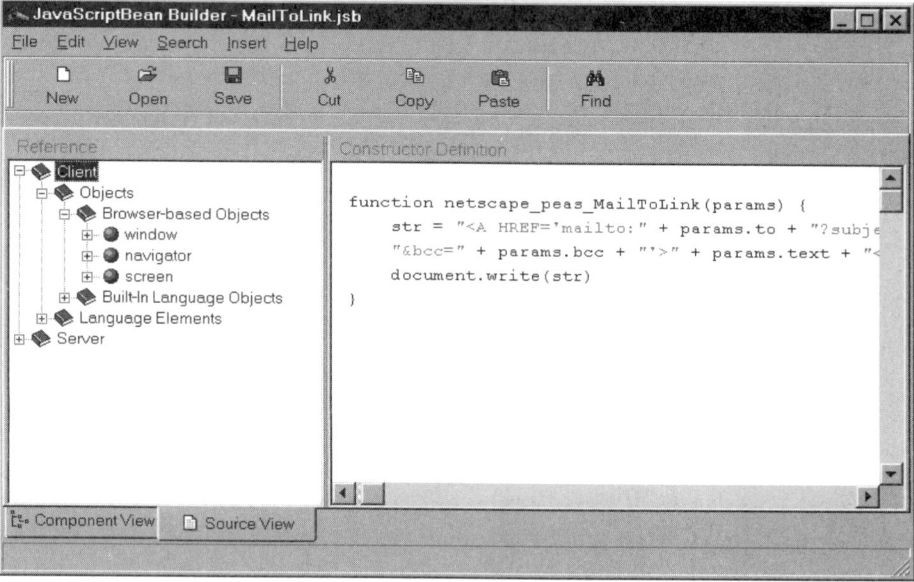

Figure B-2: The Source View mode of JavaScriptBean Builder.

Creating a Bean With Bean Builder

You use the following steps to create a JavaScript bean with the JavaScript Bean Builder:

- Create and name a new component: Choose New from the menu or using the New icon. Enter the name of your component in the New dialog box. You may have to qualify the name, entering any path and package information. You may recall from Chapter 8 that JavaScript beans are often places in packages. After you create and name the new bean, the Bean Builder will display your bean in component view.
- Define attributes: A JSB file starts with a <JSB_DESCRIPTOR> tag specifying the name and various attributes of the component. Use the attributes pane in component view to define the descriptor attributes for the JavaScript bean. When the JSB file is saved, this information will be converted to a <JSB_DESCRIPTOR> tag.
- Define component descriptors: You can add properties, methods, events to the component by using the toolbar. The attributes pane lets you edit and adjust these fields.

- Write the constructor and other methods. The source view mode contains a source code editor. Use this editor to enter JavaScript code for your constructor function and any other methods needed. All of the code is converted to a <JSB_CONSTRUCTOR> tag when the component is saved to a .JSB file.
- Save your new component: There is a Save button on the toolbar (or a Save option in the File menu). Enter the name of the .JSB file. This will save your new component to a JSB file.

Drag-&-Drop Features

In source view mode, JavaScriptBean Builder implements a *JavaScript Language Reference Tree*. In this tree-view display, various JavaScript statements and their hierarchical relationships are displayed (see Figure B-3). The *Objects* node contains built-in JavaScript objects such as window and document. The *Language Elements* node contains JavaScript statements such as loop and if. You can drag and drop various JavaScript language constructs into your code, making coding easier and more accurate. This feature was not fully implemented in the Version 1, PR-2 software.

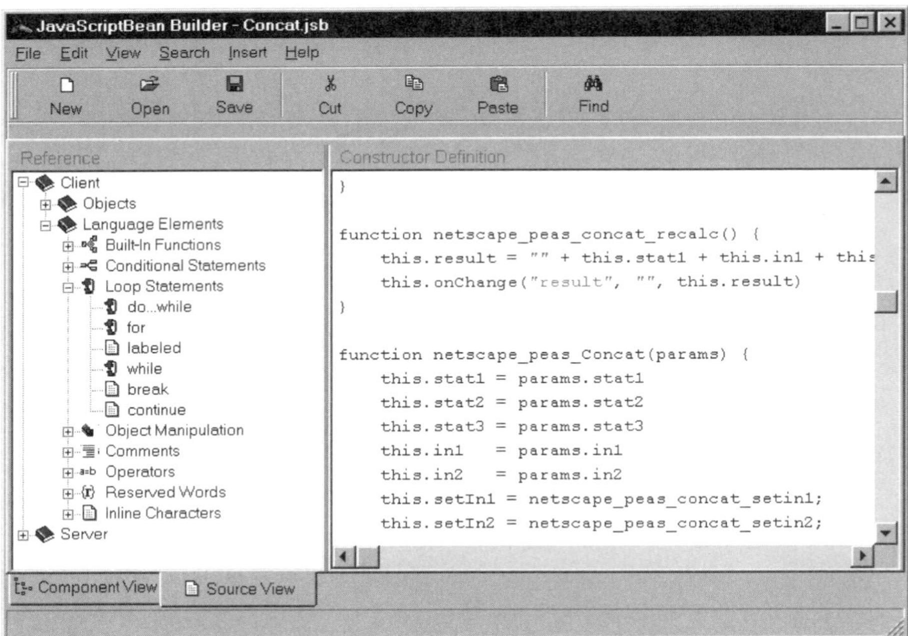

Figure B-3: The JavaScript Language Reference tree expanded to show the loop statement.

Glossary

API See **Application Programming Interface.**

Application Programming Interface (API) A set of routines that makes available to a programmer a group of (usually) related services. The set of routines made available by the libraries distributed with Java can be called the Java API.

bean A JavaBean. A component developed in Java in accordance with the JavaBeans component specification.

business object In client/server systems, an object providing services to accomplish a common business task.

broadcasting Notifying all registered listeners that an event has occurred.

Common Object Request Broker Architecture A product of the Object Management Group. A specification for cross-system middleware that can provide object services regardless of operating system or location.

CORBA See **Common Object Request Broker Architecture**

customization In component architectures, the ability to vary a component from the form in which it was delivered, changing the properties or appearance of a component.

Customizer In JavaBeans, a class that provides a GUI representation for modifying a component. Customizer classes implement the Customizer interface.

data hiding Data encapsulation.

deadlock A routine cannot return because it is waiting for a resource that is not free.

deprecation The term used for methods in use in Java 1.0 whose use is discouraged in Java 1.1.

design patterns In Sun's JavaBeans specification, a standard naming convention used for certain bean classes and methods. See **introspection**.

early binding In programming languages, when decisions about which methods or functions to call are bound at compile time. See **late binding**.

embedded plug-in Plug-ins that are embedded in an HTML page with the EMBED tag or the OBJECT tag. They appear in the page where they are placed, having the Height and Width specified in the tag.

encapsulation Hiding the implementation of data or methods from clients using the code, and providing the clients with the interface only. For example, a Java class's variables are protected from being accessed by other objects by declaring them private or protected.

event In a Graphical User Interface (GUI), events are used as a form of notification; an example of a GUI event is a mouse click or a button click.

getter A public method used to get the value of a property. See **setter**.

Graphical User Interface (GUI) A computing environment that represents data and information graphically. An end user often interacts with a GUI using a mouse or pointing device.

GUI See **Graphical User Interface**.

indexed properties Properties that are accessible by indexes, as arrays are. Individual properties or the array as a whole can be accessed.

inheritance In an object-oriented programming language or system, the ability to derive one class from another, thereby reusing code and variables from the superclass, and creating a hierarchy of objects. See **superclass**.

introspection The JavaBeans process of a component container environment discovering a bean's properties, methods, and events. See **design patterns**.

Java A general-purpose computer programming language developed at Sun Microsystems. Java is an object-oriented language, and has features that make it suited for writing programs to run on the Internet.

Java Development Kit (JDK) The group of tools, including the javac.exe compiler, and Java documentation made available to Java developers by Sun Microsystems.

JavaScript A scripting language developed by Netscape. JavaScript statements can be embedded in HTML pages, and can be client-side or server-side.

JavaScript bean A component developed in accordance with Netscape's component architecture. A component implemented in JavaScript.

JDK See **Java Development Kit**.

late binding In a programming language, deferring the decision of which function or method to call until the program is running. See **early binding**. See also **polymorphism**.

low level analysis Introspection of a JavaBean by a beanbox using the core reflection API.

manifest A manifest file is embedded in a Java Archive file (Jar file) and tells which of the archived classes are beans.

method The name for a function in Java or Smalltalk. In Java, methods are bound to an object. There are no external methods (not associated with a class) in Java.

no-op From "no operation." In JavaBeans, a method that has no effect, and returns null.

Object Request Broker (ORB) The Object Request Broker is the central idea to CORBA. The ORB is a piece of middleware that mediates among systems. Requests for objects or object services are routed to the ORB, which interprets the request, finds an object to execute the request, and returns the results.

ORB See **Object Request Broker**.

page-oriented plug-in Page-oriented plug-ins are Netscape plug-ins that work with an entire HTML page. They can be contrasted with embedded plug-ins that appear in a certain location in an HTML page.

persistence Storing an object in an object-oriented system, or a component in a component architecture. Often an object is stored with enough of its "state" to make it easily restorable in a different software environment.

plug-in A code module that can be installed in Netscape Communicator to handle different file types and MIME types that Communicator cannot read.

polymorphism In a programming language, when a decision about which method will actually execute is delayed until run time. ("Many shapes.") See **late binding**.

property In component architectures, an attribute of a component, such as the color or size of an on-screen GUI button or text field. JavaBeans implements properties as public instance variables.

property editor In JavaBeans, a class implementing the PropertyEditor interface, providing a custom interface to properties.

publishing Making the properties, methods, and events of a component available to a software container environment. In JavaBeans, all public methods are considered to have been published.

read-only property A component property that can be read by a container application, but not written to.

read/write property A component property that can be both read and written to by a container application.

reflection The ability of the JavaBeans architecture to analyze a bean to discover its properties, methods, and events.

reflection API The Application Programming Interface within JavaBeans that contains classes to support the reflection or analysis of beans.

semantic In Java 1.1, semantic events are the opposite of low-level events such as mouse events.

setter A public method to set the value of a property. See **getter**.

superclass In an object-oriented system, in which one class inherits from another, a class that appears above another in a hierarchy. See **inheritance**.

synchronized Java keyword used to declared methods or code blocks synchronized. Synchronized code is locked while it's executing.

thread A separate process of execution in a program. The state of variables and the system state of a thread is called its context.

thread-safe Thread-safe code can successfully be executed by multiple threads without causing deadlock or races. In Java, the synchronized keyword is used to try to make code blocks, methods, and classes thread-safe.

write-only property A component property that can be written by a container application, but not read.

Index

D

E

VENTANA

Official Netscape Visual JavaScript Developer's Guide

$49.99, 608 pages, illustrated, part #: 1-56604-761-7

Windows 95/NT

Doug Lloyd (Chapel Hill, NC)

Intermediate to Advanced

- Complete guide to creating Web applications and adding features without writing code.
- Instructions for developing database applications using LiveWire and Visual JavaScript's Connection Builder.
- Practical examples of key related technologies, including Java and JavaBeans.

CD-ROM with example files, reusable JavaScript components, third-party components, AT&T WorldNet® Service software using the Netscape browser.

Official Netscape JFC Developer's Guide

$49.99, 544 pages, illustrated, part #: 1-56604-756-0

Sean Michaels

All Platforms

Advanced

- Complete coverage of all aspects of programming using Java Foundation Classes (JFC) and JavaSoft's AWT.
- Highlights CORBA/IIOP, enabling JFC programmers to use the distributed architecture common to Netscape products.
- Provides real-world examples focusing on issues for intranet professionals.

CD-ROM with sample code from the book, JFC SDK, JDK 1.1 and Netscape Constructor.

Official Netscape Software Deployment With Object Signing

$49.99, 400 pages, illustrated, part #: 1-56604-834-6

All Platforms

Reaz Hoque

Intermediate to Advanced

- Provides complete instructions for creating digital signatures to safely deploy software over the Internet and intranets.
- Shows how to use Java and JavaScript to create secure applications for Internet deployment.
- Explains how to use Netscape's new cutting-edge tools to reach out to thousands of customers more efficiently.

CD-ROM with all sample code from the book, demos and shareware.

VENTANA

Official Netscape JavaBeans Developer's Guide

$39.99, 400 pages, illustrated, part #: 1-56604-825-7

Doug Nickerson
Windows 95/NT, Macintosh
Intermediate to Advanced

- Focuses on the nuts and bolts of Beans technology and how to quickly get up to speed.
- Explains Netscape's support for JavaBeans and how Beans fits in with Netscape ONE.
- Includes integrated code examples illustrating JavaBeans & Java 1.1 API features and concepts.

CD-ROM with The Java Development Kit (JDK), The JavaBeans Development Kit (BDK), Netscape's Component Development Kit, example source code from the book.

Official Netscape Crossware Developer's Guide

$49.99, 544 pages, illustrated, part #: 1-56604-768-4

John R. Vacca
All Platforms
Intermediate to Advanced

- Shows how to modify Netscape ONE starter applications (Java, JavaScript, HTML, LiveConnect and LiveWire Pro).
- Explains how to create and submit applications to the AppFoundry environment.
- Packed with sample code and application development examples.

CD-ROM with sample AppFoundry applications.

Official Netscape ONE Developer's Guide, Second Edition

$49.99, 500 pages, illustrated, part #: 1-56604-710-2

Luke Duncan/Sean Michaels
Windows, Macintosh
Intermediate to Advanced

- Covers all components of Netscape ONE—Java, IFC, LiveConnect, JavaScript, plug-ins, JRI, IIOP and HTML.
- Spotlights Internet/intranet application development with Internet Foundation Classes.
- Provides an example plug-in project showing how to use ONE components together.

CD-ROM with sample applications from the book, Netscape ONE SDKs.

VENTANA

Official Netscape JavaScript 1.2 Programmer's Reference

$39.99, 496 pages, illustrated, part #: 1-56604-757-9

Peter Kent/Kent Multer
Windows, Macintosh & UNIX
Intermediate to Advanced

- Complete reference to all JavaScript expressions, objects, properties, methods, statements, reserved words and color values.
- In-depth explanations and examples, including syntax and usage.
- Encyclopedic listing, extensively cross-referenced for quick access to information.

CD-ROM: Searchable hyperlinked version of the book.

Official Netscape Server-Side JavaScript for Database Applications

$39.99, 544 pages, illustrated, part #: 1-56604-745-5

Luke Duncan
Windows NT & UNIX
Intermediate to Advanced

- Designing and implementing Internet/intranet applications for Netscape Enterprise Server 3 using server-side JavaScript.
- Using Java with LiveConnect to create browser-independent applications.
- Troubleshooting tips, advanced topics and productivity-enhancing examples.

Official HTML Publishing for Netscape, Second Edition

$39.99, 800 pages, part #: 1-56604-650-5

Windows 95/NT, Macintosh • Intermediate

Make the Most of the Latest Netscape Features!
Learn how the latest developments in Netscape Navigator and HTML enhance your ability to deliver eye-catching, interactive Web pages to a broad audience, and how to harness new technologies to create a compelling site. Includes:

- Playing to Navigator's hottest features, including tables, frames, plug-ins and support for Java applets.
- Guidelines for designing great Web pages.
- New material on style sheets, sound, multimedia and databases.

The CD-ROM contains an example Web site on the Net, sample JavaScript, clip objects, backgrounds and more.

Official Netscape JavaScript 1.2 Book, Second Edition

$29.99, 592 pages, part #: 1-56604-675-0

All platforms • Beginning to Intermediate

Brew up instant scripts—even if you're not a programmer!
Learn all the skills you need to perk up your Web pages with multimedia and interactivity. Fully updated for Netscape Communicator, this bestseller now includes:

- Basic programming techniques.
- Tips for using existing scripts and building your own from scratch.
- Nearly 200 script samples and interactive tutorials online.

Official Netscape FastTrack Server Book

$39.99, 432 pages, part #: 1-56604-483-9

Windows NT • Intermediate to Advanced

Turn your PC into an Internet/intranet powerhouse!
This step-by-step guide to the hottest server software on the Net provides all the instructions you need to launch your Internet or intranet site, from technical requirements to content creation and administration. Learn how to exploit FastTrack Server's high-performance server architecture to easily create and manage customized web sites. Plus, enhance your site with FTP and Telnet; ensure security for online transactions; and import and convert documents.

VENTANA

Java 1.1 Programmer's Reference

Daniel I. Joshi, Pavel Vorobiev
$49.99, 1000 pages, illustrated, part #: 1-56604-687-4

The ultimate resource for Java professionals! And the perfect supplement to the JDK documentation. Whether you need a day-to-day reference for Java classes, an explanation of new APIs, a guide to common programming techniques, or all three, you've got it—all in an encyclopedic format that's convenient to refer to again and again. Covers new Java 1.1 features, including the AWT, JARs, Java Security API, the JDBC, JavaBeans, and more, with complete descriptions that include syntax, usage and code samples. **CD-ROM:** Complete, hyperlinked version of the book.

For all platforms • Intermediate to Advanced

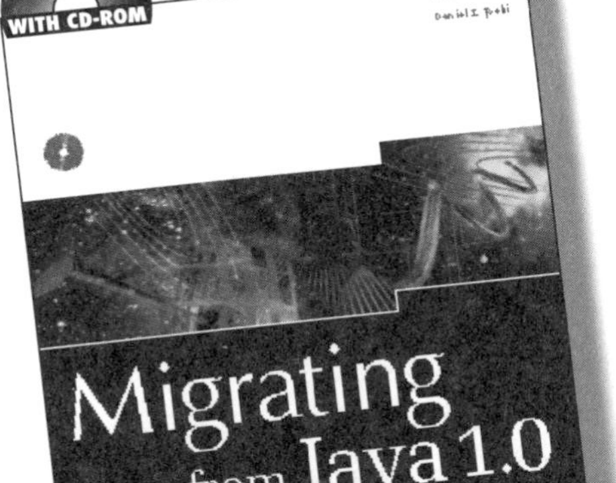

Migrating From Java 1.0 to Java 1.1

Daniel I. Joshi, Pavel Vorobiev
$39.99, 600 pages, illustrated, part #: 1-56604-686-6

Your expertise with Java 1.0 provides the perfect springboard to rapid mastery of Java 1.1 and the new tools in the JDK 1.1. Viewing what's new from the perspective of what you already know gets you up to speed quickly. And you'll learn not only what's changed, but why—gaining deeper understanding of the evolution of Java and how to exploit its power for your projects. **CD-ROM:** All the sample Java 1.1 programs, plus extended examples.

For Windows NT/95, Macintosh, UNIX, Solaris
Intermediate to Advanced

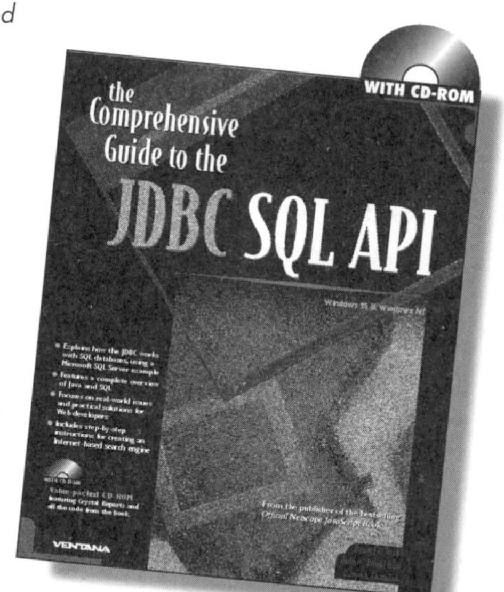

The Comprehensive Guide to the JDBC SQL API

Daniel I. Joshi, Rodney Runolfson
$49.99, 456 pages, illustrated, part#: 1-56604-637-8

Develop high-powered database solutions for your Internet/intranet site! Covers the basics of Java and SQL, interface design with AWT and instructions for building an Internet-based search engine. **CD-ROM:** OpenLink Server-side JDBC driver, SQL databases and tables from the book, sample code, JDBC API specification and example sites.

For Windows 95/NT • Intermediate to Advanced

Official Netscape Enterprise Server 3 Book

Richard Cravens
$49.99, 480 pages, part #: 1-56604-664-5

- Detailed examination of web-site security issues and benefits.
- Complete coverage of installation, configuration and maintenance, along with troubleshooting tips.
- Shows how to enrich web sites with multimedia and interactivity.

CD-ROM contains sample HTML editors, HTML references, current Netscape plug-ins.

For Windows NT & UNIX • Intermediate to Advanced

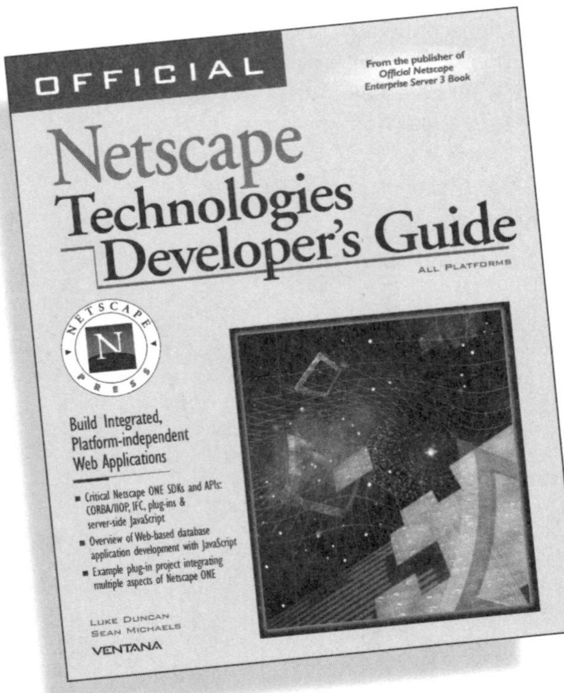

Official Netscape Technologies Developer's Guide

Luke Duncan, Sean Michaels
$39.99, 352 pages, part #: 1-56604-749-8

- Guide to the most critical ONE SDKs and APIs—CORBA/IIOP, IFC, plug-ins and server-side JavaScript.
- Overview of Internet/intranet application development with IFC.
- Example plug-in project to integrate multiple aspects of Netscape ONE.

All Platforms • Intermediate to Advanced

To order any Ventana title, complete this order form and mail or fax it to us, with payment, for quick shipment.

TITLE	PART #	QTY	PRICE	TOTAL

SHIPPING

For orders shipping within the United States, please add $4.95 for the first book, $1.50 for each additional book.
For "two-day air," add $7.95 for the first book, $3.00 for each additional book.
Email: vorders@kdc.com for exact shipping charges.
Note: Please include your local sales tax.

Subtotal = $ ______________
Shipping = $ ______________
Tax = $ ______________
Total = $ ______________

Mail to: International Thomson Publishing • 7625 Empire Drive • Florence, KY 41042
☎ US orders 800/332-7450 • fax 606/283-0718
☎ International orders 606/282-5786 • Canadian orders 800/268-2222

Name ______________________________
E-mail ______________________ Daytime phone ______________________
Company ______________________________
Address (No PO Box) ______________________________
City ______________________ State __________ Zip __________
Payment enclosed ___VISA ___MC ___ Acc't # ______________________ Exp. date __________
Signature ______________________ Exact name on card ______________________

Check your local bookstore or software retailer for these and other bestselling titles, or call toll free:

800/332-7450

8:00 am - 6:00 pm EST

Sun Microsystems' JDK 1.1.4 is on this CD-ROM:

All technical support for this product is available from Ventana.

The technical support office is open from 8:00 A.M. to 6:00 P.M. (EST) Monday through Friday and can be reached via the following methods.

World Wide Web: http://www.netscapepress.com/support

E-mail: help@vmedia.com

Phone: (919) 544–9404 extension 81

FAX: (919) 544–9472

America Online: keyword **Ventana**